ORAL HISTORY ON TRIAL

ORAL HISTORY ON TRIAL
Recognizing Aboriginal Narratives in the Courts

Bruce Granville Miller

UBCPress · Vancouver · Toronto

21 20 19 18 17 16 15 14 13 12 11   5 4 3 2 1

Printed in Canada on FSC-certified ancient-forest-free paper (100% post-consumer recycled) that is processed chlorine- and acid-free.

Library and Archives Canada Cataloguing in Publication

Miller, Bruce Granville, 1951-
Oral history on trial : recognizing aboriginal narratives in the courts / Bruce Granville Miller.

ISBN 978-0-7748-2070-7 (bound)
ISBN 978-0-7748-2071-4 (pbk.)

1. Native peoples – Legal status, laws, etc. – Canada. 2. Evidence (Law) – Canada. 3. Oral tradition – Canada. I. Title.

KE7709.M55 2011   342.7108'72   C2010-908004-1
KF8205.M55 2011

---

e-book ISBNs: 978-0-7748-2072-1 (pdf); 978-0-7748-2073-8 (epub)

Canadä

UBC Press gratefully acknowledges the financial support for our publishing program of the Government of Canada (through the Canada Book Fund), the Canada Council for the Arts, and the British Columbia Arts Council.

This book has been published with the help of a grant from the Canadian Federation for the Humanities and Social Sciences, through the Aid to Scholarly Publications Program, using funds provided by the Social Sciences and Humanities Research Council of Canada, and with the help of the K.D. Srivastava Fund.

UBC Press
The University of British Columbia
2029 West Mall
Vancouver, BC V6T 1Z2
www.ubcpress.ca

For Todd Andrew Miller, of brave heart and sharp wit

Contents

Preface

My exposure to the Canadian legal system over the last twenty years has led to this book about an issue of considerable public interest and of great importance to Aboriginal peoples: the ways in which Aboriginal oral narratives, commonly called oral histories or oral traditions, have been used in Canadian courts. The Indigenous Bar Association and a panel of elders from across Canada have met on several occasions, sometimes with federal justices and other officials and interested parties, including myself, to query the conditions under which oral narratives can be entered as evidence, and Aboriginal elders can appear in court. Many other people, Aboriginal and otherwise, have expressed their own deep concerns both in print and in private. The overriding worry is that without oral narrative evidence, Aboriginal people cannot adequately present their own evidence in litigation.

My interest is in the larger issues rather than the views of particular people, although I consider many individual views in detail within these pages. I have used, at length in some cases, opposing approaches and points of view not to be critical of their authors, but rather to explore the conflicts and identify possible resolutions that employ the best scholarship and social responsibility to all the parties involved.

Acknowledgments

Many people have kindly helped me think through this project, although any errors in fact or judgment are my own. Perhaps foremost among these are my UBC colleague Julie Cruikshank, my talented research assistant Molly Malone, my brother Todd Miller, and legal historian Allan Grove, who initially brought me into this issue. Others who have given their thoughts on the issues within include members of the Indigenous Bar Association (IBA), Catherine Twinn, David Nahwegahbow and Sharon Venne. In addition, my thanks to David Courchene, the leader of the Turtle Lodge, located on the Sagkeeng First Nation in Manitoba, site of a meeting of IBA members and a panel of elders to discuss the problems of elder testimony in Canadian courts, and to the IBA for inviting me to the event and to their conversations. Ed Molstad, another participant at the meetings, provided his thoughts on elder testimony and the courts. Thanks, too, to the elders gathered there for their spirited commentary. I also thank Chief Rocky Wilson of the Hwlitsum First Nation, Kathy Sparrow of Musqueam, Sonny McHalsie and Tracey Joe of the Stó:lō Nation, Tia Halstad, Carole Blackburn, Pat Moore, Bill Angelbeck, Eric McClay, Keith Carlson, Wendy Wickwire, Ace Forsythe, Dan Boxberger, David Milward, Michael Blake, Joseph Weiss, Bill McKellin, Laraine Michalson, and Charles Menzies. Special thanks to the very talented UBC Press editors Darcy Cullen, Sarah Wight, and Ann Macklem. Also, my thanks go to the perceptive anonymous reviewers.

ORAL HISTORY ON TRIAL

Introduction

At one time, in conducting their legal affairs, the ancestors of the people who created English common law depended on the performance of actions that appealed to the human senses of touch, smell, hearing, and taste. The swearing of an oath in some instances included a kiss or a gesture. The anointing of a king, or the legal claim of a noble title, involved the smell and feel of a particular oil and the distribution and eating of food. The transfer of land required riding a horse to legally "see" and thereby acquire the land. Law itself was sometimes created in verse and intended to be sung (Hibbitts 1992). Perhaps most famously, the Bayeux Tapestry shows the powerful nobleman Harold Godwinson touching two reliquaries while promising to support the claim of William the Bastard (later William the Conqueror) to the English throne in the eleventh century (929). This form of oath swearing was recorded not in writing but rather in memory or, in this case, in textiles that could be understood by illiterates, which were wound around the interiors of churches of the medieval period. Often, multiple senses were drawn into legal affairs, and law was not so much said, sung, gestured, or felt, as holistically performed (945). In these earlier times, the performance of law required a speaker and a hearer, someone who touched and someone who was touched.

Today, law is found in documents that can exist independent of the sanctioning of second parties or the knowing associated with touch. Well-established, firmly entrenched law is commonly referred to as "black *letter* law." We have developed the means to interpret the world as text, and we diligently translate action into writing. What we take to be the permanence of writing is associated with serious intellectual activity (perhaps a reason for the disinclination of some academics to place weight on apparently ephemeral electronic journals). The common-law legal world now generally associates the oral and the sensory with fraud (Hibbitts 1992, 896), a dramatic change from the times vividly depicted in the medieval Icelandic *Njal's Saga* (1997), when men who were the oral historians of law occupied the highest position of honour. Performance-based legal systems such as Njal's have come to be thought of as primitive or uncivilized.

But times are always changing and in the 1980s and 1990s courts and tribunals in Canada and other jurisdictions began to seriously consider the relevance of Aboriginal oral narratives – including what are often called histories and myths – to legal proceedings. Indeed, the Canadian Specific Claims Tribunal, which hears Aboriginal land claims cases, is now empowered to receive and accept any oral historical evidence as it sees fit, whether it is admissible before a court or not (*Specific Claims Tribunal Act,* 2008, c. 22, s. 13(1b)). Barry (2009, 4) notes that internationally there is growing acceptance of what he terms "unconventional forms of evidence" in land claims and declaration of rights of Indigenous peoples, even when it would be dismissed as hearsay in other categories of cases. He writes that the South African *Restitution of Land Rights Act, 1994* permits the admission of evidence considered relevant and cogent to the case, whether admissible in any court of law. This act, however, fails to show how the courts might handle such evidence.

This book is an effort, in part, to closely examine significant assertions about oral narratives that have been made by the Canadian Department of Justice, which has faced the task of defending Canada in litigation brought by Aboriginal communities. I hope to broaden the dialogue beyond technical legal arguments about evidence rules and how these might accommodate oral narratives, and the speakers of them, to consider what these narratives are and how they can be evaluated from other disciplinary and Aboriginal perspectives. I argue that there is common ground among the various parties interested in the incorporation of oral narratives into legal proceedings, and that there can be mutually acceptable means for doing so.

Why Include Oral Narratives?

The Canadian court has properly understood that Aboriginal people are at a significant disadvantage if a major source of their knowledge, transmitted orally, across time, and in a distinctive style, cannot meaningfully be entered as evidence, with the same consideration as written historical evidence. Mr. Justice Addy, for example, writing in *Blueberry River Indian Band v. Canada (Department of Indian Affairs)* (originally known as *Apsassin v. Canada*) in 1988, noted the importance of the performative aspects of evidence. He found that he was surprised by the differences in the way he understood transcripts of testimony and videotapes:

> The spoken word and the visual impression are both preserved as part of the record to explain and at times to modify and even upset the conclusions that one might otherwise come to by a mere reading of the transcript. Having read the transcripts previously, I was quite surprised to note the degree to which some of my original impressions as to the effects of the evidence were either modified or completely changed upon viewing the actual videotaped recordings. (*Apsassin v. Canada,* 39-40; quoted in Hutchins et al. 2008, 23)

There are a number of important reasons why Aboriginal oral narratives should be included in the proceedings of Canadian courts, many articulated by members of the highest court. Canadian Supreme Court Chief Justice Antonio Lamer wrote, "The laws of evidence must be adapted in order that this type of evidence can be accommodated and *placed on an equal footing with the types of historical evidence that courts are familiar with, which largely consists of historical documents*" (*Delgamuukw v. British Columbia* [1997; *Delgamuukw III*], para. 87, emphasis mine). Further, as Chief Justice Lamer pointed out, treaty obligations demand that attention be paid to Aboriginal forms of the transmission of knowledge:

> This is a long-standing practice in the interpretation of treaties between the Crown and aboriginal peoples ... : To quote Dickson C.J., given that most aboriginal societies "did not keep written records," *the failure to do so would "impose an impossible burden of proof" on aboriginal peoples, and "render nugatory" any rights that they have* ... This process must be undertaken on a case-by-case basis. (ibid., emphasis mine)

Chief Justice Lamer noted further that in *R. v. Van der Peet,* "I held that the ordinary rules of evidence must be approached and adapted in light of the evidentiary difficulties inherent in adjudicating aboriginal claims" (*Delgamuukw III,* para. 105). His ruling advanced his own argument in *Van der*

Peet (para. 68): "The courts must not undervalue the evidence presented by aboriginal claimants simply because that evidence does not conform precisely with the evidentiary standards that would be applied in, for example, a private law torts case."

The present chief justice of the Canadian Supreme Court, Beverley McLachlin, writing in 2001 in *Mitchell v. M.N.R.*, pointed to a test for the inclusion of oral narratives, namely, their contribution of new evidence that is both useful to the court and reasonably reliable. She suggested that the protection of Aboriginal rights, as dictated by the Canadian Constitution of 1982, was tied to the admissibility of oral narratives and underscored the problem of the imposition of non-Aboriginal notions of fact. I take up this issue in more detail in Chapter 1.

> Aboriginal rights claims give rise to inherent evidentiary difficulties. However, the rights protected under s. 35(1) should not be rendered illusory by imposing an impossible burden of proof. The rules of evidence must therefore be applied flexibly, in a manner commensurate with the inherent difficulties posed by aboriginal claims. *Since claimants must demonstrate features of pre-contact society in the absence of written records, oral histories may offer otherwise unavailable evidence of ancestral practices and aboriginal perspectives.* Oral histories are admissible as evidence where they are both useful and reasonably reliable, subject always to the exclusionary discretion of the trial judge. In determining the usefulness and reliability of oral histories, *judges must resist facile assumptions based on Eurocentric traditions of gathering and passing on historical facts.* (*Mitchell,* para. 27, emphasis mine)

A few years earlier, Chief Justice McLachlin had noted still another set of Canadian values enshrined not in the constitution but in legal practice, with direct significance for the incorporation of oral narratives. Writing in *R. v. Marshall* she observed that "*the honour of the Crown* is always at stake in its dealings with Indian people. Interpretations of treaties and statutory provisions which have an impact upon treaty or aboriginal rights must be approached in a manner which maintains the integrity of the Crown ... *No appearance of 'sharp dealing' will be sanctioned*" (para. 49, emphasis mine; but see Culhane 1998 concerning the honour of the Crown in litigation). Honourable dealing, in brief, required the court not appear to disqualify the practices of the cultural "other," Aboriginal peoples, in a period of official reconciliation, public apologies for historical wrongdoing, and the funding of programs aimed at alleviating Aboriginal poverty, ill-health, and other consequences of colonialism.

In *Mitchell,* Chief Justice McLachlin pointed out that without the inclusion of oral narratives the precise nature of Aboriginal rights would be difficult to determine. These narratives provide evidence of ancestral practices where none might be otherwise available, and they provide evidence of ancestral perspectives on rights – what Aboriginal people thought at the time relations with the Crown were established (*Mitchell,* para. 32). One observer optimistically noted that this line of thought in *Mitchell* might mean that whatever the Mi'kmaq heard in treaty negotiations in 1760–61 trumps what the British wrote down about it (Howes 2005; and see Niezen 2003, 3). And, in 2005, Mr. Justice Binnie of the Supreme Court noted that Aboriginal law's fundamental objective "is the reconciliation of aboriginal peoples and non-aboriginal peoples and their respective claims, interests and ambitions" (*Mikisew Cree First Nation v. Canada (Minister of Canadian Heritage),* para. 1).

These are all important arguments for the inclusion of Aboriginal oral narratives in legal proceedings. However, although Canada is the only common-law jurisdiction providing constitutional recognition and protection of the rights of Aboriginal peoples, it does not yet have specific rules regarding elders' oral history testimony (Hopkins and Nahwegahbow 2008, 2). In part this deficit reflects the serious concerns about the proper way to engage oral narratives and the potential pitfalls of engaging them improperly. The immediate barrier to allowing Aboriginal community members to give oral narratives as evidence is the ancient English common law practice known as the hearsay rule, which effectively bars lay witnesses from presenting what they have heard from others (except the fact that they have heard it) and substantially limits both what bearers of these oral materials might present and the importance given them (Roness and McNeil 2000, 68). Exceptions, however, are sometimes made.

In addition, Chief Justice McLachlin cautioned that, "The laws of evidence must ensure that the aboriginal perspective is given due weight but consciousness of the special nature of aboriginal claims *does not negate general principles governing evidence.* Claims must still be established on persuasive evidence demonstrating validity on a balance of probabilities." And, she noted that rules of evidence regarding Aboriginal cases *"cannot be strained beyond reason"* (*Mitchell,* para. 32, emphasis mine).

These decisions, *Mitchell* and *Marshall,* and several that followed, marked an effort by the Canadian courts to work out in more detail what to do with oral narratives, and, arguably, the start of a retreat from the importance given them in *Delgamuukw III,* a landmark land claim decision widely heralded in Canada and in Commonwealth countries taking note of Canadian affairs (Milward 2009, 1; Mildon 2008, 85-87). In brief, the Supreme Court mandates legal principles that pull in two directions: one toward generous treatment and the other toward strict application of evidentiary law.

Other Perspectives on Oral Narratives in Court

The issues around oral narratives are not just the concern of legal practitioners. Those whose oral narratives are entered as evidence (and appear to be put on trial) have quite different perspectives from the court and Crown regarding evidence and legal procedures. Antonia Mills, an anthropologist who gave expert testimony on behalf of the Wet'suwet'en people in the original *Delgamuukw* trial, wrote that the hereditary chiefs met repeatedly to determine how their cases should be presented (Mills 1994, 10-11; and see Mills 2005, Daly 2005). They wanted the court to operate in Aboriginal style, as a potlatch. The Wet'suwet'en believed that the chiefs were the proper people to present the case on behalf of the matrilineages, the historical land-holding units of their society. Mills further notes that *Delgamuukw* set a precedent by having the chiefs act as prime witnesses, unlike other cases in which there is an "implicit understanding that the court system can better understand these issues when they are expressed through the idiom of western culture," that is, by outside expert witnesses. The chiefs, however, decided not to wear their ceremonial button blankets, as they would to their own ceremonial and legal processes in the longhouse, because they believed the regalia would not be honoured in the courthouse (Mills 1994, 13).

The two litigants in *Delgamuukw,* the house chiefs of the Wet'suwet'en and the Gitxsan nations (these spellings have changed since the time of the trial), have oral narratives that detail their origins and subsequent histories. These oral narratives are recited by chiefs and are central to the transmission of rights to a territory (Mills 1994, 16). The lawyers for the Crown defence opposed the recitation of these formal oral narratives (known as *kungax* among the Wet'suwet'en and *adaawx* among the Gitxsan) because they are oral and unwritten, and therefore are "hearsay." The trial judge agreed to make an exception in this case and to hear testimony directly from the chiefs. However, in the reasons for judgment, the judge held that the oral narratives were without weight (17).

Richard Daly, another anthropologist who offered expert testimony, argues that the judge's position was a refusal of the gift of knowledge: "I submit that the plaintiffs and their experts deployed their respective gifts in the *Delgamuukw* case. They sought to gift the public with particular knowledge and information, and to give what is at the core of all gifts, namely, ideas and relationships." And further, poignantly, "The contents of *Our Box Was Full* [his expert report] was given to the court and returned unopened" (Daly 2005, 47). I consider the responses to the repudiation by the trial judge of the testimony of Mills and Daly in Chapter 1.

Canadian courts have attempted to refine the understanding of what oral materials are, how they can be evaluated, the procedures associated with them, and the weight they should be given by the presiding judge. But, I will argue, the courts are far from the best venue to work through the complex issues associated with oral materials. Insufficient serious attention has been given to just what role Aboriginal oral traditions might have in courts or, more generally, in Canadian society. Debates about oral traditions deserve more consideration than can arise from positions taken in an adversarial legal process, particularly contentious cross-examination. First Nations legal scholar John Borrows writes that the inherent time limits to litigation mean that there is not enough time to comprehend oral narratives (cited in Simpkins 2000, 141). The judgment in *Samson Indian Nation and Band v. Canada* that the interpretation of oral material is too slow for the court underscores Borrows's point. Historian and veteran expert witness Arthur Ray points to another courtroom problem:

> The adversarial nature of the process greatly enhances the challenge they [the courts] face. Although expert witnesses are there to assist (educate) the court, their evidence and testimony is challenged (tested) directly by opposing counsel through cross-examination. Cross-examining counsel normally are assisted by their own team of experts. In hotly contested cases, experts often find it difficult to avoid taking such challenges personally and becoming emotionally involved. From the beginning, the adversarial nature of the process frequently has had a divisive impact on the community of experts who have taken part. A key reason is that opposing lawyers often explore the limits of the theoretical differences that exist among experts. *Consequently, expert witnesses are often pushed or pulled towards the boundaries of currently acceptable historical interpretation.* (Ray 2003, 269, emphasis mine; and see 2008)

Ray's commentary echoes the broader conclusion drawn earlier by Clinton (1986) that the adversarial system in the United States pushes historical evidence into extreme positions. Richard Daly has reached the same conclusion as Ray regarding the low likelihood of thorough and careful treatment of Aboriginal oral historical evidence in litigation itself, but on somewhat different grounds. In fact, he criticizes Ray's argument (2003, 273) that historians acting as experts in Aboriginal rights cases must not only be guided by the highest ethical standards and professional standards but also bear in mind that their primary responsibility is to the court rather than to their clients. To Daly (2005, 5, 9), this is merely a tacit acceptance of the current power imbalance in society and "positivistic administrative way of thinking based on fixed text-based categories for containing data rather than context-based categories developed from various evidentiary sources, including the oral."

Legal scholar David Milward (2009, 18) notes that the legal realist position argues that the minimization of oral narratives by the court allows the subordination of Aboriginal interests. Writing in 1992, McLeod claimed that Canadian evidentiary rules are used as "tools of oppression" of First Nations. The "best evidence rule," he writes, has this effect, as do other rules and practices. The "parole evidence rule," in which courts interpret agreements put into writing to determine the terms of the agreement, he writes, was applied in *R. v. Horse* case, wherein the trial judge did not consider the transcript of negotiations between the Crown and First Nations in the Treaty Six area because he did not consider the treaty to be ambiguous. Further, McLeod notes that the assigning of weight to evidence by trial judges allows the disregarding of oral materials, as in *Delgamuukw,* which I consider later.

McLeod and Daly's positions, in common with some Aboriginal critics such as Milward, point to a need for a thoroughgoing, rather than piecemeal, revision of some features of our current legal system, at least as it relates to rules of evidence. Mr. Justice John Bouck (interview, 2008), formerly of the Supreme Court of British Columbia, has argued that legislatures, rather than courts, should change some features of the common law. He points to the practice in the US executive branch of convening hearings, in which affected parties can participate, to consider how legislative change might be undertaken, as a model for Canadian practice. Milward, on the other hand, observes that the Supreme Court of Canada itself must account for the importance of oral histories as forms of evidence critical to establishing the basis for Aboriginal rights in Canada under section 35(1) of the *Constitution Act, 1982*. He concludes, "It has therefore fallen upon Canadian courts, the Supreme Court in particular, to develop principles in the law of evidence that address the admission and weighing of oral histories as evidence in support of Aboriginal rights claims," although he says the Supreme Court has provided little guidance to date (Milward 2009, 5, 8).

In this spirit, instead of limiting my discussion to the debate in law and to long-held standards of evidence at trial, I consider oral narratives in a wider perspective and contemplate what they are and how they might be treated in the long process from their transmission by one person to another, their placement in archives, their handling by Crown and tribal/band researchers, their performance in a courtroom (outside of their cultural context), and finally to their evaluation by trial judges as forms of evidence. In the Canadian context these questions take on significance because the Crown has argued that oral materials are *transformed* into documents and hence are amenable to standard historiographic methods. A Crown witness on oral tradition described what he took to be the route from elder testimony to trial record and concluded, "Under such circumstances, it cannot be seriously suggested that oral tradition should continue to be understood and evaluated within its original context rather than as a document purposefully introduced into a new setting by an Aboriginal party or their legal counsel" (von Gernet 2006a, 6). I believe this position creates a false dichotomy and implies a subordination of oral materials to written historical ones and of Aboriginal epistemology to that of North Atlantic sensibilities, a position in contradiction to that of the Supreme Court of Canada.

Julie Cruikshank (personal communication, 2007; cited in Simpkins 2000, 138) has pointed out that oral narratives should be treated as parallel to history, but are not understood as such when they are looked on as merely repositories of data. This is a significant consideration because Crown researchers and litigators in a series of land-claim and related Aboriginal litigation since *Delgamuukw* have treated oral materials in this way, as I show in Chapter 1. Further, British Columbia Chief Justice Allan McEachern's idea in the original *Delgamuukw* trial that the absence of writing in Gitxsan and Wet'suwet'en societies marked them as primitive surely implies that the means of transmission of knowledge in such a primitive society, oral narratives, are inferior to those of societies with writing (Miller 1992b). I suggest that the nature of oral materials poses empirical and theoretical questions not considered by the Crown. What *does* happen to oral materials along the path to the courtroom?

To study this process, I rely on published materials and on my own interviews with oral historians, tribal archivists, Crown researchers, and others.

Little previous work on oral narrative has pointed in this direction. Ames (1990), however, has observed the importance of archives and their connection to relations of power as a "political institution," referring to mainstream societies' holdings of material about Aboriginal people. Ames is concerned with the principles underlying the production, storage, and distribution of images of Aboriginal people, and the relevance of understanding archives. Consequently, my approach parallels his.

I have also consulted scholars recording oral materials with Aboriginal consultants, academics who have presented oral material in court, attorneys-at-law, and judges. I believe that there is common ground among these disparate sets of people, all of whom have some role in the production and reproduction of oral materials, and suggest that they might benefit from considering the various components of the process leading to the courtroom. It's certain that anthropologists, historians, tribal oral historians, archivists, and legal personnel of all sorts have not yet gained clarity about oral narratives and their legal role. Nor do these practitioners have sufficient insight into the activities of those in other disciplines, though it would be helpful it they did. As legal scholar Michael Jackson (2005, xi) has noted, "Law and anthropology ought to be on speaking terms."

The Crown's Arguments

The Canadian courts and the Crown have raised crucial questions about oral materials, and these merit close consideration. They include questions that arise routinely about any sort of evidence entered into court simply by virtue of the existing rules of evidence in common-law courts. Are the historical conclusions drawn from oral materials supported by other evidence, and especially by documentary evidence? Are there multiple versions of oral materials, and if so, are they consistent? If there are not multiple versions, is the oral evidence widely known and accepted in the community? These questions go to the legal issue of reliability. There are also other very specialized issues. One Crown expert (von Gernet 1996), drawing heavily on the work of Africanist historians, especially Jan Vansina, has raised the issue of whether the process of flattening of oral histories, referred to as a "floating gap," creates significant and legally meaningful inaccuracies. For example, genealogies of many generations of kings or chiefs entered as evidence might be telescoped into a more limited number, cutting out some, including others, and unduly emphasizing particular ones. This process might arise from the political demands of the moment, such as the need to create legitimacy by demonstrating genealogical closeness to important ancestors and, similarly, erasing from the record poorly regarded ancestors. As a consequence, oral narratives are routinely said by the Crown to be weak evidence.

There are several ways to understand these issues, as I will point out. Bahr (1993, 48), for example, considering mythology (one form of oral narrative) from a literary rather than a political perspective, notes that the floating gap is about something altogether different. The floating gap separates myth times (the prior, other world) and the present, thereby emphasizing the collective. No single individual can trace back to the myth times. Canadian Aboriginal oral historian Sonny McHalsie makes a related argument in Chapter 3.

The Crown has also suggested that Aboriginal people in Canada sometimes misunderstand culturally important materials, such as the origins and meaning of a two-row wampum belt with a purportedly incorrect attribution. More ominously, the Crown has implied that Aboriginal people outright misrepresent oral traditions to gain advantage in legal proceedings (von Gernet 1996). Such claims are neither new nor local. Strang (2006, 990) references *Kartinyeri v. The Commonwealth,* in which an anthropologist was threatened with a lawsuit and publicly accused of colluding in the invention of evidence in a land claims case with an Indigenous community for whom she acted as consultant. The anthropological evidence was eventually accepted by the Australian court, but the circumstances acted to suppress both anthropological and Indigenous knowledges. These issues, as they are presented in litigation, merely highlight the difficulties inherent in understanding oral materials rather than providing clarification.

But first, a prior question: What does one need to know before making legal claims about oral materials? Because one primary purpose here is to examine the steps along the way to the court, this is not the place to articulate the contemporary theories regarding oral materials in detail. It is valuable to point to the signposts, however. Current anthropological theory has moved far beyond simply debating whether Aboriginal oral materials are truthful, and therefore something like Western histories and available to being disassembled and refitted to historical analysis (Julie Cruikshank, personal communication, 2006). Historians may commonly have more of a focus on issues of reliability, given, in the majority of cases, their greater distance from the oral historical practice (e.g., Allen 1979, 111).

Newer social science approaches are concerned with examining the ways in which contemporary peoples use these narratives to think through and comment on the current situations in which they and their communities find themselves, and the ways in which communities remember and characterize some events and processes and discard others (see, for example, Gordillo 2004). These approaches feature collaboration between scholars and Aboriginal people (who are sometimes themselves scholars or employ scholarly methods), rather than being the production of scholars working with materials removed from communities.

As a starting point regarding what oral traditions are, I employ Cruikshank's working definition, "Broadly speaking, oral tradition (like history or anthropology) can be viewed as a coherent, open-ended system for constructing and transmitting knowledge," and her conclusion concerning "the evolving recognition that oral tradition anchors the present in the past" (Cruikshank 1994b, 408, 407). For Cruikshank, oral transmission of stories is pan-human and probably the oldest form of history-making (2005, 60). Perhaps even simpler is Schneider's concise notion (1995, 189) that oral traditions are all accounts important enough to be passed along in the collective memory of a group.

However oral materials articulated by Aboriginal people are understood in the scholarly community, when they enter the courts they are entering a foreign legal domain with its own considerable history and formal practices. For many, perhaps most, practitioners of the law in Canada, the introduction of Aboriginal oral narratives as a sort of testimony outside the conventional application of rules of evidence, perhaps even as expert testimony, into legal proceedings would surely be a great shock. At first blush, it would appear to violate the bedrock legal standard of the right to cross-examine the witness to an event. This is certainly the view of mainstream practising lawyers and judges I have interviewed whose work has not generally engaged Aboriginal issues.

Some work therefore has to be done to clarify how oral materials might enter into the practice of common law other than simply noting that to fail to do so would place Aboriginal people at a disadvantage and that fair dealing requires it. Scholars have pointed out that the common law, by its very history as an aggregation of local legal regimes shaped into a larger, national body of law, can and does accommodate Aboriginal law (for example, Borrows 2002, Russell 2000, Milward 2009), but this stops short of clarifying the particular problems of evidence law and the creative arguments that might be made regarding the compatibility of Aboriginal oral materials and Canadian courts. There are interesting conceptual legal arguments both for and against the use of oral traditions in Canadian courts. My purpose here is not to advance particular legal practices that may work in Canada, although

Chapter 5 considers these. Rather, I hope to entice legal scholars to engage this topic in light of the broader issues I will raise.

Because the oral history debate, as I have noted, is not confined to legal scholars and the court, it's useful to look at the arguments generated by anthropologists, historians, and other academics, particularly by those interested in or engaged in court testimony. These scholars have written concerning why oral narratives are or are not compatible with the methods and conclusions of their own disciplines. In response to the trial court decision in *Delgamuukw,* I edited a collection of essays that was published in 1992 as a special issue of *BC Studies* (vol. 95), with contributions by historian Robin Fisher and anthropologists Dara Culhane, Robin Ridington, Julie Cruikshank, and myself. Dora Wilson, a Gitxsan and a member of the litigation team, added a commentary. These essays raised questions about how and if Aboriginal perspectives can be heard in the court, and the nature of obstacles to this happening. This edited volume was one of the opening salvos on this topic. The Crown expert on oral histories, in his summary of the literature, cited this collection of papers as among the few to comment directly on the use of oral materials in court (von Gernet 1996). Others, in a variety of fields, have since offered new opinions.

Some, such as the archaeologist Ronald Mason (2000, 2006), argue from the position of normal science to find against the suitability of oral materials in court. These arguments focus on the incommensurability of science and Aboriginal ways of knowing and communicating. Others in the same discipline, for example Andrew Martindale (2006), conclude the converse and present compelling empirical evidence of oral materials persisting in communities over millennia as well as sophisticated theoretical explanations of why this is so. To some extent, all of these debates turn on the issue of fact as it is understood in the court, and reflect the different definitions of fact in legal and academic domains (Kandel 1992).

These issues are not simply Canadian issues, and other legal jurisdictions have something to contribute. Newman (2005, 242) went so far as to observe,

> In certain self-congratulatory moments, Canadian law might think of its response on Aboriginal oral history as having much to teach the world and little to learn from elsewhere. And, of course, *Delgamuukw* [the position regarding oral narratives given in Delgamuukw III] has been an inspiration to lawyers operating outside Canada as well. However, the achievement of

> *Delgamuukw* in this context ought not to, in the process, insulate us from learning from others. It is sometimes almost forgotten that the Supreme Court of Canada's openness to oral history in *Delgamuukw* was not an entirely novel attitude, even though previous Canadian cases had already begun the process of opening to oral history evidence. We can, moreover, also sometimes see a pragmatic use of oral history evidence in even earlier cases elsewhere.

But I think Newman is a bit uncharitable here. The Zuni land case he cites as case in point *(Zuni Tribe of New Mexico v. United States)* involved only the living memories of people, many or all of whom were not trained tribal oral historians. These are nothing like the formal chiefly narratives of clan history presented in *Delgamuukw,* nor are the issues involved in their deployment as evidence the same as in the Canadian case. The evidence did not require the consideration of exceptions to the hearsay rule.

The Narrator

I wish to make clear my own engagement with the issue of oral narratives and their incorporation in legal affairs. For twenty-one years I have worked as a university professor, and a little longer as an anthropological practitioner. I have provided expert testimony (which has included oral narratives) in various courts, tribunals, and commissions in both Canada and the United States. Sometimes the oral material came from my own interviews with tribal elders and other community members, and in other circumstances I have relied on recorded oral materials, occasionally, but not always, transcribed. I have been interested in the evolving standards regarding these materials, particularly the ways in which they have been tested and weighed in court. I have attempted to educate my own graduate students about the many issues related to oral narratives, and especially to point out to them the need for care in questioning, in recording context, and in making clear the limits of their own knowledge regarding the materials.

I have also attempted to broach serious issues regarding evidence directly with the Canadian Department of Justice, giving an invited talk to the National Aboriginal Law Litigation Conference in February 2004, and an invited talk at the Green College, University of British Columbia, Thematic Lecture Series entitled "The Shifting Culture of Conflict," attended by the chief justice of the Canadian Supreme Court. I have spoken on evidentiary issues, particularly oral narratives and governmental record keeping, at university law school classes and before the 11th Annual National Land

Claim Workshop, hosted by the Union of BC Indian Chiefs, in October 2003. I was invited by the Indigenous Bar Association to address a gathering of elders and Aboriginal lawyers regarding issues of oral evidence in March 2010.

In 2008 I travelled to Brazil to investigate, among other things, the ways in which oral narratives might be incorporated into a legal system based not on the English common law, but primarily on Roman law. I met with colleagues in Brazil, including the staff of the federal Ministério Público, the equivalent of a deputy attorney general's office, with members of the Brazilian anthropological association, which has a formal research relationship with the state, and with senior officials of FUNAI (the federal agency in charge of Indigenous affairs). I also taught a graduate seminar at the University of Brasília that included a federal employee of FUNAI who heads the federal process of the demarcation of lands. This is a process in which the lands belonging to the Indios are determined. I found that there is, effectively, no way for Brazilian Indigenous people to represent their own oral narratives directly in legal affairs. Rather, their narratives are filtered and tendered through anthropologists and other experts in reports to FUNAI. This is at the other end of the spectrum from the Canadian interest in oral narratives, and an issue of concern to the Ministério Público. The circumstances in Brazil reflect its tradition of civil, as opposed to common, law. But as in Canada, oral narratives of Aboriginal people are "cherry-picked" to support the legal narratives of other people (Cristhian DaSilva, Brazilian anthropologist, interview, 2008).

Together with Julie Cruikshank, I organized a graduate ethnographic field school, in conjunction with the Stó:lō Nation, spending portions of nine summers residing in a Coast Salish earth-floor longhouse. From this base, graduate students have fanned out into the mountainous Fraser Valley to carry out research, often involving oral narratives, with Stó:lō people. I also continue to carry out my own field research with Coast Salish peoples, interviewing members of several communities and helping to develop an understanding of their historical and contemporary practices and viewpoints. One such project, begun with the Stó:lō and then broadened to include other communities, culminated in a book about historical justice practices in the Coast Salish world.

More recently, I was engaged to examine the work of the anthropologist hired by the Crown as an expert on oral materials in a series of cases stretching across Canada and including several distinct Aboriginal cultures. As part of this work I read the Crown's expert reports and many hundreds of pages of testimony under cross-examination. I provided my ideas on this as a consultant and, in one case, submitted a rebuttal report to the court. Anthropologist Julie Cruikshank provided her insights to me in this work.

Meanwhile, I spoke at a conference, *"Sui Generis,"* organized by the Canadian Department of Justice to bring together various participants, particularly judges, litigators, and experts, to discuss how to proceed with oral narratives and other questions about Aboriginal litigation. I present a précis of my paper in Chapter 4. Personally, I found this and related conferences insufficient and frustrating. Some speakers openly expressed their anger, including noted historians Arthur Ray and Jim Miller, dissatisfied by the present state of Aboriginal litigation in Canada, and many grumbled in private about the disinclination of the Crown to be truly open to new ways of thinking about the very questions that were the inspiration for the conferences. There was also fear of revealing too much to the other side. Nowhere were the sorts of issues I raise here addressed in these conferences, particularly those that challenge fundamental ideas about oral materials used in Crown conduct of Aboriginal litigation against the state. I applaud the Department of Justice for hosting these events but suggest we push further forward into a discussion of the nature of oral narratives and their engagement with legal proceedings that is both broader and more specific.

Recently the Department of Justice and the federal judiciary have entered into dialogue with the Indigenous Bar Association about the treatment of elders on the stand and the procedural issues regarding oral testimony, although this conversation has not raised many of the issues I address here (IBA 2009). Suggestions have been made that justices might intervene in the case of confrontational and disrespectful cross-examination of elders and that oral histories be presented without interruption, for example. Many participants in the 2010 Indigenous Bar Association meetings in Manitoba felt that there is no way for elders to give testimony in the current environment.

This book is organized to reflect the continuing dialogue, albeit a frustrating and discouraging one, among those interested in oral narratives and their role in the civil life of Canada and elsewhere. It is also personal, in that I have had a direct involvement and a small role in this dialogue over several years. I find it helpful not to erase my own involvement and I include my own oral history of involvement and the development of thinking on this topic. I wish to record something of the history of Crown practice. And, I don't believe that the box of Aboriginal knowledge need remain unopened, as Daly (2005) so aptly put it.

Organization of the Book

The first chapter is concerned with a series of issues that help to establish the questions I raise here, and reveal in more detail the differences and overlaps that exist between the various disciplinary practices that engage oral narratives. First, I consider the role of anthropology in the debate about oral narratives. Then, I examine the conceptual problems inherent in defining oral materials. Should they be called traditions, histories, narratives, or something else? Since there are different sorts of oral materials, no one term will serve all purposes. And each term reflects a particular vantage point and introduces its own problems. I think of oral materials of all sorts as narratives, and I argue that legal strategies and presentations in court share something in common in that they, too, depend on the construction of a storyline (Amsterdam and Bruner 2000).

Then the focus shifts to examining the different training academics and legal personnel receive and the consequent vast differences in their understandings of the idea of *fact*. I further consider what some Aboriginal peoples of Canada make of fact, and the sort of training many of them have undergone historically and contemporaneously. Is there a common ground here? I point to many overlaps in perspectives that might be better mined in coming to mutual understandings.

Next, I consider the issues before the court as they arise in the anthropological world, including sociocultural anthropology and archaeology. Noted archaeologists have written spirited position papers, arguing in all directions, regarding the nature of oral narratives and their suitability as evidence for understanding culture history, and, since many archaeologists give expert testimony in court, in courts themselves. Some archaeologists give compelling accounts of oral narratives that, they argue, accurately capture many centuries of changes in the environment, movement of ancestors, and so on. Others dispute this out of hand. These are the same questions raised in the court and belong to the larger conversation.

Then, I move to another anthropological venue, social-cultural anthropology, and examine the work of Andrew Wiget, an anthropologist, and his thoughts about testimony in the US case known as *Zuni*. I suggest that his approach is not a way forward, despite his considerable success in a US court. Still, academic commentary on *Zuni* suggests that oral narratives and anthropology were more successful in presenting evidence there than in the *Delgamuukw* trial. Wiget has argued that presentation in a deposition form rather than in a more free-flowing form of direct testimony helped to make the evidence more persuasive to a court.

Chapter 2 is entitled "The Social Life of Oral Narratives," and it introduces ideas heretofore entirely unknown in the dialogue about oral narratives and courts. I discuss an interview with tribal archivists about transformation. I ask, do oral narratives actually become documents, and if so, does this happen in the archives? The archivists provide a nuanced answer, suggesting that their thinking is more complex than conventionally understood and that the oral narratives they work with both have a form of life force and are open to revision by their authors. They associate the oral materials with culturally specific forms of ownership.

Next, I look at how Crown researchers use oral materials in Aboriginal litigation. These researchers reveal in interviews that decisions about the nature of particular oral materials are made *before* the court proceedings. This is part of the framing of a case and the creation of a storyline for the Crown litigators. In some instances, or perhaps most, information is assessed rapidly, data cherry-picked, and complex Aboriginal understandings missed entirely – even when there are both goodwill and ethical practices. The plaintiff's legal teams have their own ways of engaging oral materials, and the issues and problems are not entirely the same. I consider the views held by experienced legal practitioners working in Aboriginal litigation, as presented in an international conference.

Chapter 2 begins the consideration of Aboriginal perspectives in the discussion of tribal archives, but Chapter 3 engages them more fully. First, I examine what might be called the radical critique of Canadian law. By radical I do not mean views that call for an end to the Canadian state, although some may verge on this, but, rather, those whose propositions for change question some elements of the authority of the state or suggest that there may be more than one sovereign (others being First Nations themselves). Winona Wheeler and other Aboriginal scholars have presented their views to the court on oral materials, without success. But Wheeler's expert testimony remains a sophisticated, energetic, comprehensive view of the larger problem, and I consider her arguments, prior to concluding that their very complexity gave rise to the court's preference at that point for the approach taken by the Crown.

Then, I talk with an oral historian, Sonny McHalsie, whom I have worked with over the last twenty years. I ask *him* about his views of the key issues about oral narratives as understood by the Crown witness. His responses reveal grounds not anticipated by the Crown and show, sometimes indirectly, the ethnocentric bias in the Crown position. He responds to the view that

Aboriginal oral historians' testimony might be excluded if they have read the published materials about their communities by anthropologists and historians (sometimes called the problem of contamination) by pointing out that his concern is not *what the anthropologist or historian has written but how the scholar has distorted what he or she has been told.* He entirely refocuses contamination and other questions raised by the Crown.

There are other sources of insight outside of Canada into the question of integrating oral narratives into the court. The United States has a system of tribal courts that hold significant civil and criminal jurisdictions, although with contested limitations. While some literature claims that even tribal courts have little room for oral narratives, this is not entirely the case. Finally, I look at how oral narratives have been deployed in other jurisdictions.

Chapter 4, "Court and Crown," concerns the responses of both the Canadian Crown and the court to the problems that have arisen in implementing a new approach to oral narratives. I begin by considering recent shifts in the Canadian court's positions on oral narratives. Then, I present a précis of my own talk at the federal *"Sui Generis"* conference, held in February 2007. I argue that academics engaged in the use of oral materials in court must acknowledge the nature of our own non-Aboriginal systems of education, knowledge, and authority, just as McHalsie acknowledges his own Aboriginal education. I suggest that some elements of our Western systems are concealed in the way testimony is constructed and presented, to the detriment of the express purpose of expert witnessing, which is to be of help to the court (in this instance, regarding oral narratives). Next, I briefly sketch the activities regarding oral history testimony of the major Crown witness and present questions he was asked to answer in preparing a background report for the Department of Justice on this topic. This report concerning oral materials (von Gernet 1996) has underwritten the Crown position in more than a dozen cases. It is, in effect, the Crown theory of oral narratives. I refer to this report in Chapter 4, and my work here is in dialogue with this Crown report.

I then consider a Crown expert report, itself built on the 1996 Crown document. Because the Crown has a fiduciary and moral duty to the Aboriginal peoples of Canada, I take careful note of the arguments, and in some instances my own reading of the sources leads me to different conclusions about oral materials.

In Chapter 5, I turn to the nature of evidence, the rules of evidence, and the means by which evidence might be evaluated. I examine Canadian law, not from the vantage point of a legal practitioner, but from an anthropological perspective. I suggest some potential resolutions to problems regarding evidence, as I understand them from interviews with legal professionals and from the literature, and move to a review of where the Canadian court's opinions on these topics seems to be going.

Finally, Chapter 6 points to ways in which we might reconceptualize the problems around oral narratives. In particular, I suggest we move beyond a simple notion of oral historians as mere reproducers of narratives passed along to them by another generation. Instead I suggest that we understand recognized oral historians as something like Western historians inasmuch as they, too, use the materials available to them to work through intellectual problems regarding the past and present of their communities. Such people can and should be incorporated into the Canadian legal system as experts.

Throughout this book I use various terms to refer to people and groups whose ancestors (some or all) predate the arrival of Europeans to North America. In Canada, the terms *First Nations* and *First Peoples* are commonly used to refer to some of the communities of peoples who are aboriginal to the territory. Other terms include *Inuit* (for the northern peoples of the Arctic) and *Métis* (for those descended from mixed communities that arose in the nineteenth century and were composed of Aboriginal peoples and various of the settler populations). Sometimes the term *Métis* is used for those who are simply of mixed descent. The terms *Aboriginal, Indigenous, Native,* and *Indian* are used in daily life in particular parts of Canada, but not in others, and not in all circumstances. Each term carries connotations that are unacceptable to some of the Aboriginal peoples of Canada. I use *Aboriginal* as a cover term for all three groups. Federal legislation refers to *Indians,* and I use that term when referring to legislation and the language of government agencies. Today, the terms *Aboriginal* and *Indigenous* are commonly capitalized in Canada.

In some instances I use the term *Indigenous* to emphasize *priority,* the circumstance of being somewhere before the land's colonizers, and the legal entailments following from that priority, including rights and titles to lands and resources. The term *Crown* originally referred to the authority of the monarch; today in Canada it refers to the apparatus of government and specifically, here, to the Department of Justice and the legal teams engaged in litigation against the First Nations and other Aboriginal peoples. Finally, the process of colonization in Canada has led to the grouping of Aboriginal peoples into small units with formal relationships with the Crown. These are called *bands,* and when bands group themselves together they are commonly called *tribes* or *tribal councils.* The term *nation* is also sometimes used by Aboriginal peoples in Canada to reference the state-to-state relationship they commonly desire with Canada. Finally, I use the term *state* to refer to institutions of governance in countries other than Canada. I use social science conventions of citation, rather than legal ones, because I am writing as a social scientist.

1 Issues in Law and Social Science

The Role of Anthropology

My discipline, anthropology, has its own role in the present conundrum and has failed to adequately present information about the ways in which oral narratives operate. This is of major concern because one could argue that the strength of sociocultural anthropology is both the study of deep local knowledge and the production of comparative ethnography (ethnology), which, taken together, create contextualization. This contextualization is sometimes antithetical to the adversarial procedures and the rules of evidence in Canadian and other courts. However, anthropology has a role to play in creating context for the court.

Denny writes, "Western thought has only one distinctive property separating it from both agricultural and hunter-gathering societies – decontextualization. Decontextualization is the handling of information in a way that either disconnects other information or backgrounds it." He observes that all societies use context and differentiation, but argues, "Higher differentiation is making more distinctions *within* a thought unit, whereas higher contextualization, as implied above, is making more connections to *other* thought units ... different cultures make some of these thought patterns fluent and automatic, whereas the opposite pattern remains unusual and cumbersome" (Denny 1991, 66).

In a wry, cutting, and deeply contentious 1996 commentary on the original decision in *Delgamuukw v. British Columbia* published in *PoLAR*, an anthropology journal, Robert Paine laid part of the blame for the failure of oral narratives as evidence in court at the feet of anthropologists, those most associated with the recording and entry of oral narratives into court. He demanded a closer look be taken at how expert testimony is engaged in litigation and how oral narratives are contextualized, and called for closer cooperation between disciplines in working out the intellectual and practical problems:

> Now, our discipline has itself wrestled with the epistemological riddle of belief as a kind of fact. Boas and Lowie, early in this century, both rejected oral tradition as "history." Then, post-World War I, came the Malinowskian historical "charter" mode of interpretation. This was followed, post-World War II, by the literalism of Vansina *(Oral Tradition)*; and in recent years by the critique of the "error of literalism" and so on.
>
> I'm drawn to the simple (but not, I trust, simplistic) conclusion that some "backgrounding" – for the court and the judge – as to how anthropology has tussled with this issue would have surely helped. Thence one should proceed to an *interpretation* of the Gitksan and Wet'suwet'en "faith-as-fact" as testimony with evidentiary value. As it was, it seems to have been assumed the judge knew little of all this and would "buy" what he was told by an expert witness (for it also seems to have been supposed that's what "expert" means). In fact, the Chief Justice was left to draw his own conclusions. More's the pity that they were largely wrong conclusions. (Paine 1996, 59)

Paine continues immediately:

> *Issue §2: Oral Testimony*
> Similarly, it falls to the anthropologist as expert witness to explain the exegetical process involved in oral narration. Julie Cruikshank, a specialist in the field, tells us: Each narrative *contains more than one message.* The listener is part of the storytelling event too, and a good listener is expected to bring different life experiences to the story each time he or she hears it and *to learn different things* from it at each hearing (Cruikshank 1992, 33; my emphases). "More than one message" – what place is there for that in lay persons' (let alone in Western jurisprudence's) idea of truth? Similarly, we cannot expect judges, juries (or, in the future, parliamentarians?) to be comfortable with the "veiled language of cosmological symbolism" in which oral testimony may be encoded (Willis 1980, 31).

> In *Delgamuukw,* the plaintiffs and the judge, it seems, each ended up imputing a literalism to the other. In McEachern's view what the Gitxsan and Wet'suwet'en were claiming as literally true is not so, it is "only" myth; and the Gitxsan and Wet'suwet'en felt McEachern rejected their myths because (I suppose them to say), "He says they are not literally true and yet we do not present them as literal truths in the way the judge means when he speaks of something being literally true or not." There are different denotations of *literal* here; for the Gitxsan and Wet'suwet'en, their myths are "literally true" in the sense that they carry an "*ipso facto* truth" (Brown and Roberts 1980, 8); but for McEachern, "literally true" means *factually true* in a proven sense (in written documents preferably). Expert witnesses, *led by counsel,* should untangle this. It appears not to have happened. (Paine 1996, 61)

If, as Paine observes, oral narratives contain more than one message, how is a trial judge to understand and meaningfully evaluate the evidence?

The problems Paine describes sometimes arise from wildly different perceptions of science and the humanities. These differences, and their significance, became apparent at a 1995 meeting of anthropologists. The original *Delgamuukw* decision, and its treatment and rejection of oral narratives and anthropological testimony, caused so much consternation among Canadian anthropologists that I organized a session to talk about it. This session was entitled "Anthropologists On Stage and Back Stage: Expert Witnessing in First Nation Litigation," presented at the twenty-second Annual Meeting of the Canadian Anthropology Society (CASCA), Learned Societies Conference, in May 1995. The session generated impassioned, even angry, exchanges, especially about the position taken by Robert Paine, introduced above. Another, open session at this meeting brought together a large crowd of anthropologists to consider what to do in light of the failure of testimony to be meaningfully heard and weighed in *Delgamuukw.*

The question was raised: If anthropological testimony regarding Aboriginal culture and society (itself heavily reliant on oral narratives) was rejected because anthropologists are too close to the communities they study, as the trial judge in *Delgamuukw* said, what could be done (Mills 1994, 18)? Anthropologists Antonia Mills and Richard Daly had each spent three years living in one of the communities that brought suit in order to learn, in detail, information about the communities prior to offering expert opinions that incorporated oral narratives. Both have written their own frank accounts of their fieldwork, evidence, and testimony (Mills 1994; Daly 2005; and see Trigger 2004, 26, about this issue in Australia). Historian Arthur Ray (2003,

260) observes that the judge rejected the testimony of Mills and Daly because he did not understand the participant-observation method.

Someone suggested that anthropologists should provide testimony only about communities with which we have not worked. I have seen this done elsewhere (for example, in *United States v. Washington,* in which I offered testimony in its second phase), and the expert on oral narratives had not worked with any Aboriginal communities. However, this position inconveniently leaves the "expert" part out of "expert witness," and participants at this meeting gave no support for this suggestion. As Mills and Daly believe, published information reveals only part of the story about a community, and fieldwork is fundamental to gaining detailed understanding. Mills and others have criticized Crown expert witnesses who have testified concerning Aboriginal communities in which they have done no original research (Mills 1994, 19). This position is congruent with the notion that fieldwork is essential to understanding the context and meaning of oral narratives. The oral narratives are always more complex than what is written about them, shorn of the context of delivery, and what is written is inevitably a truncated version of a much longer piece.

Eugene Arima's study (1976) of Inuit recall, for example, gives striking evidence of the importance of detailed knowledge of a community as a prerequisite to evaluating the reliability and constancy of its body of oral historians and its oral narratives. Arima evaluated language (which he believed was constant over several centuries), details of technology (such as particular design features of kayaks), folklore, and historical material. Arima knew intimately the details of kayaks (he had learned to expertly construct them) and other features of technology, and, significantly, pointed to local concepts of evaluation of narratives. He noted, for example, Inuit awareness that their own recall of traditional, formalized materials may outlive "empirically 'self-conscious' historic" narratives (33). Arima's work shows the value of local practices of assessment, as does Sonny McHalsie, a contemporary Coast Salish oral historian, whose views are considered later in this chapter. In light of such work it is difficult to imagine social scientists offering testimony about oral narratives without fieldwork-based intensive knowledge.

Defining Oral Tradition/History/Narrative

One of the major problems in integrating oral traditions into the court is simply defining the term and its cognates. Too many of the definitions, or manipulations of definitions, appear to have been created by those without direct experience with them, or are too focused on a limited inventory of examples and types. My argument follows that of Cohen (1989) in emphasizing the diversity of types, and their frequently mundane nature. In addition, the role of Aboriginal intellectuals in working with the oral traditions from their own society is largely unexamined. Since many of these Aboriginal oral historians *are* historians, I suggest that their oral narratives, at least some varieties, should be referred to as *oral histories*. The more conventional use of the term *oral history* refers to a "research method where a sound recording is made of an interview about first-hand experience occurring during the lifetime of an eyewitness." *Oral tradition* is sometimes used to refer to either "a body of material retained from the past" or "a process by which information is transmitted from one generation to the next" (Cruikshank 1994b, 404). Neither term as presently conceived leaves space for recognizing the process of thinking and analysis undertaken by Aboriginal intellectuals.

Cohen (1989, 9) in arguing against a "rigidity of thinking" put it this way: "This paper points to flaws in formalist definitions of 'oral tradition' ... Historical tradition in regions ... is not lodged in a distinctive series of texts read as 'oral tradition' but is engaged in and derives from the everyday critical, lively intelligence which surrounds status, activities, gestures, and speech." Cohen cites Rosaldo (1980), noting his objection that current expectations and definitions hamper our ability to hear what is being said (and see Cruikshank 1994b, 409; Rosaldo 1989).

Oral tradition, says Cohen (1989, 9), has been thought to have its own specialized characteristics and its own "separate processual and cultural life." A reified oral tradition, he writes, has become part of the conceptual equipment of Africanists, notably Jan Vansina, and at a cost. This, I believe, is one of the problems of relying on the work of Africanists when encountering the work of Aboriginal peoples in North American courts, as the Canadian and American courts have done. Wiget (1982), a careful observer of American Indian oral narratives, notes two differences between the content of the oral narratives and the approach of the academic practitioners. One is Vansina's (and others') reliance on "fixed form" testimonies with culturally prescribed formal controls, whereas North American Aboriginal communities more frequently have "free form" testimonies (181). Second, Vansina and Henige's view that the introduction into oral narratives of publicly shared symbolic content is "distortion," Wiget argues, can be supplanted by paying attention to the metahistorical framework that supports the narrative (197). Daly (2005, 39) describes such a framework for Gitxsan oral histories: "These figures [House crests] and events overlap to an extent with the narratives and crests of certain other Houses and clans, such that a web of oral historical association is woven over the feasting area."

Cohen (1989) cites Henige (1980), in particular, for advancing formalist definitions and for rejecting materials that failed to conform to his own approach. This has been a serious problem in the Canadian courts. Cohen also notes the work of Cunnison (1951), who argued for a bifurcated approach, contrasting local with national histories, in his work with the Luapula. Local folk's considerable knowledge of the past is embedded in and part of social processes, which gives a "firmness and utility transcending the more general histories focused on throne and nation" (Cohen 1989, 11). Cohen writes of oral traditions that result from elder group processes, with each elder providing some of the documentation based on a "very broad knowledge of present and past contexts" (ibid.). He observes that among the Smaraka of Suriname, "straight-forward storytelling" is "rather unimportant," but, importantly, points to the idiosyncratic and continuous assemblage of expert knowledge in numerous settings. The historians there play an active role, listening, doing research, constructing their knowledge, and becoming experts. They are, in a word, historians who operate in an oral venue. They hold no formal status as historians, but their knowledge is entered into juridical practices (12).

Renato Rosaldo is one of the best-known scholars to have criticized over-formulaic views of oral narratives. In particular, he critiqued Vansina's early work (1965), which "overlooked a number of central methodological issues" (Rosaldo 1980, 89; and see Beidelman 1970). Rosaldo (1980, 92) observes that skipping lightly over the narrative form of texts is like studying sonnets while ignoring their poetic form. He argues that Ilongot historical consciousness, the subject of his own research, differs from our own; the job of cultural analysis is to provide an account of how they perceive their own history rather than to deny their version of how their lives have changed over the years. History, he says, is a cultural construct, and "plundering other people's narratives by sifting them into degrees of facticity – true, probable, possible, false – risks misunderstanding their meanings" (91). To grasp the message, he says, you have to work through the medium.

Most significantly, he writes,

> Because the Ilongot have neither specialized historians nor centralized political authority, they also lack a single memorized official version of their past. Thus Vansina's methods for studying fixed and undistorted group testimonies simply do not apply for he has made the ethnographic error of

> regarding rather rare forms of society and history as if they were more generally representative. I would submit that people in all human societies recall the events of their own lives and therefore method in oral history ... insofar as it purports to have general validity – should begin by studying what is most widespread. (Rosaldo 1980, 91)

He notes that Ilongot stories "mapped onto each other" and that "a larger history could be pieced together from the assemblage of personal accounts" (ibid.). This is, I might add, the work of community historians as well as outsiders.

Cruikshank questions whether there is a basis for generalization about oral narratives. Current theory "destabilizes" the simple idea *"that there is a prescriptive, cross-culturally valid method for assessing their historical value"* (emphasis in original). Further, she writes, "If there are broad pan-North American similarities in storytelling traditions, they probably have more to do with epistemology than with content." She observes that Indigenous people who grow up with these traditions believe that rather than subjecting oral narratives to formal analysis, one should absorb successive personal messages in repeated tellings. Storytelling, she writes, should be studied as a practice that is part of everyday life and provides a "framework" for understanding both historical and contemporary issues (Cruikshank 2005, 60).

A sustained example of the development and work of such an oral historian in a North American Aboriginal context is the work of Stó:lō Nation cultural advisor Albert (Sonny) McHalsie, which I recorded and published as a chapter in a book I edited (McHalsie 2007). McHalsie has other published written work, but this chapter is essentially an oral product, tape-recorded and transcribed to paper. McHalsie made revisions and I edited for minor errors, mostly mumbles. His chapter reveals many of the features presented by Cohen. McHalsie listens, thinks, and synthesizes information learned from a variety of community elders and others, and, over the space of a few decades, became a recognized expert in the history of his community.

McHalsie (2007, 82) observes that an important Stó:lō cultural teaching is that learning is a lifelong quest, and an oral historian is expected to continue to learn. In addition, McHalsie continually relies on his own insights, oral histories given by others, and the work of academic and amateur ethnographers and archaeologists, including their field notes. He relies on these in different ways, and is aware of the deficiencies and advantages of both material from his own community and outsiders.

The following reveals something of McHalsie's understanding of the limitations of the work of academics and the sort of connections he makes in his own scholarly work:

> Look at the word *S'ólh Téméxw*. The last syllable in *Téméxw* is *méxw* – "to do with like the dirt." What do we call ourselves? We call ourselves Xwélmexw. Not only that, our neighbours, who are considered to be part of the Salish, have that as part of their word that describes themselves – Lillooet-Stl'atl'imx. It's a little bit different, there's an "mph" in the sound. And you have the Nlaka'pamux. And you have the Secwepemc. They all have that little mexw sound at the end of their name, just like we call ourselves Xwélmexw. Not only are we Stó:lō, the river people, but we're also Xwélmexw. And so we're connected to the dirt and to the world.
>
> Our burial practices were very important. We had the burial mounds and we had the tree burials. When I talked about tree burials with the late Rosaleen George and Elizabeth Herrling, they said there was a tree burial across from Frank Malloway's house, across from Yeqwyeqwi:ws. Rosaleen was saying that at that tree burial place, when they used to put the people up in the trees, it was usually the large maple trees that were used. And that the branch had to be touching the ground when they put the people in there. The branch had to be touching the ground, that was an important part of it. It had to be connected to the ground. And the one tree burial that was up in Skw'átets, Elizabeth Herrling talked about that. There was a platform that extended across from one maple tree to another.
>
> *Researchers do not ordinarily include these kinds of connections in their work* [emphasis added]. For example, linguist Brent Galloway was talking about how he'd collect the name and the meaning to the name. And that was the scope of his work. He wasn't interested in any other context that could be provided. For instance Agnes Kelly – I was talking about how I'd missed out on doing that final day of work with Agnes Kelly – there are probably more specific details I could have gotten out of her. There's one rock with a story of a young maiden who was transformed to stone and all Brent collected was the name and the meaning of that name, but he never asked "Why was this young girl transformed to stone?" or anything like that. So there's no adequate context for this story. It's very limited. As for me, I'm interested in those sorts of things. And the other example is amateur ethnographer Oliver Wells. I just get so frustrated reading his transcripts because he was only interested in language. So every single time

> where he writes in his book, "Oh okay. That's very ... that's very nice! I'll come back and talk to you about that." Every time, you know the elder's just going to tell him something, wants to tell him something that's just *so important!* And then Wells cuts him off and says, "What's the word for this?" You know – "what's the word for this" or something. That's all he was collecting, was the language. He didn't realize that what these elders were trying to do him was provide him with a context that would enable him to understand – it's not just about the language and the meaning of the words. Oliver Wells contributes a lot to our understanding if you read the transcripts, but it's just so limited. If he had been more interested in those stories and realized their importance, he would have said "Yeah! Tell me that story!" or "Tell me the story in your language!" or something like that. But quite often, you go through those interviews, and you come to where he says, "Oh. That's a nice story, I'll come back to you." And of course, he never does. All those stories are lost, and the elders, his informants, were ready to tell to him. There were important stories that we'd have a lot of use for today, but they're lost (McHalsie 2007, 108-9).

McHalsie's extended account of learning about a Stó:lō memorial site illustrates how he learned from listening to his elders and the importance of connection to place in the production of historical understandings. The strength of his historical interpretations is a consequence of the growth of his own knowledge:

> The other thing, too, is that at Í:yem there's the Eayem memorial, there's a monument. It's a memorial to the Stó:lō people: they've got the sign right there. It says "Eayem memorial 1938 AD Erected by the Stallo Indians in memory of many hundreds of our forefathers buried here. This is one of six ancient cemeteries within our five mile Native fishing grounds which we inherited from our ancestors. R.I.P." That memorial is set up at the cemetery there at IR [Indian reserve] 22, also known as Bell Crossing. It was set up by my great-grandfather Dennis S. Peters along with the help of Isaac James, who was his brother-in-law. And they set that up in 1938. I always wondered about the connection of that to the Great Fraser Midden Cairn, which was erected in the same year. I always wondered if my great-grandfather had seen that one and wanted to do that up there – I don't know. It's something that I've always wondered about because they were both erected in the same year, in 1938. When you look at that memorial what are the key messages? To me, my great-grandfather wanted to make sure that we remember

the cemeteries that are up there. He wanted to make sure that we remember the name of the place, the Eayem memorial. It was erected by the Stó:lō, so the Stó:lō is an important part there. He wants to make sure we remember our ancestors – "many hundreds of our forefathers buried here." It is "one of six ancient cemeteries" so that makes you go, "Where are the other five?" The other five would be the one right at Yale, or Xwoxwelá:lhp, the one at Xelhálwh, the one at Q'aleliktel, Aseláw, Í:yem, and the one at Lexwts'okwá:m. Those are the six. This is one of those six. These are located "within our five mile Native fishing grounds," so that's the other key message: we are not to forget about our fishing grounds "which we inherited from our ancestors."

There are a lot of teachings just in the wording of that memorial. It's only last Saturday that we had a memorial for my cousin, the late Herman Peters or Siya:mia. In preparation for that I wanted to find out a little more about his name because it comes from one of my ancestors. And it's an important name because it's a leader's name. I had known that, over the years: I had seen references to it, but I had never really looked at them. I find out that Siya:mia, the very first Siya:mia, was from Í:yem. That's one thing I've learned as well – that it's really important to have personal connections to places. And I didn't really have a personal connection to Í:yem; it's a place where I don't go fishing. I know my grandfather fished just upriver from Í:yem where Rita Pete fishes now. My grandfather fished there. And then I know that Dennis Peters erected that memorial, our great-grandfather erected that memorial. I often wondered, "Why did he do that?" I looked at the different teachings contained in the memorial itself, but at the same time, wondered what personal connection he had there? I often wondered that, so when I found out that Siya:mia – that's Dennis S. Peters' name as well, I think he was number three, Siya:mia number three. And then the original Siya:mia was right there from Í:yem and actually lived in one of those pithouses there. So I thought, "Wow! So that's the personal connection!" That's probably the personal connection that he had to the place and he wanted to do something. That was his memorial. Not only was he taking care of his own personal connection to the place but also he was taking care of the Stó:lō, remembering our ancestors and the burial grounds and the fishing grounds.

I think that is really important to actually have a connection to place. Because you have to look at the oral history and how the oral history is shared: it's called sxwóxwiyám. Sxwóxwiyám are the stories about when Xexá:ls, the Transformers, travelled to our land to make the world right. The three bear brothers and bear sister who were orphans, were Transformers. They were children of Red-Headed Woodpecker and Black Bear.

> They travelled from the head of Harrison Lake down to the Fraser, up the river to the sunrise, through the sky to the sunset to back upriver again. (McHalsie 2007, 91-92)

Both of these excerpts reveal several elements of Stó:lō historical practice. McHalsie provides his genealogy, a demonstration of the grounds on which he may, in part, claim his stature as an oral historian, and also of his limitations, in that he is not the descendant of other people with other knowledge. His work incorporates both the spiritual and the otherwise insignificant and mundane. He also reveals how his knowledge is thematically organized around the idea of *S'ólh Téméxw*, translated as "taking care of the land." (Thematic organization is an issue I address later in this chapter concerning Wiget's work with the Zuni.) Further, the oral histories, and his own interpretations, are related to "teachings" (McHalsie 2007, 85), by which he means core, widely understood cultural notions of appropriate behaviour and, in some instances, knowledge particular to one's own family.

Significantly, the McHalsie chapter (2007) also addresses two of the issues raised by the Crown in its effort to counter oral histories in court, and in Chapter 3 of this book he addresses many of the others in an interview. These are the problem of differences of opinion among Aboriginal oral historians and what to make of an apparent failure of chronology in oral histories. Archaeologist Ronald Mason (2000, 2006) has argued, as I discuss later in this chapter, that chronology is essential to history and that without proper chronology, there is no history. But McHalsie's work shows a sort of history that simultaneously incorporates stories operating in various time scales. It takes someone trained in the historiographic methods of this community to understand this practice, although it need not be a Stó:lō or other Aboriginal person. And, concerning the contention that oral histories fail as histories because they are particularistic and not open to outsiders, McHalsie's work reveals a historiographic sensibility open to others. The University of Saskatchewan historian Keith Thor Carlson, with whom McHalsie often works, arguably, is one of these. Julie Cruikshank, professor emerita of anthropology at the University of British Columbia, is certainly another. There are still others.

McHalsie describes a Stó:lō approach to chronology:

> The other thing, though, I always like to talk about, is how when you look at that story or listen to that story and they talk about the sores on the body, Wilson Duff actually looked at it. But he didn't look at it as a story about

> smallpox, I mean based on the stories he was told. He said that, based on the genealogy of Mrs. Bob Joe and the origin of the *sxwó:yxwey,* he estimated that the *sxwó:yxwey* must have originated around the 1780s. Now, if you look at 1782, that's when the very first smallpox epidemic happened. None of the elders has ever said that the sores on the young boy were smallpox. But I think it was smallpox. One of our other biggest teachings is that whenever there's something bad, there's always got to be something good. It's kind of a balance, you never really know. An encounter with a *stl'aleqem* could be bad – it could harm you. Or else you could get something good out of it, like the encounter with the water baby. You could learn something or you could die from it! My mother, when she saw little people, she was told by her grandfather, "Next time you see those little people you might die." It could be that tragic. But at the same time, you could also learn something from it.
>
> I keep that in mind when I look at the story of the *sxwó:yxwey*. I can imagine if those sores were smallpox, and the huge devastation that that had on our people – nine out of ten people dying – that something good had to come out of it. And when you ask elders today, depending on who you talk to, some elders will say, "Oh the *sxwó:yxwey* is only a couple hundred years old." Some elders will say, "No, the *sxwó:yxwey* is thousands of years old." And so while you try to disprove or try to prove one of them, you really can't. You can look at the genealogies of some families and say, "Oh yeah, that must be around 1780." But then what about the other ones that are saying it's thousands of years old? Well, they're partly correct as well because after the smallpox epidemic there were certain teachings that needed to be retained, and elements of those teachings that were retained were inside the *sxwó:yxwey* story. That's what's made it real so that it could be believed and could become a sacred part of our culture and our tradition. So those old teachings are encompassed in there. To me, that's why I think that an elder says it's thousands of years old is right because there are teachings within the story that are probably thousands of years old. Within this story that's only two hundred years old. (McHalsie 2007, 116-17)

McHalsie's narrative shows that Aboriginal oral historians have their own approach to characterizing oral narratives and the role of oral historians. Val Napoleon (2009, 36), an Aboriginal legal scholar, for example, emphasizes a particular feature in defining oral history as "formal legal theory information, pedagogy as legal reasoning, and as representing Gitksan people's enduring connections to the land."

Fact in Law and Academia, and among First Nations

A related fundamental problem facing those who wish to use oral narratives in court is the existence of very different ideas of fact, evidence, credibility, and truth held by the court, by social scientists and historians, and by Indigenous peoples themselves. Some observers fear that oral narratives will be continually classed as belief and not as fact (Simpkins 2000, 188; Roness and McNeil 2000, 70). Others are concerned that oral narratives may be "cherry-picked" for "facts," by virtue of an inadequate approach that considers these narratives as broadly homogeneous data about "what really happened" (Cruikshank 2005, 60; Cristhian DaSilva, interview, 2008).

Sometimes these differences simply manifest themselves in confusion, annoyance, and muted contempt for the ideas of others. Daly (2005, 5-6) describes this phenomenon:

> The actors in the courtroom arena coexist uneasily. They are ultimately coerced to conform to the procedures and views of the judiciary. The officials of the judiciary, in general, neither accept nor acknowledge what is the *aqua vita* of both everyday life and the anthropological universe; namely an awareness of the importance of grasping the contextual complexity as it arises out of alternative cultural and historical trajectories of social action. The litigants and their arbitrator, the judge, play by a set of rules central to the organization of the nation-state – rules often little understood by other actors in the courtroom field of action.

Daly movingly describes the responses of a "hypothetical" Gitxsan female chief, a woman of reputation in her own community, giving testimony: "But here on this witness bench she is not accorded the smallest scrap of respect. Any old lawyer can interrupt her words whenever she or he likes. The Judge does the same. Then they ignore her and argue fiercely about her words [oral narratives] or the 'justice' of admitting them into the evidence" (6-7).

The court can be the location of culture shock for both judges and Indigenous elders. These differences make it difficult to *hear* and comprehend the perspective of others and to evaluate what they say as evidence. They can also complicate the preparations for trial or make them inadequate, as in the case of the Chagossians living in the UK, which I discuss below. This situation is not a two-way street; rather, it is more like a four-way intersection of lawyers, judges, experts, and plaintiffs. Because judges and lawyers are trained in the same systems of thought and for the most part come from similar ethnic and class backgrounds, I will consider them equivalents for the sake of this discussion.

In my own experience, these epistemological differences are rarely addressed directly. In contrast, Pandey, an expert who gave testimony in *Zuni Tribe of New Mexico v. United States,* found the trial judge interested in Zuni mythology and what it indicated about claims to land (Wiget 1995). However, my own expert testimony about Indigenous oral history and cultural and social practices has more than once elicited comments by the trial judge that I was interesting and that he would like to drink a beer with me on some future occasion. In one memorable case, a judge told me that he wished me to translate my comments about sacred sites into something that he, as a good Catholic boy, could understand (Miller 1998). I tried to do this, describing Coast Salish sacred sites as something like European cathedrals, and he responded by telling me the sites were more like the Holy Grail. In these cases, I intuited that the judges found the testimony quaint, folklorish, romantic, ethereal, and concerning stories about days gone by, but *not* important in the real and present world.

Mills (1994, 29) describes giving testimony before an unbelieving judge in *Delgamuukw,* and characterizes the judge's response to her testimony as a variety of culture shock (30). To these judges, ideas about Aboriginal culture are interesting enough to potentially spend time hearing about in a pub, beer in hand, but they remain simply lore. They aren't really something relevant to the court and they aren't *true* in a legal sense. The significance and the epistemological basis of these ideas is invisible to the court. It's helpful to hear that this was not the case in *Zuni,* nor need it always be. Such cases point to disciplinary differences in reasoning and in determining the relevance of evidence.

Another example of the issue of disciplinary differences arose in *Delgamuukw* concerning how historians understand fact, and, hence, history as evidence. Gover and Macaulay report that

> counsel for the plaintiff objected to a distinction made by McEachern C.J. between what does and does not qualify as historical fact and therefore what is and is not admissible under the exception to the hearsay rule for notorious facts of history. In so doing, plaintiff's counsel pointed out that such a distinction was contrary to the way historians approach their discipline. He cited an academic paper in which the author espoused the view that a fact may acquire status as an historical fact if scholars of good repute

are satisfied with the accuracy of the source material and its relevance to other historical facts or theories and restate it in their historical writings. In rejecting this argument, McEachern C.J. pointed to the *differences between the disciplines of lawyer and historian:*

> [H]istorical facts are always open to dispute and revision and history is frequently being rewritten. Testimony in litigation, on the other hand, once admitted into evidence and interpreted by a court, becomes fixed inter-parties even though the same evidence out of the context of the litigation could, as an intellectual exercise, be given a different interpretation by subsequent scholars or upon other facts emerging to change the context ... *[My] answer to ... [his] submission is simply that we legal people have our own discipline and I think we must stick with it.* (Gover and Macaulay 1996, 5, quoting *Delgamuukw,* 689-90, with emphasis added)

Chief Justice McEachern was also concerned with the differences between legal facts and Aboriginal concepts. He observed that he rejected the oral historical testimony of elders not because he believed that they were untruthful but "because he had a different view of what is fact and what is belief" (Asch and Bell 1994, 542). (Roness and McNeil [2000, 71] note that he was later criticized for this view by Chief Justice Lamer, who noted that the wholly distinctive nature of Aboriginal concepts demands a unique, *sui generis,* approach.)

The justice's use of oral narrative, historical, and anthropological data led to an immediate response by academics who condemned his treatment of the testimony and evidence presented by members of their own disciplines (Miller 1992b; Cassidy 1992; Niezen 2003, 13), and retorts by an anthropologist (Ridington 1992) and a historian (Fisher 1992) that experts need to become more aware of the assumptions of judges. The Crown expert (von Gernet 1996), in turn, wrote deploring these expressions of discontent. Asch (1992, 227), contra to Chief Justice McEachern's comments about history, observed that anthropological testimony *can* potentially fit into legal contexts concerning findings of facts, but that McEachern's judgment uncritically accepted information as factually accurate that was most likely the product of ethnocentric bias. Asch was here referring to the sociocultural branch of anthropology. Howver, several archaeologists (among them Anyon et al. 1997, 83), scholars from another branch of anthropology, took a more narrow view and noted that science relies on disproving hypotheses, a process that may not be acceptable in the use of oral traditions in legal settings.

The issue runs deeper than the results in one or two trials, however. In arguing that social scientists would find more success in the courts if they were aware of the ways in which logic is used in legal settings, Kandel (1992), a law professor with a doctorate in anthropology, has succinctly summarized six key differences between the thinking of anthropologists and members of the legal profession. She is writing from a natural science model of anthropology rather than from the humanistic wing of the discipline, which features understanding rather than explanation.

Kandel observes that law is focused on locating liability, fixing social responsibility so that direct action can be taken to correct, punish, ameliorate, or recompense. Beneath these actions lies a moral imperative that is essential to legal thought. The search for liability, then, "guides the scope, content, and quality of truth, information, and explanation in a virtually teleological fashion" (Kandel 1992, 1-2). Social sciences, on the other hand, create non-teleological explanatory analysis. Second, while anthropology is best practised non-judgmentally, ordinarily within some version of cultural relativity, the law explicitly seeks to render judgment to resolve disputes. Law, she writes, is normative and judgmental (3).

Third, law works through concrete, specific disputes. In law, abstract principles are applied to specific cases. Anthropology, on the other hand, produces explanation that is systemic, holistic, and abstract. It transcends the individuals and the case studies that are frequently the subjects of research. In the fourth instance, in the law "the meaning of causality is inseparable from the concept of responsibility. The search for legal causality is not a scientific search" (Kandel 1992, 3). The law seeks to isolate the parties responsible. For anthropology, causality is commonly statistical and probabilistic in nature and is not focused on isolating a particular individual. This is the distinction between discrete and multifactorial causality.

Next, she points to differences in the meaning of truth and fact. Here she considers the narrativity of the courtroom, where truth lies in the outcome of a battle between competing viewpoints framed for the court and determined by peer evaluation. In the law, then, truth lies in the story told by a witness to a human act. The concepts of credibility and objectivity do not overlap between the disciplines of law and anthropology. In social sciences, *objective* is what is "outside the observer" and *subjective* is what is inside. But, Kandel writes, "Legally when a jury is told to apply a 'subjective' test it means to apply the standard of what the person on trial thinks – the 'outsider' standard. By contrast, when a jury is told to apply an 'objective' test, it means the jury should apply the standard that the jury thinks the community or average person subscribes to – an 'insider' standard." Hence, the credibility of a witness is not synonymous with objectivity in a scientific sense. Equally important is the distinction between the legal idea of fact and that in social sciences. In the law, a fact is "not an element of raw data" but, rather, a finding made within a moral and normative context (Kandel 1992, 3).

An interesting feature of Kandel's analysis is the emphasis on the narrativity in the court. Facts are the outcome of peer evaluation of narratives, of the sort described by Crown researchers (see Chapter 2). This is oddly parallel to the construction of fact in some Aboriginal communities, in which peers, the community of relevant elders and others, evaluate the oral narrative (or, as it is alternatively called, the oral history) on several dimensions. These evaluative features include the appropriate citations (as in oral footnoting), the standing of the speaker (which parallels the establishment of expertise in the English common law system or, perhaps, the Islamic sharia court's use of oaths by men of standing and reputation), and the appropriateness of the fact to the occasion at hand. This, in turn, parallels the legal notion of fact-in-context, that facts are not being established for abstract scientific reasons, but for a particular case.

And, if what is legally "objective" is what the community thinks, then, this, too, overlaps with Aboriginal practice. Consider the case of a potlatch, an important ceremonial event among any of the Northwest Coast nations of Canada and the United States: what is "fact" (for example, that a particular person has properly assumed the position of chief) is so because the community found the narrative presented by his side in support of his chiefly attributes to be more compelling than any alternative narrative at the potlatch. Indeed, potlatches are sometimes described as having law-like functions, as quasi-jural processes of adjudication, and as instruments to register changes in status (such as the assumption of a chiefly name), and to proclaim the law publicly (Miller 2001; see Culhane 1998, 120). There are parallels between these diverse systems of thought and practice as well as divergences.

Rigby and Sevareid (1992) write that lawyers and anthropologists are trained in different intellectual traditions and work within different intellectual cultures and, in consequence, their approaches to fact are different. Asche (2004, 56) refers to "a difference in epistemology between lawyers and anthropologists." But Paul (2004, 145) argues that history and law have "a shared tradition of positivist, empirical notions of evidence," to her, an old-fashioned sort of history from the period before the changes in the discipline in the 1960s. She observes that working with lawyers and talking history "can feel like time travel."

I'm not fully convinced by Rigby and Sevareid's conclusions, in part because law students ordinarily enter law school with undergraduate training in disciplines such as history, anthropology, and literature. And all law students are exposed to the same media. Rigby and Sevareid claim to demonstrate these differences by the varying reactions to a classic anthropological film, *Dead Birds,* produced in 1963 by Robert Gardiner. The film is an account of the Dani, a Papuan people in the central highlands of New Guinea. In Rigby and Sevareid's words (1992, 5), "The film shows two confederations of Dani men throwing spears at each other. They fight only in the daytime and stop if it begins to rain (so their feathers will not get wet). They fight until one person is killed and then adjourn for a month, one side to celebrate, the other to mourn and cremate the dead." It's important to add that there is a spiritual dimension to the fighting.

Rigby and Sevareid found that law students accept the film as portraying facts that they use as evidence to argue for a Hobbesian view of human nature, which must be contained, and the consequent need for systems of law. Anthropology students, they say, "react differently. Their first reaction is to question the 'facts.' Does the film accurately portray Dani warfare? Is it indigenous or a product of colonialism? Has the filmmaker imposed Western categories?" These differing responses "reflect differences in epistemology between anthropologists and lawyers," and these differences, they claim, lie in their training (Rigby and Sevareid 1992, 5-6).

I informally tested this theory by showing the film to two classes of senior undergraduate anthropology majors and two classes of law students studying evidence law, all at the University of British Columbia. Then, with the help of note taker Joseph Weiss, we engaged the students in an open-ended conversation about the film. I found little support for the theory; the law students reflected a broad interest in "fact" as understood through prior training in cultural and other studies and a widespread awareness of criticism. For the most part, they sounded like social scientists, although a few outliers conformed to Rigby and Sevareid's characterizations and eagerly adopted and embraced legal language and thinking. In all fairness to these scholars, my experiment was perhaps fifteen years later and conducted in a different country. But my experience indicates that there is not such a clear distinction in viewpoint between the groups.

Rosen (2006, 92-93) observes that the creation of fact in legal systems, including the common law, is, at its core, a cultural process, and one with considerable flexibility. Law students, it turns out, are influenced by the general North American culture of cynicism and critique. And the expectations of differences in epistemology among the groups in question – Indigenous oral narrators, academics, legal people – need to be undertaken with caution, due to considerable overlap in thinking and in categories. There are legal personnel with training in social sciences, Aboriginal people with law degrees, social scientists with long exposure to and interest in Aboriginal perspectives. The unexpected hybridity and the interpenetration of categories is part of the interest in working with Aboriginal litigation. (In Chapter 4, I consider in more detail another feature of the socialization into the disciplines, namely, the systems of training and authority on which expert witnesses' knowledge is based).

Niezen (2003, 11), an anthropologist, questions where judges get their ideas about the tenuous anthropological concept of culture, arguing that in the current Canadian court these ideas come in part from anthropological and historical expert opinion, but are more connected to the idea of "fact," to international human rights standards, and, possibly, to public opinion. Public opinion, he writes, includes the view that Aboriginal culture is defunct and deployed simply to gain advantage in resource competitions, such as the salmon fishery (18). He points out that judges are more oriented to "facts" than to developing or elaborating new theoretical paradigms.

Culhane (1998, 95) observes that judges prefer to rely on their own "common sense" in evaluating Native testimony, and, presumably, culture, as opposed to what the members of these societies themselves say. This is the case, she writes, "before and after" the ruling by Mr. Justice Mahoney, who presided over *Hamlet of Baker Lake v. Canada (Minister of Indian Affairs and Northern Development),* a 1980 Canadian federal court decision in an Inuit land claim case that required the litigants to prove "that they and their ancestors were members of an organized society." All of this is particularly important because Canadian law, since *Ontario (A.G.) v. Bear Island Foundation* in 1985, sets a legal test for Aboriginal title that requires an Aboriginal right be "integral to the distinctive culture." Aboriginal culture was thereby defined and codified by the law (Culhane 1998, 104).

But Rigby and Sevareid have more to say regarding the thoughts of lawyers and anthropologists. Lawyers and judges, they write, come to see themselves as pragmatists and empiricists. They adopt the "twin myths" of judicial neutrality and legal reasoning, which together compose the "rule of law." The rule of law, "a concept more 'sensed' than articulated by American law students, is rooted in the metaphysical belief that law is 'natural' (as in natural law theory) and not the mere 'command of the sovereign' (positivist jurisprudence)" (Rigby and Sevareid 1992, 6-7, quoting Friedmann 1967, 258-60). Law therefore is independent of people or society and can be discovered by the process of reasoning. The myth of judicial neutrality, then, depends on a belief in an open mind, free of preconceptions, and the ability to reason correctly. Incorrect reasoning will not enable the judge to "find" the law because of a failure to move between the major facts and the controlling principles of law. The notion of a lack of bias is derived from the concept of natural justice. Contemporary anthropology, on the other hand, is fixated on observer bias and the problems of reflexivity, they write. Rigby and Sevareid are no doubt overstating the importance of natural law in the thinking of law students, who intermingle their thoughts with ideas of positive law – that is, law created by human lawmakers. They are perhaps closer to the mark regarding the perspective of many contemporary anthropology students.

Rigby and Sevareid (1992) further describe legal reasoning as operating syllogistically, with a major premise, a minor premise, and a conclusion, in an Aristotelian mode. A well-known example is "All men are mortal, Socrates is a man, therefore Socrates is mortal." The syllogism itself depends on compare-and-contrast reasoning, rather than strict logical deduction. But the two authors note that the Socrates syllogism is one in which the premises are unquestionably true. This is not always the case, and law students, they claim, are primarily trained to critique the syllogistic reasoning of judges in appellate court case opinions rather than the less accessible process whereby raw data become the significant facts of a case. The students don't study the trial transcripts or the pleadings to see what event has triggered the lawsuit. And they have not observed the events themselves.

Rigby and Sevareid (1992, 8) describe briefly the journey from the "raw phenomena of experience to legal fact." Their description of this journey interests me because it parallels the journey of oral narratives from narration to possibly becoming legal fact, or to legal neglect. Little attention is paid to this part of the story of the legal system, although scholars of law and society have a renewed interest in examining the "lenses" through which the stories, the initial narratives, of lay people are translated into legal narratives and legal proceedings (e.g., Ewick and Silbey 1998). Rigby and Sevareid tell us that in the first stage of the journey of raw phenomena, facts are selected on the basis of their relevance to the issues in a case. Other facts are rejected on the same basis. The story at this point is beginning to have shape, an outline. The evidence presented before the jury or judge is already highly selective. Then, in the next stage, the trier of fact draws from the pool of evidence the "ultimate" facts, those that will be used in forming the court's decision. The raw phenomena thus become a work product of the trier of fact and "law," which, in yet another stage, can be directly imported into another case as established fact. The law students study the end product rather than the sort of data studied by anthropology students, but, the authors claim, the law students are not usually aware that their facts are selected abstractions (Rigby and Sevareid 1992, 8-9). In brief, legal training directs lawyers to ignore context and the normative aspects of decisions.

The Crown and sometimes the court have largely overlooked the context and normative aspects of oral narratives. In one instance, in 2005, *Samson Indian Nation and Band v. Canada* [*Samson*], the court has ruled that court time need not be spent on hearing interpreters of the narratives, which plaintiffs have requested so that their context, and ultimately their meaning, be clear to the court. Perhaps this decision reflects a difference in approach to fact as well as the great differences between training for the law and the work required to become an oral historian. These differences may be a key source of difficulty and of the claims of incommensurability or impracticality coming from both sides of the debate over oral narratives in court. For oral historians, it is all about context, and their credibility in the community depends on this.

Finally, Rigby and Sevareid claim that litigators, those practising law, are pragmatists with an approach to facts grounded in nineteenth-century English positivistic empiricism. I believe this is what Chief Justice McEachern (above) was referring to in his comments about the differences between the methods of historians and judges; he was reaffirming his commitment to positivistic empiricism. This approach to facts assumes an independent existence of events and state of affairs, assumes that true statements are those that correspond with facts about these events and state of affairs, and further assumes that knowledge of these is possible and that specified standards of proof exist for statements of fact about them. In this approach, present knowledge is partial, and therefore establishing the truth about past events is a matter of probabilities or likelihoods. Finally, allegations about the past are based on a stock of knowledge that includes, in a descending scale of probability, generalizations accepted by the scientific community, the opinions of experts, and, finally, "common-sense" generalizations (Rigby and Sevareid 1992, 10-11, following Twinning 1984).

It's worth adding that the common-sense generalizations can be interjected through judicial review, a process whereby a judge can notify the court of reliance on his or her own body of knowledge. It was this component of the judgment in *Delgamuukw* that was disturbing to some scholars, such as historian Robin Fisher (1992) who wrote of judges as amateur historians, or my own complaint about "common sense and plain language" (Miller 1992a), the idea that what is held to be common sense embeds unexamined and often biased viewpoints. In the Australian context, Paul (2004, 146) objected to the same sort of legal "common sense" view of history and the view that documents "speak for themselves" and do not need interpretation.

Legal logic, in short, derives from the contradictory philosophic traditions of the metaphysical belief in natural law and the strict empiricism of John Locke, who believed that ideas are derived from experience (Rigby and Sevareid 1992, 11), but it also includes classical Greek syllogistic thought. Rigby and Sevareid conclude that lawyers believe they can look at facts without preconceptions and judges believe they can be objective and neutral, and see "true" facts among competing discourses. Scholars in the interdisciplinary field of "law and society" have reported a range of judicial approaches – including those who "uphold the law," the legal positivists Rigby and Sevareid comment on, those who attempt to bypass the law to effect a reconciliation between parties, those interested in writing new law, and so on (Conley and O'Barr 1998, 89).

My own interviews and conversations with judges over several years confirm this plurality of attitudes and aspirations on the bench, despite whatever commonalities may have been in their training and backgrounds. Often, the differences are idiosyncratic. One judge, through his own experience, doesn't trust police testimony, another was the first woman in her area on the bench, another the first Aboriginal person. But Rigby and Sevareid write that judges first must have a theory of the case, which they hold consciously or otherwise. They can then reason from this major premise to reach the minor premise and conclusion (Rigby and Sevareid 1992, 20). Although there are differences in the approaches of judges, they all must have an underlying theory of the case, or, rephrased, a frame, as these authors suggest. What Rigby and Sevareid describe as a theory of the case must emerge from the individual's own judicial consciousness. Furniss (1999), for example, wrote that Chief Justice McEachern's views in *Delgamuukw* reflected widespread, conventional beliefs supported by multiple epistemologies. The judge's reasons for his judgment included what she has termed the "frontier myth" of empty land, and a struggle of white values of self-reliance, democracy, and competition against opposite and degraded Aboriginal values.

Geertz's classic essay "Local Knowledge: Fact and Law in Comparative Perspective" (1983) provides anthropologists and other interested parties a lesson in comparative logic from the vantage point of interpretive anthropology, far different from the sort of anthropology described by Kandel (1992), or Rigby and Sevareid (1992). Geertz points out significant similarities between law and anthropology and suggests that law is an interpretive affair, like the sort of anthropology he practised. These similarities wouldn't appear to the practitioners of a more natural-science, hypothesis-testing anthropology Geertz sought to displace. He writes,

> Between the *skeletonization* of fact so as to narrow moral issues to the point where determinate rules can be employed to decide them (to my mind the defining feature of legal process) and the *schematization* of social action so that it can be construed in cultural terms (the defining feature, also to my mind, of ethnographic analysis) there is more than a passing family resemblance. (Geertz 1983, 170-71, emphasis mine)

Geertz points to both systems of knowledge and practice as based on local knowledge and on seeing broad principles in parochial facts. In an interesting twist, the kind of anthropology that has these points of similarity to the law is not the sort that finds favour in the courts. Judges may practise judicial review, but anthropologists cannot invoke "anthropological review," although they are entitled as expert witnesses to draw on their own experience. It's not the anthropologists' courtroom. The favoured version of anthropology is the sort that diverges from the epistemology of the law. In fact, Geertzian interpretivist anthropology has been attacked by the Crown as postmodern, as failing to affirm the tenets of positivist empiricism noted above and thereby failing to have utility in the court (von Gernet 1996). The Crown expert's approach, as I show later, was to label sophisticated work by leading scholars of oral narrative as having the failings of postmodernity, a bogeyman to devotees of normal science anthropology. Within the interpretivist framework, it is difficult to establish facts acceptable to the court. Just as the judge finds facts with certainty (although the appeals court may disagree with the interpretation of them), scientific, rather than humanistic or culturalistic anthropology, most easily finds its way in the court.

Indigenous Ideas of Fact and Knowledge

Indigenous perspectives on fact and knowledge are often different yet again from those of lawyers and social scientists, but there are also important parallels. All the Indigenous peoples of Canada or of North America do not share one single perspective on this topic. It's a mistake to think so, despite the many efforts by Aboriginal people to identify essential traits of Aboriginal people (see Miller 2004 for a summary of some of these). Such approaches seek to differentiate Aboriginal people from those of European descent, but this effort at binary logic ordinarily obscures more than it illuminates. Still, a piece by an Aboriginal scholar, Clara Sue Kidwell (1991), points in interesting directions and allows for variation among Aboriginal perspectives. She argues that historical Aboriginal modes of thought and Western science are both oriented to the same outcome: predicting events and processes in order to successfully find one's way economically and to appropriately use the environment. But the processes underlying the two modes of thought, she writes, are fundamentally different. Indigenous thought relies on observation of an animated universe to understand the particularities of the beings present there and of the other features of the environment. From this understanding comes the ability to form predictions of what may happen (without presuming that it will) and plan for the future.

European-derived modes of science (what I have referred to as normal science), on the other hand, at least since the scientific revolution following Newton and his generation, rely on controlled experiments or mathematical proofs with elements of what has come to be understood as a largely inanimate universe. These experiments or proofs allow the identification of regularities of nature that form scientific laws. This leads to the ability to predict the probability or even absolute likelihood of future events. Both Aboriginal and European (or Euro-American) thought, for example, may be concerned with the relationship between rain and flooding, but European thought looks for generalization and historical Aboriginal thought, resistant to generalization, looks for the particular.

This perspective is echoed by Naranjo (1995), who writes, concerning the relationship between archaeology and Aboriginal oral histories, that oral traditions are often axiomatic, rather than hypothetical. Science searches for exclusive and universal truths, while Indigenous oral traditions are used to obtain a *multiversal* understanding of the past that operates at multiple levels (see Anyon et al. 1997, 81).

Jean-Guy Goulet (1998) observes that Cree forms of knowledge, and theories of learning, rest on the development of individual experience. True knowledge can be obtained only through experience. This world view is resistant to generalization and dependent on direct engagement. Children learn by observation, gradually inferring meaning from stories that do not give explicit moral lessons, and by forming their character to become attuned to the natural world and all its beings. This approach is considerably different from the Euro-Canadian system of memorization of facts and theories derived by a previous generation, as in, for example, memorization and application of the Pythagorean theorem. Nor are Indigenous theories of education associated with argument by authority (for example, requirements to memorize the theorem, often independent of any context). Robin Ridington (1990) put this as "little bit know something," meaning that knowledge among the Cree is personal and often private. People don't let on what they know because it reveals private information about who they are. Knowledge is individual, unlike the universalizing and public notion of fact in Western science.

The Cree and other groups, however, are not without oral traditions that constitute a form of knowledge held by the group rather than privately by individuals. There are also important differences in epistemology and social practice between communities. Mills writes that the Wet'suwet'en giving testimony in *Delgamuukw* did not believe that they were giving hearsay evidence. Rather, they were giving *evidence,* since in their society, unlike the Cree, no critical distinctions are drawn between ideas learned from direct observation and those conveyed orally:

> The Witsuwit'en understanding of what one is empowered to talk about is not the same as the concept of hearsay in Western jurisprudence. A thorny issue in *Delgamuukw* was the willingness and ability of the lawyers for the Crown and the judge to listen to and understand the import of Witsuwit'en (and Gitxsan) oral traditions and to accept as valid evidence testimony about events that were not observed by the witness, but that he or she had the authority, under Witsuwit'en tradition, to talk about. (Mills 2005, 34)

It's easy to see how these culturally different ideas about the nature of "facts" are important to the courtroom and to the understanding of oral narratives. The work of Goulet and Ridington helps explain why Aboriginal people will commonly not speak beyond what they know directly, while Mills reveals the circumstances in which Wet'suwet'en do precisely that when they are trained in oral traditions. These scholars show why Aboriginal people may not wish to speak at all: some knowledge, even supposedly mundane knowledge, is connected to spiritual awareness and is private. The "facts" of oral narratives are understood according to one's development and capacity, rather than being accessible universally. Context and subtlety is more significant than generalization and law-like regularities. Efforts at understanding oral narratives by the Crown or in the early work of Vansina (1965; he recanted much of this earlier work [Ogot 2001, 48-49]), characterized by Robert Paine as "literalist" (Paine 1996), fall down when they seek out regularities instead of specificities. They are looking in all the wrong places and in all the wrong ways.

Anthropological Sparring

An Archaeological Debate

Ronald Mason is perhaps the leading archaeological exponent of, for lack of a better term, the "doubter's" position on oral traditions as historical data. Mason's work is important to consider in part because the Crown's expert relied heavily on it in the report submitted to the court in *Lax Kw'alaams Indian Band v. Canada* in 2007. Mason's argument is aimed at the increased use of oral materials within his discipline rather than the application of oral materials to legal settings. But he succinctly and thoughtfully raises key questions that must be considered in both domains. He writes, concerning the difficulties in incorporating oral materials, "Not least among these difficulties is that of attempting to reconcile inherently and profoundly different ways of conceptualizing the past without violating the integrity of one or the other or both ... The pro and con arguments ... raise such problems of incommensurability as to severely limit the fruitfulness and even desirability of making the attempt" (Mason 2000, 239). Interestingly, his notion of the incommensurability of oral materials and scientific archaeology echoes the arguments of incommensurability made by Aboriginal scholars who hold that oral traditions should be accounted for in court, but only within an Aboriginal epistemology and with Aboriginal interpretation (see, for example, Winona Wheeler [2001], or Deloria 1995).

These efforts to argue *for* the inclusion of oral historical materials on the basis of incommensurability have been rejected by the courts. In its extreme form, the problem of incommensurability would, on practical grounds, exclude Aboriginal thought, however it is expressed, from legal proceedings, because it could not be understood and applied. Other approaches focus on distinctiveness and difference within a framework of partial mutual comprehensibility. This latter position is what I argue here and is, I think, compatible with that of the Aboriginal legal scholar John Borrows (2001). Bahr (1993) advances the contrarian view that archaeology and mythology might be compatible but that archaeology has claimed the subject matter of myths and offers a bad deal to Aboriginal people.

Mason (2000, 239) takes the position that incompatible oral traditions, in common with other lines of evidence, should be excluded from archaeological work unless they can be shown "to enjoy preponderant weight." (This is not the test the court created in *Delgamuukw,* which created space for oral historical materials and the obligation of the court to consider oral testimony.) Mason's position can be considered to be that of normal science. He says that the enabling assumptions of archaeology as a science

> include the existence of a real world independent of observers regardless of how we construe what we apprehend; the conviction that the world is in principle knowable ... ; that it is sufficiently orderly to have permitted the growth of testable knowledge, knowledge that builds on itself (even by paradigm shifts) and facilitates the posing and investigation of questions previously beyond imagination; and that the procedures and findings of all sciences are ultimately mutually compatible. They cohere. (239-40)

Among all of these properties of science, Mason (2000) focuses most heavily on coherence, which refers to, in part, the mutuality of logic, the adherence to canons of evidence, and the suspicion of unsupported assertions. He clarifies that coherence cannot be confused with scientific omniscience. He worries about, but discards, accusations of ethnocentrism regarding the Western way of knowing and rejects the relativist idea that all knowledge claims ought to have equal status (240), noting that this position has led to claims both that Aboriginal oral histories ought to be included in the "universalist paradigm of science" and, in the opposite direction, to the rejection of science. Mason, like many in this debate, roots his view of oral history in the work of Jan Vansina, itself a source of problems as I have noted, although he has read more widely in the literature.

Regarding what seem to be the key questions, the veracity and applicability of oral traditions, Mason (2000, 242) provides a summary of pro and con arguments deployed by archaeologists but also ethnographers and ethnohistorians. He presents the following pro arguments (in abbreviated and slightly altered form):

1 Oral tradition is as valid as any other kind of information about the past.
2 Those who made their own history know it best.
3 Oral traditions, being emic, are unchallengeable by outsiders.
4 Much of the past survives only in the spoken word.
5 Verbal traditions and Western historiography access different kinds of knowledge and address parallel realities, each valid.
6 Archaeology and oral traditions overlap and in combination supply a richer view of the past.
7 Archaeology is ethnocentric and must be balanced by alternative histories.

Mason (2000, 242) reduces the con arguments (reasons *not* to use oral traditions in archaeology) to four propositions:

1 Oral traditions are not trustworthy because they are dependent on memory and verbal transmission.
2 The genre is more an artifact of contemporary culture than a record of the past.
3 Oral traditions are closed belief systems, beholden to authority and impervious to external challenge.
4 Oral traditions in their entirety or in part are sacred and therefore not accessible to outsiders, and their release depends on their guardians.

Mason (2000) notes that taken together, pro arguments 1 and 2 form the notion that oral traditions *transcend* scientific knowledge, thus eroding the idea of the equality of different ways of knowing. Science is thereby placed in an inferior position and universalism is defeated. His case appears to depend on the idea that proponents of the validity of oral traditions and the position that Aboriginals know their own history best move inevitably to the proposition that science and oral histories are irreconcilable. Mason doesn't so much object to religious and other views concerning oral traditions as believe that those with "pre-scientific metaphysics are not required to jettison their beliefs for those of scientists, *unless they presume to work at science*" (244, emphasis in original).

In this debate one rhetorical position is exchanged for another, and those Aboriginal people and their friends arguing for the exclusivity of knowledge joust with others arguing for the exclusivity of science built on an evolutionary perspective that regards Aboriginal metaphysics as merely "pre-scientific." I believe this argument echoes that of the Canadian Crown, which similarly placed oral traditions in a position subordinated to that of historical analysis. In the end, none of this debate goes beyond political posturing, although Mason explicitly sought to exclude this.

The third pro argument regarding emic phenomena and their supposed unchallengeable nature as forms of evidence is countered on the grounds that oral traditions are not simply the products of ancients, but, rather, are utterances of contemporary people. The pro argument depends on the idea of a distinctive enculturation into a particular Aboriginal value systems that non-Aboriginal archaeologists have not experienced. The current funding system for academic research, argues Mason, often contains imperatives regarding Aboriginal participation and demands the inclusion of Aboriginal knowledge.

In making his fourth pro argument, that much of our knowledge is only spoken, and therefore oral traditions must be relied on in archaeological science, Mason cites Lowie's conclusion that oral traditions cannot be regarded as true if they are not corroborated (Mason 2000, 245). Mason believes that Lowie is difficult to refute, quoting Lowie's 1917 notion that because we do not accept Aboriginal astronomy, biology, physics, and so on, we should equally not "exalt" Aboriginal history. Lowie's view, however, is far out of step with current views of Aboriginal astronomy and other sciences, which have attracted immense attention from the Western scientific community and lengthy debates over how to employ what has become known as "traditional ecological knowledge" (sometimes referred to as TEK; Julie Cruikshank, personal communication, 2006).

Mason raises the interesting questions of reliability: do all accounts tell the same story, and what do we do if they do not? He asks, if oral traditions are highly symbolic, how do we get to questions of fact? These are good questions, but there are reasonable answers beyond quoting Lowie, acknowledged by Mason as notoriously closed to oral traditions, to the effect that "many contemporary versions of traditions are to some extent the debris of an obliterated past" (Lowie cited in Mason 2000, 246) and suggesting that well-known contemporary scholars such as Bahr and Clifton have reached the same conclusions as Lowie. Mason (2000, 246) quotes Clifton's remarkably acerbic work (1989, 30), in which he observes, "Today's tradition often enough is last year's novelty." It simply seems to me that pointing to apparent cases of the failure of oral traditions isn't sufficient to exclude the argument, which I rephrase, that some important knowledge is known only orally. As we will see, the Crown, too, argues that much of the contemporary oral narrative is something like debris, as Lowie suggested.

Mason's argument features the idea that oral traditions are, at heart, religious and emotive, and these elements cannot be included in scientific research. He writes, "However much emotion is spur to motivation and a reward of research it is a potentially treacherous companion in the exercise of reason" (Mason 2000, 247). This is arguable; indeed, many have pointed to the benefits of a scientific inquiry that accounts directly for religion and emotions (see, for example, Goulet and Miller 2007). Mason (2000, 248) concludes that the ultimate test of evidence, including oral histories, is external verification or the openness to being discredited.

Mason (2000, 248) carefully observes that it is an error to view archaeology and oral traditions as entirely binary opposites:

> There is a good bit of empiricism and logical thinking in oral traditional history, and the realm of scientific archaeology and historiography supplies ample testimony to the universal human capacity to live with compartmentalized contradictions ... There is a leakage between these modalities, and each is not as impermeable as might at first seem. The genuine contrasts are in degrees of potential and actual openness to corrections by appeal not to authority but to evidence and rigorous argument.

Mason further develops his ideas about openness to criticism in disputing pro argument 6, that there is overlap between archaeology and oral traditions. He believes that the people he calls the guardians and transmitters of traditional history are largely immune from critical questioning, and that the traditionally accepted histories change over time due to inadequacies of human memory. These changes are presumably unnoticed. The tricky part of commenting on this is that Mason (2000, 248) is writing about traditional history that "has been accepted as truth from generation to generation," which suggests that he believes there are such long-term traditional histories, a position he otherwise does not seem to hold.

I can respond only that, in my experience in Aboriginal settings where important or sacred discourses are engaged, there is certainly the potential for dispute and refutation for those who don't get it right (see Bahr 1993, 47). In any case, oral historians are not jukeboxes that may or may not be able to accurately produce a recording, but rather thoughtful thinkers who, over the course of their lifetimes, gain deeper knowledge in diverse categories and piece together their own view of things. A good example of this is the document of Sonny McHalsie, the Stó:lō cultural heritage advisor who has written how he has come to know and use oral histories (McHalsie 2007). Oral historians are open to change and refinement (a more appropriate word than *correction*) through a long process of learning and piecing together an understanding of the world. Indeed, McHalsie reveals a constant course of refinement even after he has become a masterful and widely recognized oral historian.

In my experience, oral historians are openly criticized in ritual settings even to the point of being rejected in the work they are undertaking. An example is the giving of "Indian" names in the Coast Salish world. These ancestral names are held by senior members of extended families and given to family members who are thought to have particular qualities inherent in the name; they, in effect, reincarnate the name or are reincarnations of previous incumbents. The public gathering to announce the giving of the name requires a recitation of the history of the name and knowledge of the previous holders. But sometimes errors are made and, on occasion, the ceremony itself fails and the name is not passed down. Someone in the audience is able to dismantle the oral narrative presented in the longhouse, point to its errors, and present a more accurate and suitable narrative. Family members dread this outcome because it damages their reputation generally. In brief, the problem with Mason's discussion of the falsifiability of oral histories is that he fails to consider the processes of training of oral historians, their intellectual activity, and the many opportunities for correction or even refutation of those acting in the capacity of oral historians. Mason is thinking of too narrow a notion of oral tradition, a notion identified by Cohen (1989, 9).

Finally, in critiquing pro argument 7 that archaeology is ethnocentric and needs to be balanced by alternative histories, Mason (2000, 255) claims that archaeology is "not ethnocentric because it eschews the narcissistic, ethnically-unique, quasi-religious character of the latter societies [for example, historic Aboriginal societies] in favour of a universal, *culturally transcendent* epistemology in principle open to anyone instructed in its procedures" (emphasis mine). In Mason's view, the traditional knowledge of the Zuni or Hopi, in contrast, is off-limits. I don't think Western science can escape so lightly into transcendence. This really just avoids the argument about the definition of ethnocentricity by making the claim that the product of a particular tradition transcends the others. No doubt many victorious colonial generals, say, for example, my favourite, General (Chinese) Gordon, held this idea prior to his death in battle with colonials at Khartoum. Moreover, I can't imagine why Aboriginal people would wish to work with someone who defines their society as "narcissistic," which puts me in mind of the caustic reaction of Aboriginal undergraduate and graduate students at my university to Ruth Benedict's characterization (1934) of "Kwakiutl" society as Dionysian and Zuni as Apollonian. They get Benedict's underlying idea but don't like the crass reductionism.

Mason (2000, 260) concludes that oral traditions, because they are said to be vague, weak, or erroneous regarding time, which is less featured than place in Aboriginal thinking, are not history because "'History' sans chronology is not *history*." This is perhaps an old-fashioned approach to defining history that would likely equally reject the sort of personal and social histories that beleaguered professional historians during the 1980s, along with Studs Terkel's accounts of working people (1974, 1978) and the TV series *Roots,* and that later were incorporated into the Crown testimony against Aboriginal oral traditions. This approach would also reject the work of one of the founders of the European practice of history, Herodotus, whose works on the relations of Greeks and Egyptians was chronologically vague and involved telescoping of time. This issue does not appear to bother historian Roger Axtell (1997, 17), the former editor of *Ethnohistory* (1983-90), who notes that Aboriginal histories typically lack exact dates, but still are histories.

Oral traditions sometimes incorporate "fabulous beings involved in fantastic happenings" that occur in the recent period as well as the myth period. This troubles and mystifies Mason. "Things and events that never happened," he writes, "occur here as well as things that did, things that belong earlier are brought forward, dislocated, and transformed into something else." And, significantly, "events known on other grounds to have occurred are missing entirely or have been radically disguised by reinterpretation, mistake, or ignorance" (Mason 2000, 261). It's interesting that in his treatment Mason conflates various sorts of issues, including reinterpretation (even university historians do this; often, tenure depends on it), error (such as proposing that earthen mounds in Wisconsin were made in the nineteenth century) and, as he puts it, the "fabulous" or the engagement of the mythic in the lives of humans. Each of these issues requires its own sort of responses; they are not of a single category. All of them are also characteristic of history written by Euroamericans (we refer, even in print, to "the fabulous" as *luck,* sometimes even *Lady Luck,* or slip the issue by invoking "chance"). Non-Aboriginal academics simply have a less colourful, less anthropomorphized vocabulary than Aboriginal people.

Another issue from Mason (2000) that I wish to examine here is what might be thought of as contamination. In a section titled "the evaluation of sources," Mason asks several reasonable questions, such as "How knowledgeable is the informant?" (261). However, the phrasing is a giveaway here; the speaker is not an intellectual or a colleague or a collaborator, but rather an *informant* who might offer something to the scholar, who presumably knows better what to do with it. Academic knowledge is subtly situated as a higher form of knowledge, and, by implication, the culture of the academic is situated higher than that of the Aboriginal informant. This is simply to point out that Mason's work is saturated in hierarchy, and although he disavows ethnocentrism, the privileging of one's own group's practices and views over those of other groups *is* ethnocentrism. It's not necessarily a bad thing to value one's own ideas over those of others. But Aboriginal archaeologist Roger Echo-Hawk's view (1997; see 2000) is that legitimate insights into human past are frequently viewed as the sole prerogative of Euroamerican scholarship. He also notes that archaeologists are often unwilling to defer to Aboriginal experts on oral traditions because most of these experts are religious leaders who emphasize spiritual elements and see academic analysis as inappropriate (89). It might be tricky for some archaeologists to work with some Aboriginal oral historians when the shoe is on the other foot and the question is, how knowledgeable are the archaeologists, and, if they are knowledgeable, why are they asking such disrespectful questions?

Mason (2000, 261) further asks, "How did the informant come to know?" Notably, he continues by observing, "In the majority of cases, however, oral traditions are derived secondhand from ethnographers or historical documents, or even more indirectly from ethnohistorians." It's entirely unclear to me how Mason, or anybody else, might know that this occurs in a majority of cases; I'd like to see the empirical science behind that assertion. It may be a misreading of Henige (1974, 96), who observed that feedback is the "principal mechanism by which the contents of oral traditional accounts were adapted to form new coalesced traditions." Henige further speculated that "uncontaminated oral tradition simply does not exist any more except possibly in the most remote areas of Amazonia, the Philippines, or New Guinea" (1982, 85). Henige's use of the idea of contamination here implies disease and that "contaminated" oral materials should be cured or discarded like mouldy bread.

In my own experience in the Coast Salish world of Washington State and British Columbia, prominent oral historians commonly do read the works of those who have engaged with their communities over the last hundred years or so. Several know these works well. A fine example is the recently deceased Vi Hilbert, who was an official living treasure in Washington and a classically trained (in the Coast Salish sense) oral historian (see Hilbert 1985). She memorized long oral histories as a child at the bidding of her parents (Hilbert, personal communication, 2003). Over the last few decades she worked with a number of scholars to bring important oral traditions to print. She didn't believe print distorts them, but she did believe that print versions are shallow versions of the spoken ones, lacking something of the spiritual substance, just as does Tracey Joe, a tribal archivist whose work I consider in Chapter 2. Hilbert said that community members who do not participate in the oral literature of her community are undernourished (in Jennings 1997). She believed the written versions can help in the retrieval of the oral and that this effort might be engaged with the help of the sound of the Skagit River of her homeland. One of her collaborators was the anthropologist Jay Miller (no relation), whose work on ethno-ethnohistory (1998) is dismissed out-of-hand as patently fabulous by Mason (2000, 250). Miller's decades of careful, linguistically informed work with the most knowledgeable oral historians is of no use to someone who has a different view of what constitutes knowledge.

I have learned over nine summers living in a Coast Salish earth-floored longhouse that oral historians like to compare the ethnographic and ethnohistoric accounts and, sometimes, to point out errors or interpretations that seem odd to them. They are better off for having done so, I believe, and I can hardly imagine that they would not wish to look at what is written about their community and their history. To think otherwise is to hark back to a day when Aboriginal people were thought not (or were not) able to read what was written about them and scholars could afford to be less careful with their thoughts. In my experience, being read by Aboriginal people and being more careful with my thoughts does not impose a politically correct set of blinders, but instead creates a more interesting and informed dialogue. I appreciate, rather than object to, viewing scholarship as dialogical. Some archaeologists are among the few holdouts in North American anthropology who may feel they are free from observation by the observed. From one vantage point the subjects of archaeological investigation are dead societies, and possibly dead people, a subject Mason (2000) himself describes. But archaeologists are not dealing only with the dead, and many enjoy their relationship with the contemporary communities who are successors to their archaeological objects of study (see Schaepe 2007b).

On other occasions, Aboriginal oral historians seek information from written materials or the researchers themselves, as Mason suggests, and that is also good. In one instance, for example, I was called as a guest of honour at a naming ceremony and asked to comment on the history of a name being given to a boy based on my own archival research with the field notes of an anthropological predecessor some eighty years earlier. Mason thinks this sort of interconnection between precisely the people who have worked together over the last decades spoils the party. Again, this view does not recognize oral historians as intellectuals or interested parties who seek out information where they can, understanding full well that academic accounts of their own cultural practices and discourses have their own particular qualities and flavours.

Oral history materials and oral historians do not need to be hidden from view, an idea that is a curious manifestation of the noble savage idea, and the subsequent notion that real Indians wear buckskin or pounded cedar and don't read. It also has an underlying assumption that oral materials are transmitted only in particular ways, a common fallacy among those who encounter oral histories on paper rather than in a living community (see Cruikshank 1994b and Cohen 1989 on this point). If I were to interview an elder and record a particular piece of oratory, could I not play this tape to a younger community member and thereby secure its transmission? Apparently not, in this intercultural-intolerant viewpoint. And if not, then these particular assumptions about oral traditions should be made clear. Oral historian Sonny McHalsie offers his own views of the issue of contamination in Chapter 3.

In the end, Mason's critique of an archaeology that is informed by oral histories is that it requires too much effort. Oral tradition, he says, is too unlike archaeology as he understands it; it is too particularistic and unintegrated with Western science. There isn't enough epistemological common ground: "Like religion, you believe oral tradition or you don't" (Mason 2000, 262). I find these conclusions sad but widespread in the academy and in mainstream society. The distinguished Canadian geographer Cole Harris drew a similar conclusion after reading Cruikshank's award-winning book on oral histories and related matters, *Do Glaciers Listen?* (2005), concluding that Aboriginal stories about the world are too difficult to decipher, require expertise, and, ultimately, are not worth the effort (Harris 2005/06; personal communication, 2007; and see a rebuttal by Schreiber 2008). This is the position the court took in *Samson,* that spending the time and money on oral traditions was not worth the court's time. But do other disciplinary categories of knowledge get such short shrift in court?

Echo-Hawk (1997, 89) reverses perspectives on this question by noting that the complexity of oral traditions *discourages* scholarly interest, particularly given that the intellectual and cultural heritage of Aboriginal people is commonly regarded as inferior. To this, I add, why would a scholar give up on important material unless it is thought to be inferior in some sense? This perspective seems to ask, Why can't they simply do things the way we Western folks do? It is troubling that Mason's vantage point overlaps with those arguing for incommensurability. He appears to say that in practical terms there is incommensurability even if in theory there could be common ground.

Mason's analysis in many respects simply restates Lowie's position in his famous published debates in 1914-17 with Swanton and Dixon, critiqued later by Goldenweiser (1915; and see Thornton 2008). Lowie (1915, 598) critiqued the supposed uncritical use of oral materials and concluded that oral materials have no historical value "whatsoever under any conditions whatsoever." Whiteley (2002), in disputing Mason, has argued that oral narratives have both historical and mythological features, which can be distinguished, and a form of testability. Despite the influence of Lowie and of Malinowski's theories of myth as charter ([1926] 1948), Whiteley believes ethnohistorians have long realized that oral traditions contain material that is consistently reported with strong standards of verifiability. He writes, "That message, apparently, has not yet fully crossed over the divide from sociocultural anthropology to archaeology." But there is no clear divide, inasmuch as some sociocultural anthropologists and some archaeologists fall into the extreme doubter camp. For example, Clifton (1989) has edited a book with the apparent purpose of making clear the widespread fallibility of oral tradition and the outright invention of supposedly important Indian views, such as the "earthmother."

Ethnohistory, with its birth in the effort to meaningfully present various forms of evidence in the US Indian Court of Claims, may be the bridging discipline. I think we can look at the same set of problems that Mason (2000) has so clearly engaged and come to the opposite conclusion, that oral traditions *do* have a place in archaeology. Indeed, archaeologists *do* work with oral historians and oral histories (among others, Martindale 2006, Anyon et al. 1996; McGuire 1992; Watkins 2000, 2005; Colwell-Chathaphonh and Ferguson 2007; and see McGhee 2008 for a trenchant critique). Or, more simply, we might note that there can be different sorts of archaeology, including both those that engage with oral histories (asking particular archaeological questions and connecting with communities directly) and those that do not. Many things can be known independent of oral histories, but the record clearly tells me that there are benefits to engagement. Mason doesn't overlook this issue but he does disavow it.

The stalking horse in Mason's analysis is the postmodern, or its alter ego, extreme relativism. To his credit, I think, he does not retreat directly into the argument-by-authority position that often accompanies accusations of postmodernism. Yet Mason (2000, 256) writes, "One version of philosophic nihilism currently chic in academic circles, and even archaeological squares, sees nothing in historical disputations – or indeed in all knowledge and all claims to objectivity – but ideology, politics, and self-interest." He speaks of oral histories as novelties (246) and states that "the claim of mutual interdependence of two 'ways of knowing' about the past, one reliant on verbal tradition and faith, the other on empiricism and logical argument, is a *fact*" (248). Here he seems to be sticking his finger in the eye of any postmodernists who might be lingering and willing to dispute, on philosophic grounds, what a fact is and whether we can know one. He writes of "the fabulous" and the "fantastic," of the "Alice-in-Wonderland" qualities of Aboriginal histories, of the "foolish and angelic" among archaeologists who attempt to work with Aboriginal oral materials, and the "corrosive ecumenism of the irreconcilable," and, finally, he admonishes those who "eschew all vestiges of 'hegemonism'" (262). Who else today speaks of the relativism of knowledge, disputes notions of fact, and derides hegemonic discourse other than the postmodernists? For many in archaeology and in other social sciences the invocation of postmodernism draws a line, creates a binary, one side of which is beyond the pale (McGhee 2008; Smith 2005).

I have examined Mason's work in some detail because it raises many of the issues brought up by the Crown in defending against oral narratives, but in a more developed argument. Recently, Andrew Martindale (2006) has written a critique of the Mason position, focusing on a set of Tsimshian oral narratives known as *adaawx*. Martindale refers to the oral materials as "oral records" to create a parallel between archaeology and Aboriginal systems of thought through juxtaposing oral and archaeological "records." His terminology foreshadows his position. Martindale argues that the narratives are created within a structured system, such as those described by Cohen (1989) and Daly (2005), which provides historical referents that allow archaeologists to compare their own chronologies to those within the narratives. In particular, the recording of significant moments in Tsimshian history may reflect a universal feature of cultural historiography that derives from the working of the memory. This is not new, and many others have argued for the use of "significant moments" in the creation of chronologies by academics, although without invoking universals.

But Martindale (2006) suggests that oral narratives may be historically accurate for hundreds of years and ought to be included within archaeological studies, points that Mason (2000) rejects explicitly and the Crown rejects implicitly. Martindale gives three reasons. First, since apparent conjunctions exist between archaeological data and oral records, the most parsimonious explanation is that they derive from a common history. Second, Aboriginal protocols for the transmission of oral materials allow for replication fidelity in the absence of writing. This is the case at the lineage level of transmission, not the person-to-person level. It needn't depend simply on individuals getting it right. And third, oral narratives are structured around events and people that provide an internal "architecture" such that precise words can vary even while historical accuracy is maintained. This is a point that Aboriginal author Arthur Parker (1989, xxi) made almost a hundred years ago. Moreover, in law reliability of written documents need not be indicated by exact sameness but rather by whether meaning is constant (former judge Todd Miller, interview, 2008).

Martindale (2006) argues for commensurability or, as he puts it, "commonality" or "conjunction." Individuals from different cultures can gain insight into the practices of another because there are some similarities. He refers to a universal "grammar of memory and history." In its worst form, such a position can lead to Western academic views "subsuming" Aboriginal knowledge, as Mason (2000, cited in Martindale) suggests. But Martindale pushes for finding commonality and complementarity.

Martindale (2006) cautions that oral narratives such as *adaawx* need translation because of the epistemological differences between archaeology and Aboriginal perspectives. This is Aboriginal scholar Winona Wheeler's point (2001), but her view is more categorical. Martindale claims that since oral narratives can be understood on multiple levels, simple low-level chronologies might be derived by outsider archaeologists. He divides the meaning of oral narratives into two categories: the descriptive/external and the arbitrary/internal (170). The latter, he writes, is comprehensible to fewer people, and my reading of Wheeler suggests that she believes oral narratives are largely or perhaps entirely internal and arbitrary. By arbitrary Martindale appears to mean not necessarily subject to laws of causation and to

Western scientific investigation, and therefore not universalistic, as Mason would have it. By descriptive/external Martindale specifies the observable, operational, interpretable, and the abstract. This division of labour corresponds closely to the science/non-science distinction. Wheeler and Mason take the opposite extremes on this issue, and Martindale falls in the middle.

Martindale (2006) concludes that there are two primary approaches to the question of oral narratives and academic studies within archaeology and history. One camp argues that oral records include formal systems for their production and performance, and for the transmission of texts and of knowledge across time. The second group focuses on variability within the performative and narrative practice of records. This group, according to Martindale, sees oral records as weavings of traditional metaphors and narratives into spontaneous versions according to the relevance to the situated audience. I disagree with Martindale on this partitioning because it tends to flatten the differences between the oral materials of the diverse peoples on the planet. Moreover, both sorts of oral materials might exist in a single community.

But more important to the issue at stake in this book, variability has arisen in the court only as a reason to exclude material from the court or to devalue it if entered as evidence. To the Crown, variability means something entirely onerous. Further, the Crown has argued that even the second position Martindale articulates discredits oral narratives as evidence by virtue of its cultural relativism or even postmodernism. Even though Martindale writes directly about the Canadian litigation that has invoked the question of how Aboriginal oral materials ought to be understood in court, he doesn't address the legal ramifications of his discussion. Other anthropologists, including those in *Zuni,* approach issues of oral histories explicitly in their legal context.

The Problem with *Zuni*

The research team in the 1980s US litigation known as *Zuni* developed its own methodology for the presentation of *the* (a unitary, corporate understanding is ultimately necessary for the court) Zuni view of affairs. The litigation team put on evidence in the form of direct testimony of experts and depositions by elders who could recall features of the built and natural landscape in their youths in the 1910s and 1920s. The team also used expert anthropological testimony concerning Zuni mythology. Wiget has meticulously chronicled his work for the research team in his publications (1982, 1995, 1996). A great strength of the approach is that the team sought to convey an understanding based on the statements of the Zuni informants collectively, although I will suggest that this might be for the wrong reasons. They recognized that narratives within a community are linked in particular ways that convey meaning in a manner that individual narratives do not (see Rosaldo 1980, 97). Wiget (1995, 173) notes the need to develop a method to identify and evaluate the internal structure of oral traditions composed of dozens of testimonies to "develop the shared sense of the remembered past."

Ultimately, the methods employed were successful in the case, but I think they are not a template for other litigation, particularly in Canada, because of particular flaws and potential traps, which I will describe. There are two major reasons why this case isn't a useful precedent. First, as I have already noted, the depositions by Zuni elders were limited to events and processes these people had witnessed and did not include those they had heard about. The deponents (people giving depositions) were lay witnesses and exceptions to the hearsay rule were unnecessary. Second, none of the deponents appear to have been trained and recognized oral historians, although they were apparently people of good reputation in their community and selected for their good memories.

Wiget obtained twenty depositions in 1984 totalling more than 1,300 pages of text, some in English and some in translation. He reviewed thirteen depositions from earlier cases to establish the reliability of the memory of informants deposed in two cases. He was unable for reasons of time to test these depositions against those obtained by other expert witnesses. Further, he couldn't test the narratives for validity by comparing them with other documents. In fact, Wiget deliberately isolated himself from data drawn by other members of the team, whom he refers to as "scientific experts," to ensure that his interpretation of the oral materials was not influenced, consciously or otherwise, by the other information. He believes this strategy proved helpful in "revealing the integrity of the tradition" (1995, 174). It may well have played into the courts' received notion of how science should operate, particularly ideas of "blind" and "double blind" tests.

Wiget's theory (1995) is that the past is irrecoverable and that the record of the past is partial. Efforts to recount the past by their very nature select, with some elements excluded and other included. Recall of the past is *motivated* in particular ways that structure the "past-as-remembered" (173). The past makes sense only when it is *thematized,* that is, contained within a temporal sequence supplied with a motivational or causal framework. The past is thereby put into a *narrative,* and discrete elements are related to each other (175). Wiget mentions that such is the case for either oral or written materials, and is a reason to not assume oral materials are of lesser importance than those that are written. He cites Alice Hoffman (1984), on whom he relies heavily, to position what he claims is the majority opinion of historians that oral histories are one among several primary sources, and are better when made with "knowledgeable interviewers" who can promote the best record available. Hoffman's work, however, is *not* directed to oral narratives of Indigenous peoples; indeed, she mentions many research programs employing oral history methods, as she terms it, but not Indigenous topics. In particular, Hoffman writes that without corroborating evidence, oral histories are "a bit of esoterica whose worth cannot be properly evaluated" (71).

Significantly, Wiget (1995, 175) writes that "the usefulness of any historical record depends on understanding the ways in which the motives of the maker and the circumstances of its construction have shaped the record." This effort to find context depends on three steps. First, the *veracity* of the depositions must be evaluated, as they reflect the motives and circumstances behind the record as recalled. Second, the form of testimonies must be established concerning validity, reliability, and consistency. Third, a particular tradition, such as the Zuni "golden age," which he believes characterizes the depositions he took, must be analyzed to get at the motives and circumstances surrounding the record as constructed.

He argues that one should assume the purpose of the deposition shapes testimony by forcing on the deponent a concern for relevance to the upcoming case. He observes that the deponent is never free to order the recollections as he or she wishes because there is an external order to the deposition. However, he found that deponents may have a "settled sense of the past" (Wiget 1995, 175) and may be reluctant to give some kinds of information that lie outside of this framework.

Much of my problem with the *Zuni* approach lies in the team's understanding of validity, reliability, and consistency, and how these might be measured. Wiget defers to Hoffman's definitions (1984, 69). Validity here is the degree of conformity to other primary source materials such as documents, photos, diaries, and letters. In other words, validity is a measure of external corroboration. This sort of indiscriminate triangulation appears shallow and perhaps unwittingly assigns a primacy to written materials. No mention is made of weighing the merits of the written documents against which the Aboriginal oral narratives must be measured. In the case of violent conflict, for example, what are the grounds on which an oral narrative of the butchery of women and children would have to *conform* (Wiget's term) to the notes in the diary of a soldier who perpetrated the butchery? I use an extreme example to make a more generalizable point: different sources may emphasize or fail to mention different things, as Wiget himself points out. An oral account might be more accurate and complete, or may simply focus on something other than the written record in whatever form it comes. The job of the historian is to provide, rather than remove, context, and to evaluate, rather than make equivalent, the various materials available.

Second, reliability, again following Hoffman (1984, 69), is the "consistency with which individuals will tell the same story about the same events on different occasions" (Wiget 1995, 178). To get at this, Wiget checked depositions made five years apart. But I can't think of a definition that more ably loses track of the motivations for creating oral narratives, another point Wiget makes but forgets. A commonly understood feature of oral narratives is that they are pitched to an audience and to an occasion. As Cruikshank (1994b) and many others have noted, narratives needn't be slavishly the same in each telling. In the case of oral narratives told to interviewers, different people would elicit different responses. The circumstances can never be exactly the same, and the responses elicited would also not be the same. As Wiget points out, the deposition process itself puts constraints on the deponent. Hoffman's literalist definition of reliability imposes requirements that don't account for the nature of narrativity. Wiget seems to suggest this himself, indirectly, in commenting that forms of testimony structured by a number of culture-specific rules are generally more reliable than those that are less rule-bound and structured, such as elicited testimony. Reliability might more appropriately be defined as the consistency with which the same larger message is conveyed.

A third test is consistency, which is defined as the degree to which the form or context conforms with other testimony (Hoffman 1984, 179). This is a measure of conformity between forms of evidence, rather than conformity within the tradition. This is referred to elsewhere simply as external validation.

Having established these tests of the testimony, Wiget describes the features of the Zuni testimony he elicited. He notes that testimony given with a narrow line of questioning rarely has thematic coherence or formal, performative elements (1995, 182). Significantly, he writes that the more unstructured testimonies are *the original narratives.* He develops a theory that these unthematic narratives are the most reliable (measured by replicability without change) because they lack the causal, temporal junctions needed to bind episodes together. The "crafted" testimony is less reliable, he says, taken as a whole, then the fragmented testimonies of others.

I find this to be remarkable. Wiget's notion, I infer, is that the historiography of Zuni life is solely the provenance of outsiders, those with no memory of the period in question and with limited comprehension of the society, relative to the narrators. It elides the idea that the community itself might craft histories and that these histories might coalesce and properly reflect the collective understanding, as shown by the work of Sonny McHalsie in Coast Salish territory. In the Society of Friends (Quakers), for example, this process of the coalescence of the ideas of the group is referred to as "the sense of the meeting." In what appears to me to be a form of scientific imperialism, the "scientific experts" Wiget refers to have appropriated the intellectual business of the community. I have no doubt the historiography is thinner for it. Wiget's work is now a quarter of a century distant and I do not want to be guilty of presentism, but we have since moved forward. Instead of a literalist notion of reliability, we should look for what is reliably sophisticated, in touch with the facts, but synthesized. This, of course, can't be easily measured by scientists. To me, the literalist effort to "scientize" the study of oral materials reflects the needless anthropological (and more broadly, social sciences) "science envy" frequently said to characterize the development of the discipline in North America in its formative years and still present today.

In addition, the Wiget approach rests on the mistaken premise that there is an "original story" that can be excavated with care (1995, 182). Other versions are faulty, lesser. They are "crafted" testimony, an idea that suggests to me "craftiness," rather than an intellectual project. Also, I am confused by the argument. If a structured, coherent narrative is presented as evidence, and if the evidence reflects the integration of discrete materials into a causal, chronological framework, then this must be taken as less reliable. But Wiget also seems to be making the converse point, that narratives without chronology are *not* history, a point made by the archaeologist Mason (2000) and others. Is the point that there are no authentic histories among Zuni people and no historians? And, therefore, the task of outsiders is to cherry-pick from the narratives historical information that might pass muster as legal fact? In total, this approach denies agency to Aboriginal communities.

Wiget's work with community members appears to have shown him that those who can create structural and thematic coherence in their narratives commonly end up with mono-causal explanations (1995, 183). The Zuni here cannot be trusted to produce sophisticated multi-causal explanations because they create "individual identity frames," meaning that they interpret events from their own vantage point and implying that they are unable to see a larger, non-idiosyncratic perspective. For these reasons, Wiget appeals to the historical understandings derived from the depositions as a group (184).

Wiget carefully separated his own work from that of others in his team, not wishing to be influenced in his study of oral narratives. He believes this isolation was helpful, as I mentioned. I think this is a bad precedent because our approach should be to know more, rather than less, about the communities with which we work. The Australian historian Mandy Paul (2004, 150) made a similar point regarding litigation research in her country. She called for a regular exchange of information during the research phase between those working in various disciplines such as linguistics and anthropology in order to spark new ideas and research angles. She wants an "information loop," but warns against charges of "contamination" in court against such collaborative work. If archaeological evidence is relevant to understanding oral narratives, then we should attempt to find out. Wiget's model, I believe, is derived from an applied science model. If one wanted to understand and provide evidence about why a bridge fell down, one would not work with the office of the firm that constructed the bridge; an analysis of the collapsed bridge itself would be in order. But in work with human subjects we need not practice these forms of isolation.

A better model is that of the helping sciences (Randy Kandel, personal communication, 1995). Nurses and physicians are in direct contact with their patients, ideally, and this contact is *not* seen as a source of bias in their work, which couldn't be done otherwise. There could be a forensic examination of, for example, the nursing chart of a patient, or the doctor's records, to see if appropriate care was given. But this would be the work of outsiders, not those who form their opinions and gain their knowledge directly. The forensic exam is to study the work of the professional; the direct work is to understand the patient, or in Wiget's case, the society. We don't need to isolate ourselves, a form of misapplication of the applied sciences. In addition, this kind of approach to the problem of *cross-contamination* of knowledge too closely parallels the misleading notion that Aboriginal people's knowledge of the published materials about their communities contaminates and disqualifies their oral narratives in litigation.

In sum, the Wiget approach has scored a success in court, but isn't a model because it implicitly deploys etic categories of knowledge, fact, and science. The approach appears vastly expensive in time and effort in order to approximate something like "normal" science. Expertise is located outside of the community. The critique of Aboriginal lawyer Callison (1995) that oral histories are appropriated in court seems apropos, as this seems clearly to be the case in *Zuni*. One penultimate note: a recurring issue is how elders should be treated in court. Borrows (2001), for example, observed the discomfort they experience by being treated in ways inconsistent with their standing in the community (and see Blackhawk 2004). Wiget (1995) astutely notes that the "settled sense of the past," which he says characterizes the views and narrative strategies of the Zuni elders, can be disrupted under cross-examination. For this reason he believes depositions might be a better source of information. He's pointed to a good way of talking about this issue, and a more effective one than simply noting discomfort or insult, in showing why the tension arises. I think he understates what might bother elders, however, who may have more of Callison's perspective on the use of their own stories.

I wish to make clear my admiration for Wiget's work, which these paragraphs do not suggest. I am critiquing his approach to forensic issues on the basis of what it might mean in Canadian courts. His several publications (1982, 1995, 1996) reveal a careful and thoughtful scholar who is deeply respectful of the communities with whom he works and of their narratives. Perhaps his greatest insight is that instead of simply adding confusion and distortion, when information is encoded in narrative and enters the Aboriginal public discourse articulated as statements of shared value and represented by shared symbols, then there is a high degree of durability. Further, when these narratives are properly decoded, there is a high degree of reliability (1982, 196-97). He drew these conclusions from the intensive study of Hopi and other oral materials and from a fieldwork perspective. These are important findings for the Canadian court, which has only begun to find its way to proper evaluations of oral materials. To date, I would say, the Crown has emphasized the purported problems facing the use of narratives as evidence that has complex properties.

2 The Social Life of Oral Narratives

Views from the Tribal Archives

Here I wish to step back from the legal fora and query just what actually happens to oral narratives when they leave the mouths of the community members, the storytellers, enter the consciousness of the receiver, are recorded, transcribed, archived, and, sometimes, studied by and sifted through by Crown and tribal researchers. Eventually they may be entered as evidence. But I start with their treatment in the archives.

Despite the commonly held view articulated by the Crown, oral traditions that have been tape- or digitally recorded, transcribed or not, are not inert, nor are they immune to change. Rather, they take on lives of their own, independent of the initial communication between teller and audience (Schneider 1995, 196), a view more in line with contemporary thinking regarding the "social lives of things" (Appadurai 1986). Cruikshank (2005, 78) observes, "I continue to marvel at the social life that transcribed texts [of oral narratives] gain in the communities where they originate and continue to be told." Yukon storytellers, she writes, view writing as one means to tell their stories and embed them in local social processes. The women with whom she worked were willing to tell stories in various formats that worked for them: radio, video, public presentation, carving, and books. Significantly, written versions of stories familiarize readers with narratives so that the storytellers can later do the "real shaping of narrative" to an audience. In this sense, "reading is the handmaiden of listening" (79), a viewpoint also articulated by Vi Hilbert, the Coast Salish storyteller (personal communication, 2005).

Here I consider this social life and visit the neighbourhood in which the social action occurs. Oral traditional material is commonly archived in tribal/band facilities, which are sometimes formal archives developed for the purposes of preserving documents and other objects and for making them systematically available to tribal officials and members. In other cases, what started as informal collections of materials are later transformed into a professional archive, operated by archivists. An example is the Stó:lō archive, in Sardis, British Columbia. This tribal archive holds materials from some twenty bands, including a wide range of oral traditional materials. Tracey Joe, a tribal member and supervisor in the Stó:lō Research and Resource Management Centre, and Tia Halstad were the archivists in 2008, when I interviewed them. Tracey Joe is a member of a prominent family and her father is a regionally respected ceremonial and spiritual leader. The archivists described how they understand and treat oral materials held in their collection.

This archive inherited a vast collection of recordings, including reel-to-reel tape of interviews carried out by Oliver Wells, an amateur ethnographer, in the 1960s. More recent, and of note, are the recorded interviews carried out by Sonny McHalsie, the tribal cultural historian, since the 1980s. For much of the last three decades, the Stó:lō have made determined efforts to record elders and other community members' oral historical materials. Sometimes this effort is in response to particular legal issues, but more often it is in the more general interest of preserving the knowledge of elders and the particular vantage point embedded in their own language. About half of the archive's recorded material is now transcribed and tape logged. In some cases, researchers provided transcriptions and in others, transcription was carried out by employees of the archives. Some of the oral materials were obtained in one-to-one interviews, and others in group settings, including those carried out by historian Keith Carlson concerning residential schools. Some were videotaped and others audiotaped, but all the holdings have been transferred to DVD format. In some cases, contextual information about the recording was provided by the interviewer. The tribe keeps careful control over these materials and a Referral Advisory Committee, established in 2002-03, determines questions of access. Holdings can be searched by topic, tribal research project, time frame, title, description, accession number, and the name of the interviewer. Oral history materials and other information can be accessed by the same search.

The archivists explained that the relationship between the archives (and archivists) and the Stó:lō people is not a simple one. There can be community misunderstandings about the role of the archives, particularly concerning oral materials that are regarded as family, and private, knowledge (see Boxberger 2004 and Carlson 2006). The archive, Joe pointed out, does not own its oral materials: "We don't transfer ownership – it's not our [archive's] ownership. It still belongs to the person." This is a key issue in Coast Salish and other Aboriginal communities in which oral traditions, designs, and other features of material and expressive culture are carefully guarded and maintained within the family, which holds something like copyright, but with other dimensions. Materials are carefully held within the family because of their origins, a sacred context in some cases. Many of these materials may be displayed to others only under specific ritualized circumstances, but may not be recorded or reproduced by anyone else. The role of the archivist and the archives as an institution is to help keep oral materials safe for the future so that oral traditions are not lost in the event that someone is not able or willing to "carry" them. Part of this protective function is to keep private knowledge confidential. Although the archive's approach has gradually become clearer to the community, not all are willing to share their knowledge through working with the archivists.

Joe also pointed out that the Stó:lō tradition regarding how information is relayed dictates that information *can be held outside* the family or community. In the case of a big gathering (*work*, in Coast Salish terminology), such as a naming, in which an individual is given a historic, spiritual name by senior family members, outsiders are called as witnesses to the event. These witnesses bear the responsibility to pass the information along once they return home to their own communities. In the case of a naming, speakers at the work would provide an oral history of the name and how the new incumbent came to have it. Important gatherings bring in people from a wide area, including non-Stó:lō Aboriginal people. For this reason, a portion of the Stó:lō historical knowledge is held outside the community.

Interference with private knowledge is commonly thought of as theft, and private knowledge, unlike materials under copyright in the Western legal conception, cannot be lost to the control of its possessor, or possessed by others, merely by the passage of time. Such knowledge can, however, be gifted to non-family members. The field notes of Dr. Marian Smith, who worked in the Coast Salish region in the 1940s and 1950s and conducted an ethnographic field school in Stó:lō territory, are held in the British Museum, outside Stó:lō territory. Although there are copies in the provincial archive in Victoria and the national library in Ottawa, the Stó:lō archives cannot obtain a copy because the British Museum will not permit the copying of the microfiche. This is a source of frustration to the archivists and to community members who can't access transcripts of interviews with their own relatives and ancestors. This is understood as a violation of family knowledge. Although a family member disclosed information to Smith, and this is recorded in her notes, permission to use this information does not necessarily flow to anyone who might read the notes. Halstad captured a sense of the community view of this in the phrase, "That's my family!"

Joe pointed out that "information [oral historical narratives] may exist even if it is not discovered," meaning by researchers. Halstad added that for tribal or other interviewers working with tribal permission, gaining access to oral materials "depends on asking the right person in the right setting." Joe pointed to the importance of time and place, noting that it often takes more than one interview to gain insight into a particular topic. The tribal cultural advisor "sits down over a number of years on a regular basis, at least once a week, for years" with elders. From these sessions and over time, new material often emerges, such as the example of Mómet'es, a spiritually significant transformer stone (produced in the myth period during an encounter between an ancestor and the Transformer, a spiritual figure who transformed the landscape and who turned some Stó:lō ancestors to stones that exist today) destroyed by railroad employees, which came up in weekly conversation with elders. These interviews move between the discussion of current issues and particular research questions. There are other difficulties in getting information in interviews. Halstad noted that interviews in groups keep some people from speaking out of respect for someone else present. Then a one-on-one interview is necessary. In other cases, note taking, rather than tape recording, may be necessary for an elder to discuss a particular topic.

The archivists informed me that they attempt to obtain multiple versions of the same oral histories. Halstad observed that "different people remember differently, especially with *sxwóxwiyám* (myth-age) stories, which are [inherently] different." In such cases, "it's not right or wrong. Together they make a larger picture." Joe added that Stó:lō are taught that *sxwóxwiyám* stories told within a family have to always be told the same way, but emphasis on details within the story may vary in order to express a particular lesson or a certain teaching, such as greed or mischief. This is *not* done to alter the story. Emphasis equally depends on the nature of the audience and other elements of the context of the storytelling. She added that although stories are learned in childhood, storytellers, even elders, remain learners because a story means different things at different ages.

Halstad noted that the "Stó:lō have amazing knowledge of past events." In refining this thought, Joe added that Stó:lō stories of particular events may feature the *reaction* to the event and not the event itself. For her the intergenerational transmission of information is connected to weavings, pictographs, transformer stone sites, and drumming, in addition to the more familiar oral histories. A major source of information lies in place names, which often link to mythic and historical events, such as epidemics of smallpox. In addition, history is connected to the ancestral names given to family members. Some sources of oral history cannot be recorded or brought forward publicly, in particular the songs learned by winter dancers and by masked dancers who perform at memorials and other significant ritual events.

These variables indicate that oral materials are plastic in that they are sometimes *transformed* and exist in various manifestations. Moreover, tribal archival practice encourages speakers to alter tapes and transcripts of oral historical materials after they are produced. Interviewers are encouraged to provide copies in accessible format so that they can be edited and changed by the speaker. Halstad observed that these oral histories are fixed at the time of the recording, but are *"mutable."* Joe observed that she sees them as *"transformable,"* and the interviewee may properly change, delete, or restate to ensure that they are correct. This is a different notion from the Crown's concept of unilineal transformation.

Perhaps most significantly, Halstad noted that transcripts of oral history materials (including transcripts of tapes and DVDs) are stored in an area physically removed from other archived materials and in a separate catalogued area. This is for two reasons: first, oral historical materials are sometimes private knowledge and not available to non-family members; and second, the oral materials themselves are ontologically distinct from other documents. Joe explained, "You asked, 'Is an oral transcript a document?' In my mind it holds weight as a textbook. A transcript and the oral tape of the transcript is still part of the oral interview. They are not separate. They hold the same weight. There is no difference between the audio and the transcript." She added that if the interview is about *sxwóxwiyám,* "then it has a spiritual part to it. Other topics don't have the same spiritual weight. *Sxwóxwiyám* is a spiritual story. It has *shxwelí* – everything has *shxwelí,* but *sxwóxwiyám* has even more." Halstad added, "The transcript has *shxwelí,* the elders say."

Explaining further, Joe noted that archaeological "artifacts have *shxwelí* [even after the long passage of time]. It comes from the person who made it. Even inanimate objects. It's still part of them. *It's still their words and the transcript is just another form.*"

McHalsie (2007, 103-4) provides more detail about *shxwelí:*

> *Shxwelí* is what's referred to as the spirit or the life force, and it's like everything has that spirit and everything's connected through that. I remember when I first saw the word; I first started this job in 1985 and I'd seen the word in the classified word list and I always remember, it said, "'Spirit' comma 'life force.'" I never quite understood it. I didn't really know what it was all about. It wasn't until *Xa:ytem* – the rock down there at *Xa:ytem* – was first talked about that I began to pay more attention. That's when our elder, the late Aggie Victor, said, "The *shxwelí* of those *siya:m*" – those three leaders that were transformed into stone there – "The *Shxwelí* of those men is still inside the rock." So I didn't – I still don't understand that. What did they mean? The *shxwelí.* It's the spirit or life force that's inside that rock. So I went to see the late Rosaleen George and I said "What is a *shxwelí?*" – and I've never forgotten her answer, and I always tell people because I think it's probably the best way to explain it. She put her hand on her chest and she said, "*Shxwelí* is inside of here." And she puts her hand in front of her and she says, "*Shxwelí* is in your parents." She raised her hand higher and said, "then your grandparents, your great-grandparents, it's in your great-great grandparents. It's in the rocks, it's in the trees, it's in the grass, it's in the ground. *Shxwelí* is everywhere."

The archival practice of the Stó:lō Nation reflects both the concern for private ownership of knowledge and the recognition of the *shxwelí* of the tapes and their secondary manifestation, the transcripts. These remain active and open to correction. These materials can be placed into a contemporary context and manipulated with advanced archival practice but, in the view of these archivists, one Stó:lō and the other trained in Stó:lō epistemology and archival science, the essential feature persists that renders them Stó:lō and distinct. In this sense, they can best be understood within a Stó:lō cultural frame of reference, and although they may be *transformed,* their transformation does not delete this feature. They do not simply become documents like any other documents, as the Crown has argued, and entirely amenable to analysis within the historical canon. If the job of historians is to create context, then from the Stó:lō viewpoint, *shxwelí* is a vital part of the context for these documents.

Oral Narratives in the Hands of the Crown

Oral narratives produced by Indigenous people in preparation for entry into litigation are often recorded and transcribed and then submitted to the Crown under the rules of discovery. Perhaps less common is direct testimony by First Nations oral historians. In order to clarify how these oral narratives are treated, I interviewed professional technicians who work for the Crown. I do not use their names here at their request and to protect their privacy. They have, however, voluntarily agreed to participate and went through standard human subjects procedures as mandated by fairness and Canadian policy. These Crown technicians were very careful to describe the efforts made by the Crown to proceed fairly. They were clear that they were not subject to undue pressure to use documents in a manner that would favour the position of the Crown in litigation. One noted that he was "struck by how ethical the lawyer [in one case] was and amazed at how serious the lawyer was about the spirit and the letter of a confidentiality agreement" undertaken in treating litigant evidence. The lawyer, this researcher said, "had to have it to the letter." The researchers see several sides of the story about oral narratives and theirs is not a morality tale. There are features of how the Crown litigation process works, however, that bear careful scrutiny.

According to one researcher, the discipline one is trained in influences one's perceptions of oral narratives; for those trained in history, "oral history is second best, it's used to fill in the gaps, substitute for other information, even though it's 'golden.'" The information generated by oral history projects "is golden where issues are solved and dealt with directly." This researcher commented on one case in which oral history tapes were produced in the legal process of discovery. The First Nations plaintiffs made allegations about a piece of land, but the ethnographic material was thin and the historical evidence was mixed, and consequently there was not much evidence to back up their claims. A significant member of the band produced audio-recorded narrative evidence held in his possession for some years. These tapes were copied and turned over to the Crown researcher, who listened to them and found evidence directly relevant to the case, even though the Crown attorney "didn't understand" the nature of the narrative. This evidence "added flesh to the bones" of the existing documentation.

In this case, the Crown researcher "cherry picked the relevant material – relevant to the legal issues." The research process was one of "rendering it [oral narratives] down for litigation, settlement, or determining who has the stronger case." But this researcher was able to understand how mythological accounts related to the movement of Indigenous families to particular locations. In effect, the Crown process was not simply and solely one of cherry-picking data, but also involved the application of specific training to identify the evidence and advise the Crown attorneys about its nature. All of this happens *before* the courtroom contest gets under way, and according to these researchers, some litigation is avoided in favour of a negotiated settlement. In these instances the researcher can play a significant role in determining the nature of the evidence even before Crown experts see it. Formal debates about reliability and validity are not directly engaged, because oral narratives might be deemed decisive *before* debates about how they can be used as evidence.

This is, perhaps, the positive side of the story. But there are other considerations. One is how and by whom the oral narrative is transcribed from recording devices. One researcher said that he transcribed relevant portions of the material, and it was his decision which portions were relevant. This act early in the process of transmitting narratives from mouth to courtroom is fraught with difficulty; important context could be lost or retained through transcription. But the researcher noted that "the other side could handle the material the way *they* wanted and the band had their own transcription. It was important to get it right" (referring to the Crown transcription). In another case, a researcher described a situation in which the band would not allow audio oral narrative evidence to be produced as a document. Only information recorded in the form of notes could be made public.

In the litigation process, the Crown may have material that can be used only for the preparation of background information; these materials cannot be produced on the list of documents prepared for the court, and the other party, in this case bands, may not know of it. The Crown must produce a list of privileged documents for the judge to examine even though they cannot be produced as evidence. Sealed Crown documents include government Cabinet notes, correspondence within the Department of Justice that may have solicitor-client privilege, and work products of the researcher. These work products are put into an operational file, and then into the national archives, where they are not accessible. There is no way to know exactly how the researcher actually understood and processed oral narratives. The Crown must make their storyline, their case, based on the evidence available to use in court. The Crown can also choose to waive privilege over portions of documents and produce parts of them for trial.

Other than these privileged documents, anything in the care and control of the Crown must be produced for the other side in litigation. This can be maps, documents, other archival material, and information in the possession of Crown departments. Withholding documents can be the basis of an appeal. Crown lawyers determine what confidential documents cannot be shared and what must be. However, as cases evolve, pleadings are amended, and issues shift, the Crown may have to review documents in their database for relevance. Here the researcher may play an important role in explaining how particular forms of data may link together to help develop the Crown strategy for litigation. Some materials considered marginal and not produced in discovery may become more significant later in the case.

The Volume of Oral Materials and the Problem of Technology

The late 1960s and early 1970s was a period of growth in interest in oral narratives in the mainstream community and among First Nations. New technology made this affordable and possible. No doubt thousands of tapes were produced by members of First Nations in Canada themselves or by local historical society volunteers and other interested parties. These tapes present a number of problems today. The simplest is that the technology, such as cassette players and high-speed dubbing machines, used to play or manipulate these tapes, may no longer be available or may be hard to access. More serious, Crown researchers listening to dozens or hundreds of ninety-minute tapes from decades ago cannot easily process the information. It may take weeks of full-time work to listen to and choose portions for transcription. Researchers flag portions of tapes for transcription later on. Protocol calls for another researcher to check the original work. Then, these portions may be sent on to a professional transcriber. The poor quality of tapes from the 1970s – many are deteriorating – is another difficulty inherent in working with these oral narratives.

Yet another problem is the structure of the recorded information. One researcher described "historical fact mixed in with myth, family history, and other material, all in one narrative. It's cherry-picking to haul out portions relevant to a legal issue. I'm uncomfortable with it." It is difficult to separate out relevant portions of the tape. Cherry-picking, per se, is only one issue. Another is that Indigenous people, especially those with training as storytellers, sometimes tell stories in long, circuitous routes. Probably every anthropologist who works with Aboriginal communities has experienced interviewing someone with a particular issue in mind and ending the interview with the impression that the consultant never got to the point of the interview. Sonny McHalsie (2007, 111, quoted in Chapter 1) refers to the opposite side of this issue in his comment about linguists who fail to pay attention to something an elder may wish to transmit – such as the cultural significance of a place-name, rather than merely the linguistic features of the name.

One example in my own experience was an extended interview in a coffee shop with a distinguished elder on the topic of justice practices. I left convinced that we'd never quite gotten there and was surprised and pleased to play the tape and realize that the elder had given a long, seamless answer to my question. The elegance and specificity of the elder's discourse had initially passed me by. On other occasions, I have counted on this genre of speech and consultants have spoken for many hours, in the end revealing a complex and interwoven response. What appears to be a jumble may be part of a carefully rehearsed and connected oral performance told as a story instead of a linear narrative.

The need for Crown researchers to whizz through tapes obscures, perhaps entirely, the ability to understand a non-linear story and to grasp the meaning of particular parts of the recorded narrative. Even researchers fully aware of the range of Aboriginal discourse would be unable to perceive the structure of the oral performance. None of this is news to anthropologists and others practising field interviewing. But it's important to consider when looking at the larger picture of how Indigenous oral materials become part of the court record or are filtered out entirely at the beginning of the litigation process. This research process inherently favours the Crown in that the many instant decisions about relevance mean context is missed, and with it, Indigenous meaning and understanding. Moreover, bits of narrative that might pass Crown scrutiny as simple historical facts may be invisible with rapid research methods. Indigenous perspective, including that which may not support the Crown's position, is overlooked, and the Crown may take a legal position unmerited by a deeper understanding of the evidence. It seems inevitable and no one's fault, but rather a feature of the process of litigation.

Conflicting Evidence

One researcher noted that if oral narratives, for example creation stories that tell how an ancestor came to a particular place, a familiar genre among Coast Salish peoples, conflict with historical understandings of patterns of migration and settlement, the tendency among litigators is to say, "They don't know what they are talking about." This researcher notes, "I kick in and say different families have different stories. Both may be right! They were not just moving as *tribal* collectives. They were family groups, not tribes." But many now employed at the Department of Justice "have more understanding" than previously about Indigenous culture and history. There is a convergence, he says, between those trained in various disciplines, including law, history, and anthropology, as research teams gain experience in First Nations litigation. Many now know the outlines of BC history including details of the creation of the reserve system, land removals, and scholarly sources that are widely consulted. This convergence, he believes, leads to greater insight into sources, including oral narratives.

And, the researcher claims, those working with evidence for the Crown need to know the law, such as what legal tests determine an Aboriginal right to fish for food, or how to determine the date of contact in an area. This is in addition to having intimate knowledge of records such as those created by the Hudson's Bay Company, missionaries, or governments.

Multiple Versions and Storylines

In addition to using oral narratives in evaluating whether the Crown has a case in the first place, researchers need to create a legal storyline, overall narrative, or "picture of what happened," in the researcher's terms. Multiple versions of oral narratives complicate this process; the oral narratives are weighed by their ability to fit into the overall litigation picture. But these storylines themselves change as the legal strategy changes and as the cases evolve. The storyline presented in litigation may in turn alter the way in which the oral narratives are integrated into the case and the way in which multiple versions are understood. All of this is prior to debates discussed within expert reports and in direct or indirect testimony about the theoretical nature of oral narratives. At this stage multiple versions are evaluated by their "fit" with legal strategy and legal narrative.

Researchers also use the standard social science method of triangulation. They compare evidence from various sources, including field notes and archived materials. They can point out to the litigation team if information is consistent with other records, stopping short of rejecting some materials in favour of others.

Researchers, Lawyers, and Legal Teams

Researchers collect, arrange, evaluate, and store information of many kinds. They do this based on their instructions regarding potential upcoming litigation and based on their own knowledge of records, culture, histories, and law. They also advise the litigation team. This relationship is difficult, however. One researcher told of telling a lawyer that his case narrative, or storyline, was not substantiated. Another researcher reported that he was "afraid to tell lawyers 'no' [the argument didn't hold water] although others do tell that." Another said he would say, "The case frame is not consistent with the evidence available." Ultimately, the framing of the case and the use of evidence is up to the legal team, and the team may wish to give different weight to the evidence than the researcher might think appropriate. One researcher noted that he had learned to compare the material presented by academics in their publications and field notes, where discrepancies are not uncommon. He also developed ways to evaluate contradictions in evidence when different scholars worked in the same communities, even interviewing the same Indigenous people.

Part of this evaluation involved gaining a sense of the particular informants and their place in their community. This informal evaluation might indirectly incorporate the practice of oral footnoting. It works like this: one or more academic works in a given community, selecting consultants to interview and engaging in participant observation there. These academics determine which community members they can rely on in forming opinions. If they are alert, they attune themselves to community protocols about oral narratives and they record multiple versions of narratives. Later, researchers for the Crown assess these academic assessments and report their conclusions to the litigators, who create their own impressions of what the material means and how it might be used. By this point, community protocols are long in the past and other concerns have to enter in.

In earlier periods, through the late 1950s, academics often included published notes about their informants. This practice largely stopped because, I think, it came to be seen as patronizing and hierarchical. Anthropologists may have gained a sense of the damage this might produce as Indigenous people came to read their publications more commonly. Yet others came to see their field relationship with Indigenous people and communities as not justifiable simply by the mere argument of the advancement of science, but rather, as a gift that must be reciprocated. Still, evaluations of Indigenous people persist in field notes even though they no longer appear in print. These informal evaluations of consultants published in books or journal articles, or appearing in field notes, may influence the evaluation of the scholarship. Researchers told me that they pay attention to *whom* scholars worked with in shaping their understanding of community culture and history. One scholar might be considered better than another because he or she gave more weight to those the researchers consider credible. The process is one of the multiple filters applied by the researchers.

One researcher concluded, "It's thorny for me. The legal world is at cross-purposes for oral histories. Oral history projects were to get *their* understanding. But legal processes [are] about what is relevant – it becomes evidence."

Pure Evidence and Indigenous Elder Interviews

The motivation underlying the creation of recorded oral narratives is an issue for researchers. One researcher recounted,

> Someone said that the tapes [from a particular band oral history project] are "pure," not sullied by land claims information. They were *not* for making claims in the guise of oral history. There is a danger in that. A [different tribe named] works by saying, "Let's find an elder." [Named person] talks to an elder and says, "You've heard about this [named] case – do you have any information about how we can understand [subject]?" I'm uncomfortable with that interview. [Named person] was very leading. (Here I have obscured names and other specifics to address concepts rather than the particulars of any case.)

This researcher notes that much of the evidence for the litigation involving a number of Aboriginal communities is in the form of oral narratives, which get mined for every little detail. In many cases there is little anthropological material from the early twentieth century and small amounts from the 1950s. The interviews conducted by Indigenous communities with their own elders, by contrast, can often link them back in time, even into the nineteenth century.

Interestingly, this researcher implies that both Crown and Indigenous researchers mine every available bit of evidence for litigation, scouring the same anthropological notes by the same few scholars working in the middle of the last century. But my interview with Sonny McHalsie (Chapter 3) suggests that what Aboriginal researchers do with the data generated by scholars and by their own community members can be quite different.

The Structure of the Legal Apparatus

This researcher observed that land claims in Canada have produced a huge industry of Native law, with billions of dollars generated. He joked it would "cause a recession if it ended," because many people have well-paid jobs doing this work (and see Widdowson and Howard 2008).

The "Native law industry," as the researcher termed it, is structured in particular ways that influence the use of oral narratives. One feature is the disarticulation of the efforts of the Department of Indian Affairs and the Department of Justice, each with their own Aboriginal law groups, which don't like to work together and act as rivals. Another feature is the existence of private law groups that mine federal archives for evidence of some sort of wrongdoing, which they report to tribal meetings so they can sign on clients and launch litigation against the Crown. According to this researcher, some bands similarly send researchers to federal archives to find past failures of the Crown in their relationship with the band.

The "Native law industry" is also structured by the presence of Crown resources. One consultant noted that "the Crown has huge resources and if it decides it's a big case they could get one hundred researchers from a 'standing offer' roster of available people. It takes a while to get up to speed. A committee to review statements of claim establishes the risk to the Crown and the far-reaching effects. If they can't lose the case, then they do what they can."

While the Crown doesn't pressure researchers to misrepresent the facts, according to my collaborators, the Crown does apply time pressure to the work. One technician reported working a "record twenty-one-hour day." He noted, "The litigation world is crazy. It's on schedule. They want no stone left unturned." But because the Crown "wants no surprises in trial," the senior employees go out of their way to act ethically and provide researchers under them a free hand intellectually.

The researchers themselves are organized hierarchically. Researchers have project managers who report to the representative for Indian Affairs. A committee of lawyers also manages the input and output of researchers. Ultimately, when cases go on the docket, judges themselves determine the timelines and set when documents are needed. The discovery and undertakings process is a particularly stressful time for researchers.

One of the researchers said that he is concerned with the new use made of field notes. He observes that an academic whose notes he uses "never conceived that his notes would be used this way." He says that he needs to theorize this, too. He also pointed out that in one case, "gold nuggets would be picked out for evidence, and the rest is slag, but in the next one, the slag turns to gold," meaning that as the issues change, the value of information shifts.

Another researcher reported that he is sometimes used by the lawyers to indicate how a particular discipline works and how that discipline views oral history. People from various disciplines may be asked to characterize their own disciplines for a legal research team composed of people with different training. This, too, he says, is the cause of internal struggle because academic disciplines are not unitary entities and it is difficult to adequately represent them and their internal issues.

Researchers do assist with expert witnesses, but "can't be seen to be coaching them" since the Canadian legal system requires witnesses to independently draw conclusions regarding questions put to them. One researcher said that he poses questions instead, such as, "Do you think that the field notes of [academic] are useful in this case?"

Finally, one consultant asserted, "The whole legal process is wrong – at the foundations."

To summarize the information from key consultant interviews about the production and organization of knowledge about oral narrative by Crown researchers:

- Oral narratives are processed at multiple stages, including the determination of whether the Crown should proceed with litigation or negotiate a settlement.
- Oral narratives are quickly assessed in the case of a large volume of material. Assessment of oral materials helps create the Crown "storyline" for the litigation.
- Oral narratives are triangulated with other data to calculate likelihood of help in litigation and veracity.
- Oral narratives are reframed in the case storyline as the case evolves and legal strategies and narratives shift.
- Oral narratives are cherry-picked for facts to suit the case.
- Oral narratives are deployed by researchers to advise the litigation team.
- Sections of oral narratives are selected and transcribed.
- Sections of transcribed oral narratives are shared with the other side through discovery.
- Oral narratives are decontextualized and recontextualized.
- Much of the work on oral narratives is done *ad hoc* – independent of theoretical debate presented in litigation.
- The producers of oral narratives (the oral historians and others) are evaluated by their community and by academics who work with them, all of whom in turn are evaluated by researchers.

- Oral narratives are a product of an "industry" with many well-paid workers.
- Oral narratives are evaluated regarding the motivations of the producers.

Oral Narratives in the Hands of the Plaintiff's Researchers and Lawyers

Later, of course, oral narratives go through other lengthy processes of evaluation, by the trial judge and possibly by appeals court judges. It's not solely the processes of the Crown legal team that influence the nature and value of oral narratives of Indigenous peoples in litigation. Mills (1996, 40) noted the difficulties inherent in translating Gitxsan and Wet'suwet'en concepts into a form the court would recognize in *Delgamuukw v. British Columbia*. She described her own transformation of oral narratives into new forms:

> I then wrote and revised an expert opinion report for submission prior to trial. The expert opinion report emphasized descriptions and explanations of matters I thought would assist the judge in assessing the forthcoming evidence. It described the potlatch system in clear simple language as a guide to the long complex testimony to follow. It summarized the content of the Witsuwit'en oral traditions and explained their relevance to the Witsuwit'en claim to have occupied their territory since time immemorial. The summary of the contents of the oral traditions was intended to aid the admission of the oral tradition by explaining its relevance as encoded oral history. (42)

Jeffrey (2006, 231) found something similar in a case heard in the UK involving a group who were removed from the Chagos Islands in the Indian Ocean and treated unfairly:

> I start by arguing that collective narrative and standardized history have become the two central features of Chagossian historical narratives ... I go on to demonstrate that, during the production of legal evidence for the court, the processes of transcription and translation concealed the collective and standardized character of Chagossian historical narratives from their legal team, resulting in witness evidence that the judge criticized on the basis that it was neither consistent nor individual eyewitness evidence.

In particular, Jeffrey comments on the issues of admissibility and consistency in evidence. She wonders, "As trained lawyers, did the Chagossians' legal team not recognize that the collective and standardized character of their Chagossian clients' historical narratives could potentially pose serious difficulties for them in court if the case was heard by a judge with particular interpretations of the laws of evidence concerning admissibility and consistency?" (231).

The legal team for the Indigenous plaintiffs have their own views about the nature of oral narratives, how they might be used in court, and what the issues are regarding rules of evidence. My comments here reflect the emerging state of the law following the decision in *Samson* previously and my concern that the new and rather difficult standards that oral narratives must pass might not be achieved. These comments are, in effect, advice to anthropologists and historians serving as expert witnesses, and to oral historians themselves. In my own experience as an expert witness in Indigenous litigation in Canada and the United States, the plaintiff's legal team, like the Crown team, are keenly interested in oral narratives, but their focus appears to be on how these are understood in the court. The lawyers, after all, are members of the bar. Several lawyers who act in First Nations litigation spoke at a forum organized by legal historian Allan Grove and myself at the 2006 Society for Applied Anthropology meetings in Vancouver, an academic gathering of some 1,800 people, which I co-chaired. The following comments are from my notes of that meeting.

Canadian lawyer Craig Bavis described the then current situation regarding the use of oral narratives. He pointed to the difficulties of demonstrating an "unbroken chain" of the transmission of narratives, which he said must be shown. He commented that "contaminated" narratives will be rejected and that oral history will be attacked by documentary evidence. Further, he stated that oral histories may conflict with other First Nations testimony and therefore a legal team must determine what *other* First Nations were saying. Legal teams, as a consequence, need to know the details of competing claims. (Recall tribal archivist Tracey Joe's observation concerning members of other bands holding information about her band history). All of these circumstances are linked to the Crown position advanced in a number of cases and already accepted by the court.

Anthropology, Bavis continued, needs *proper interviewing* techniques practised over a long period with internal cross-referencing. Anthropologists must test the *reliability* of the oral materials with the internal archival record. They will have to find out *who* the last informants were to speak about a particular issue, place, or event. They can reduce the risk of decontextualizing the anthropological work by

- setting off the kind of work, and showing its limitations
- "not theorizing about stuff that is not your own research. Or if it isn't, say so"
- "list[ing] restraints of the research. Time, mostly"
- resisting sweeping statements, and *not straying from the focus*
- including oral history in their work
- showing the context of interviews
- being cautious in reporting an erroneous viewpoint from the academic literature
- leaving a *footprint* in their work – showing their identity. An alias can't be checked.

He added that oral history rejected in one court may emerge in other litigation.

Bavis's comments point to the growing difficulties of using oral narratives in litigation since *Delgamuukw*. This is particularly the case since, in British Columbia, many tribes remain engaged in the treaty-making process with the provincial and federal Crowns (organized through the BC Treaty Commission). The Treaty Commission position has been that tribes might hope to receive Crown land or equivalent compensation of up to 5 percent of their own historical land. This process pushes tribes to show even joint-use areas as falling within their historical homelands and to support these claims with evidence, including oral narratives that feature their own ancestral use and occupation of the territories. This situation, which effectively pits band versus band, virtually mandates conflicting oral narratives without a clear means to clarify why this is so and how to meaningfully understand conflicting oral narratives (a topic I explore in Chapter 3 through an interview with oral historian Sonny McHalsie). Further, there is no meaningful way to show that narratives are not "contaminated," since this information would not be ordinarily available, and the burden entailed is a great one since the ability to present important evidence may rest on it.

Canadian Aboriginal lawyer Gary Campo pointed to similar problems that had emerged in the developing arena of oral narratives. The use of these narratives in *Tsilhqot'in Nation v. British Columbia* required the compilation and presentation of material gathered in contemporary fieldwork. It also required a thorough search of archives to compare to the oral histories and a review of academic literatures in archaeology, history, and anthropology. Old tapes and transcripts, including the sort produced by local historical societies and by tribal communities themselves, had to be searched. Significantly, he observed, "Almost without fail the oral truth corroborates the archival record." Campo observed that his message was that "anthropology is taken out of context and in the future [anthropologists] must take care in how they write." They must, he said, find ways to *create* their context.

Campo noted, "Courts give deference to anthropologists, so what's the problem? The problem is the wide spectrum of expertise and [the issue of staying in] focus. Going outside [of one's area of knowledge] can be used against [the litigants]. First Nations [people] are experts and anthropologists may qualify if First Nations and history is not available." Here Campo is pointing to inadequate expert reports written by anthropologists, a problem also cited by Crown researchers, one of whom mentioned "the abominable quality of some of them [reports]." Campo also pointed out a problem of "changing dominant theories."

Legal historian Al Grove similarly commented, "The government uses fringe scholars whose work wouldn't be accepted" in academic circles. These experts aren't clear about their limits or knowledgeable about the records. Grove also noted that researchers "need to know the legal theory of the case." And, as the Crown researchers pointed out, historians and anthropologists must check each other. Anthropology, Grove said, is "about creating context, it's concerned about creating a regime of truth." Anthropologists are better trained at challenging received wisdoms than providing court testimony. Courts, he noted, are adversarial, not academic. He cautioned that anthropologists who enter the court as advocates and distort the truth will find this practice will come back to haunt them. Like the Crown technicians, Grove observed, "It doesn't serve any purposes by holding back information."

Historian Ken Coates also spoke, pointing out that "legal processes are killing First Nations communities and turning their best [people] into lawyers." He said that communities need fewer cases and more negotiations, and cases need to be assembled so that government will negotiate. Crown technicians share this viewpoint also, pointing out that their work with oral narratives can help convince litigators that a strong case is not available. Finally, Coates pointed out that it is rare for First Nations to be funded to fight the Crown.

A few key points emerge from these veterans of First Nations litigation. First, the standards for establishing oral narratives as containing evidence of real merit are continuing to rise. It is unclear what is left after "contaminated" narratives, and those that conflict with others, are omitted. In any case, the intensity of the research effort continues to grow and now requires teams of researchers. Any thought of simple testimony by an elder standing as evidence is long obsolete. As Jeffrey (2006) found regarding the Chagos Islands case, the British court effectively imposed formalisms that created barriers for the attorneys of the litigants attempting to employ community narratives. The changing standards make it more and more likely that some stone previously left unturned will be discovered and that surprises await in court.

3 Aboriginal and Other Perspectives

The Critique

I've not yet dealt with the more radical critique of the case law and legal handling of oral narratives. Aboriginal scholars such as Val Napoleon and John Borrows emphasize that, in the end, Aboriginal thought is evaluated in Western terms. They might simply be incommensurable. Napoleon (2005, 152) gives a snippet of testimony from the original *Delgamuukw v. British Columbia* in 1991: "Mr. Goldie: Now my friend [attorney Stuart Rush, acting for the plaintiffs] says that history is not static. Well, I agree with that. He says it's a growing event. Your Lordship will appreciate that if that principle is accepted, the *adaawk* can be reshaped by recent views to support a particular point of view, and thereby the principle of reliability and trustworthiness is lost."

Napoleon (2005) advances the idea that the *adaawx* (spelled variously), the oral traditions of the Gitxsan, are not frozen in time but are the living statement of Gitxsan law. If they are frozen, and accepted as reliable, then they are not compatible with a vibrant Gitxsan culture. If alive, they might not pass muster in court. She fears that oral tradition is decontextualized in legal processes; in being heard in a courtroom it is "fractured into slices by both direct and cross examination" (137). She is concerned that, in the end, "as Borrows points out, the *adaawk* is a fundamental challenge to the legitimacy of the western legal system. *Delgamuukw* really was about one legal system (western) judging another (Gitksan)" (154).

Napoleon appears to be foregrounding the incommensurability of the two systems of law and the power relations between them. Still, her persistent efforts to point out the problems with Canadian justice and the value of the Aboriginal contributions suggests that she may see some hope in the legal system.

Non-Aboriginal anthropologist Andie Palmer (2000, 1045) adds her own related critique arising from differences in epistemology. She notes that although Chief Justice Lamer, writing in *Delgamuukw v. British Columbia* in 1997 [*Delgamuukw III*], states that he wishes to "come to terms" with the oral histories, he undermines his own point by claiming that in the absence of written records, conclusive evidence of pre-contact practices could not easily be produced. However, to the Gitxsan, *the adaawx are regarded as the authoritative record of the past in feast halls.* She does not conclude that the judge's failure to accept them as such is the result of incommensurability, but rather of the education system's failure to show children something of the viewpoint of First Nations people.

John Borrows is also not quite as pessimistic as Val Napoleon. But he is clear about where he stands and, further, is clear that oral histories are inherently controversial, not because of their genre as a form of speech but because of their content:

> The mere presentation of Aboriginal oral evidence often questions the very core of the Canadian legal and constitutional structure. In many parts of the country certain oral traditions are most relevant to Aboriginal peoples because they keep alive the memory of their unconscionable mistreatment at the hands of the British and Canadian legal systems. Their evidence records the "fact" that the unjust extension of the common law and constitutional regimes often occurred through dishonesty and deception, and that the loss of Aboriginal land and jurisdiction happened against their will and without their consent. These traditions include memories of the government's deception, lies, theft, broken promises, unequal and inhumane treatment, suppression of language, repression of religious freedoms, restraint of trade and economic sanctions, denial of legal rights, suppression of political rights, forced physical relocation, and plunder and despoliation of traditional territories. As such, oral tradition is controversial because it potentially undermines the law's claim to legitimacy throughout the country due to the illegality and/or unconstitutionality of past actions. (Borrows 2001, 10)

Additionally, Borrows (2001) points to another source of controversy, namely, the existence in Canada of other legitimate normative orders in the form of Aboriginal law. This law, he says, stems from an independent source of authority and invokes a "strong vision of legal pluralism," which challenges Canada's monopoly on law. Borrows fears that, given all of this, and unless the court changes the entire approach to the "reception, interpretation, and use of evidence," Aboriginal oral histories *may* not be able to be accommodated like other forms of evidence (10). As Napoleon and others have pointed out, the evidence offered in oral histories would still be interpreted by those from a different culture who may not be able to receive the message. Borrows fears non-apprehension and misinterpretation. He appears, however, to place some hope in the ability of judges to comprehend, or be trained to comprehend, the symbolic aspects of Aboriginal forms of communication (see Simpkins 2000, 158, and Ray 2008 regarding the educability of judges).

Borrows (2001) observes that Aboriginal people must participate in the interpretation of oral narratives, along with others, including *amici curiae* and counsel knowledgeable in Aboriginal culture and practices. Oral traditions (his term) will not be properly accommodated otherwise. Finally, Borrows points to the problem of the treatment of elders in court, who often endure treatment inconsistent with their status in their own communities that discredits their knowledge and standing. Their questioning by counsel and judges appears ignorant and disrespectful (11). For these reasons, I am apprehensive about the development of quite elaborate processes of questioning by Mr. Justice Vickers in *Tsilhqot'in Nation v. British Columbia* and the suggestion for yet more tests of elders by Newman (2005). As Borrows mentions, the overwhelming difficulties faced by today's elders, including the residential school experience, make this problem particularly onerous. Everyone, Borrows says, dislikes being the subject of aggressive cross-examination, but its implications are not the same for all.

Borrows (2001) acknowledges, and indeed celebrates, the "transsubstantiative" qualities of oral traditions. He believes that they will often provide important factual information to the court and on other occasions may mislead. He worries that oral histories will be discredited generally while the problems he points to are being worked out. He thinks that a more careful examination by the court of Western forms of inquiry and knowledge can lead to a better appreciation of oral traditions. He's asking for fair-minded introspection, for seeing beyond our own Western cultural blinders. He hasn't given up, just as his elders and ancestors have not, a point he makes clear.

Catherine Twinn, a member of the Indigenous Bar Association involved in *Sawridge Band v. The Queen*, expresses her concerns that the Canadian federal court has procedurally disadvantaged Aboriginal litigants through "death by process" (personal communication, December 13, 2009). She is afraid that proposals advanced by the Crown in a draft position paper in 2009 to require "will-say" statements, in which testimony by elders giving oral traditions will have to be written out "prior to trial will become a tool to exclude evidence and to make findings that we [Aboriginal elders and the lawyers for Aboriginal litigants] deliberately breached court orders. It creates a chilling environment." Further, "It becomes another tactic to exclude oral history evidence." She, too, is worried about the direction of Canadian law, but hopes for a better resolution.

Yet another Aboriginal lawyer, then a law student, Cynthia Callison (1995, 167), writing in dismay and barely disguised disgust following the original *Delgamuukw* ruling, attempted to show the legal grounds on which oral traditions could have protection from "cultural appropriation" by outsiders. She decried the use of oral narratives as evidence in court even by the communities that have produced these narratives, arguing that oral traditions collected as evidence are subject to interpretations influenced by passions and prejudice. Anthropologists, she wrote, are used merely as cultural translators to support the legal arguments. I believe this opinion misrepresents the positions of the particular anthropologists who gave evidence in the *Delgamuukw* trial, Richard Daly (2005) and Antonia Mills (1994). There is no evidence that they simply performed the tasks assigned by the litigation team; that, in effect, they distorted or lied for the litigant; or that they have any obligation to distort on behalf of clients under the terms of professional ethics, issues I have raised elsewhere (Miller 1992b). But, more significantly here, Callison's opinions provide grounds for eliminating the use of oral narratives as evidence. She states that Aboriginal oral narratives are misused by the Aboriginal litigants for the purposes of litigation. In a case of curious bedfellows, her views overlap with those of people who I believe have no real appreciation for the nature of oral narratives, such as the late Chief Justice McEachern. Her argument is compelling evidence of how issues can be read very differently when seen from different angles. Callison isn't writing directly about oral traditions as evidence; rather, she is concerned about their appropriation in *any* setting.

Callison's argument (1995) is one of incommensurability; oral narratives just can't be heard by outsiders without the risk of appropriation and manipulation. Others take positions of near-incommensurability but on different grounds. Among these are Aboriginal scholars who have had their say, not only in academic writing, but in the court itself and in goodwill events sponsored by the Department of Justice.

Aboriginal Expert Opinions on Oral Narratives

The Crown has repeatedly presented its understanding of oral narratives generally, in addition to reports specific to particular cases. Tribes in litigation have used their own experts to provide another theoretical perspective on oral narratives. The courts have commonly preferred the views of the Crown, but these Aboriginal experts provide a perspective that can usefully be reconsidered, particularly that of Winona Wheeler, a professor of Indian studies at Saskatchewan Indian Federated College. Her 2001 report in *Samson Indian Nation and Band v. Canada (Samson)* is a long (162 pages), sophisticated, and interesting examination of what she calls Indigenous "oral tradition histories." The paper is wide-ranging, and although she has her eye on the arguments presented by the Crown expert, she provides a deep critique of why non-Aboriginal scholars and institutions, including the court, misunderstand Aboriginal knowledge, and especially oral narratives. To Wheeler, Western history is trapped in the belief that non-Western people simply lack a historical consciousness. She points in particular to the "fetishism" of facts that developed in the nineteenth century in the effort to escape national histories based on myths of oral tradition. (She doesn't give an example of a European oral national history, but here is one: in the middle ages, Scots developed the now unacceptable idea that the first Scots were the descendants of warriors from the Trojan war who encamped in Spain for a while prior to heading north). She presents Voltaire, author of *Candide,* in his guise as a cynic, as an exemplar of this trend toward the creation of a common-sense view of history.

She argues that Western historiography is tied to an implicit cultural evolutionism in which literacy is the marker of civilization. She critiques Walter Ong's prominent work on literacy for perpetrating the age-old prejudice against oral societies. Instead, she notes that literacy is a form of power that creates the ground for the sort of "intellectual colonialism" described by Frantz Fanon and Edward Said. Some of anthropology has held a similar stance. Lévi-Strauss's idea of "hot" and "cold" societies, for example, evokes an opposition of the modern and historical with the traditional and timeless. Other anthropologists, she observes, have rejected the oral tradition–history dichotomy, including Robert Brightman (1993) and Keith Basso (1996). But, problematically I think, she points to Aboriginal scholar Angela

Wilson's view (1997) that oral histories constitute a web from which secular history cannot be picked out from the sacred, since stories must be understood in relation to other stories. Meaning, to Wilson, is layered. But in rejecting a clean dichotomy between oral histories and histories, a new version of incommensurability arises.

For these reasons I suspect that Wheeler's approach was not effective in the context of *Samson;* the court preferred the much simpler and reductionist arguments of the Crown. Wheeler's report was perhaps overly nuanced and detailed, with too much historical analysis of Western traditions of oral history. Jackson (2005, xii) notes something similar in the original *Delgamuukw:* "The chief justice also found Daly's report [his expert report on Gitxsan society] 'exceedingly difficult to understand' because 'it is highly theoretical and I think, detached from what happens on the ground.'"

Wheeler's argument is complicated by her running critique of history as a discipline, and, to a lesser extent, of anthropology. She devotes considerable space to making a comparative argument as to why oral traditional histories are held to a different and higher standard than historical materials. She notes that historians since Herodotus and Thucydides have relied on oral histories in their work. She writes that historians are guilty of the sort of presentism that is used to discredit oral narratives, for example in Ruth Finnegan's observation (1996) that oral narratives are subject to current interpretation and contemporary politics when they are elicited by interviews rather than spontaneous narratives (Wheeler 2001, 83). She points to historian E.H. Carr's view that history is value laden. Perhaps her most trenchant observation is that historians who say that oral history must be rejected because it doesn't adequately present a notion of chronology (and therefore gives rise to telescoping and foreshortening) overlook the idea that time itself, as it is currently understood, is a modern Western invention. Vansina, she points out, observes that each culture has its own sense of time and that oral historians frequently use significant events to create a sense of time. This sense, she says, would be understood only by immersion in the culture. Local knowledge is needed to understand the temporal sequence (108). She critiques the Crown for arguing that this view is merely extreme relativism.

In advancing her case for what oral tradition history *is,* Wheeler makes the argument that the study of oral traditional histories is very complex, much more so than historical methods permit. Indigenous societies, she writes, have distinct intellectual traditions, including their own historical consciousness and historical methodologies, which can be understood only from within Aboriginal society. She doesn't argue, however, that only Aboriginal people can do this, and she frequently cites in favourable terms the work of non-Aboriginal anthropologist Julie Cruikshank with Tlingit and Athabascan Aboriginal women, and historian Gordon Day's research involving oral materials about the American revolution. She does specify that training in these intellectual traditions must come from within the Aboriginal community.

Wheeler concludes that oral materials do not simply become documents, amenable to standard historiographic methods, once transcribed on paper. Instead, in a position similar to that held by Stó:lō people interviewed for this book (Chapter 2 and below), she believes that oral narratives have a spirit, a quality that makes it impossible for them to become simply documents.

Wheeler's entire argument connects the "deprecation of Indigenous intellectual traditions" with the larger colonial enterprise, which itself depends on negating Aboriginal practice so that a new order can be imposed. She evaluates the Crown's position regarding oral narratives from this position and concludes (here I abbreviate):

- Indigenous societies have their own notions of history, historical consciousness, and methodologies.
- Indigenous perspectives on any historical issues can be ascertained only from within the Indigenous context – through oral tradition histories.
- These oral tradition histories can reliably inform an appreciation of Indigenous perspectives on treaty-making (the specific legal issue at hand in the case for which she tendered an expert opinion; presumably this would also be true for other issues, such as land claims).
- Oral tradition histories must be placed on an equal footing with historical documents.
- But this does not mean that they are historical documents.
- Indigenous oral tradition histories cannot be understood outside their own intellectual traditions and cultural contexts.
- Western historical methods are useful in the study of oral tradition histories in tandem with Indigenous methods.
- Oral tradition histories are *heard* stories and the fullest meaning can be acquired only when equipped to understand.
- Training to understand is acquired only within the cultures themselves.

Wheeler's work, to me, is compelling and merits careful consideration.

An Oral Historian Addresses the Issues Directly

Indigenous academics such as Wheeler are no doubt well versed in the oral narratives of their own communities. But they are not necessarily oral historians, so here I shift focus to such a person. Albert (Sonny) McHalsie was introduced in Chapter 1. He is from the Stó:lō nation, a tribal council composed of member bands situated along the Fraser River in and adjacent to the Lower Mainland of British Columbia. McHalsie is in his fifties, a young elder, and a grandfather. He received an honorary PhD from the University of Victoria in 2011. He has spent the last twenty years learning the oral narratives of people throughout the Stó:lō Nation. Some of these he encountered within his own extended family and others through his work in the domain of culture for the tribal council. He is now widely known in both the Aboriginal and non-Aboriginal worlds for his knowledge and thoughtful treatment of oral narratives. I discussed with him some of the debate about oral narratives in Canadian courts since *Delgamuukw* (interview, August 26, 2008). Some of the questions were foreign to him and caused considerable introspection. It is the very foreignness of the way outsiders, particularly the Crown, understand and manipulate oral narratives, that is startling and puzzling to McHalsie, and reveals the considerable gap between Aboriginal perspectives and legal ones. McHalsie has not testified in any court about oral materials, and his views of oral materials are specific to the practices in his own Stó:lō and Coast Salish communities.

The Question of Definitions

According to McHalsie, Stó:lō oral histories fall into several categories, the first of which are *sxwóxwiyám,* stories of the time when the world was mixed up and not quite right. The Transformer, Xexá:ls, made the world right for humans, and his actions are written on the land like a constitution, in the form of transformer rocks and gashes in the stone where Xexá:ls engaged in spiritual fights. This is an idea McHalsie first heard from Stó:lō member Steven Point, now the lieutenant governor of British Columbia, and appears to echo the idea of "charter myths" espoused by Malinowski, except that McHalsie refers to physical manifestations. These stories provide a perspective on the land. *Shxwelí,* a life force or spirit, is an important part of the stories of this period. There are also *sqwelqwel,* or true stories held by families. Every Stó:lō person has his own, distinct set of *sqwelqwel,* since everyone has both a familial and a personal identity, and these are handed down, in part, by scolding younger family members to pay attention to what they hear and experience. Finally, there are histories that may not be distinctly

Stó:lō. For McHalsie, the term *oral historian* refers to those telling *sqwelqwel,* and *oral tradition* is a general term for all categories.

Oral narratives (my term) depend on the practice of oral footnoting, or "who told us." If the story is told in the narrator's home, they "must say it the way they heard it" because the family members will know how their ancestor said it. The listener will realize that it is not something made up, but passed down. They will know who told it before that. Telling the story connects to the *shxwelí* of the deceased previous teller, it draws them in. This is similar to the idea of name taboos for four years after a death, a Coast Salish practice that allows the ancestors to take the recently deceased away from the living. To invoke the name is to hold onto that person, and so is *stingy.* The deceased person's rightful place is elsewhere.

"They're right here with me [indicates his shoulder] when I mention their name. It's a strength. It can be a source of power to mention their name [in oral footnoting], but you must say it [the story] the way they said it. Both kinds of stories [*sxwóxwiyám* and *sqwelqwel*] have the same degree of *shxwelí* and provide the foundations of the belief system. We are connected through *sxwóxwiyám* and *sqwelqwel,* we are joined by both." McHalsie mentioned as an example the T'xwelátse story (Schaepe 2007a). T'xwelátse is both the "Indian" name of a senior ritualist among the Stó:lō, Herb Joe (father of Tracey Joe interviewed in Chapter 2), and the name of a stone carving unearthed near the international border and subsequently sold to and held by the Burke Museum of the University of Washington for a century until it was transferred into the hands of the Joe family in 2007. Evidence presented in support for the claim of the family to the carving was in the form of a *sqwelqwel* particular to the Joe family and Herb Joe himself. T'xwelátse was held on behalf of the family in the Museum of Anthropology at the University of British Columbia. On the instructions of the family, and based on the understanding of the statue as an animated being, an ancestor and namesake to Herb Joe, the statue is clothed and fed. This practice by museum professionals makes sense only if the context of the *sqwelqwel* itself is understood.

Variation in the Content of Stories

"Elders can't discard any versions of a story. They would have to mention what others said. For example, the Halkomelem [the language of the Stó:lō] word for the town of Hope – some say it has to do with trees. Tilly Guiterrez says it has to do with a bare rock. Everyone told the story, maybe some not the whole story." McHalsie provided as an example of the issue of variation in stories his own work concerning stories about the Transformer, Xexá:ls.

He initially thought he had gathered all of them and could get all of the details and produce a single, master account. Instead, now, for an upcoming Stó:lō Heritage Trust publication, he will orally footnote differences in accounts. A primary reason for this is that "one of my biggest teachings is respect for other teachings so I look at the sincerity and meaning of the tellings. It's important for someone to tell the story and they can't be cast aside, even short, non-detailed stories."

McHalsie's approach seems parallel to the search in law for reliability as established by the reputation and the careful practice of oral historians. Although the Crown would have it that variation indicates failure of memory and lack of credibility, to McHalsie, credibility is measured in different ways. Rather than regarding variation as outside of legal practice and in noncompliance with what the Crown hoped was standard historical methodology, the convergence with the law and even with history are apparent.

Contamination of Stó:lō Narratives by Foreign Stories

I recounted for Sonny a claim by the Crown that foreign stories could be incorporated into Aboriginal (including Stó:lō) narratives by a practice, presumably, of borrowing, and because of thematic parallels between stories of widely divergent societies. This view follows on from the nineteenth-century practice of categorizing narratives into recognizable types, such as evil stepmother stories or star-child stories. Can Stó:lō narratives be regarded as inauthentic or, perhaps more humbly, partly not of Stó:lō origin, because of the intrusion of Western stories, such as those in the Bible or Grimms' Fairy Tales? McHalsie observed,

> *Sxwóxwiyám* are sometimes referred to by others as fairy tales or legends. I prefer to use the proper term. I don't think stories [from other cultures] can be entered in [to Stó:lō stories]. There can be parallels but it doesn't mean they can infiltrate. Stó:lō rules and protocols would keep these out. It's not to say some elders need to make it more exciting and [therefore] embellished their stories. One young fellow studying stories for theatre looked at Harrison Lake [part of which is Stó:lō territory] and found a huge gap – he wanted to make up the gap! [by making up new stories].

More than a decade ago, McHalsie and others working for the Stó:lō Nation began work on a story intended to show something about Stó:lō life and help educate outsiders as well as community members. The book is entitled

I Am Stó:lō, and McHalsie said, "I thought we would make up fictional stories for the book, fictional names of people, and other details. But it was going against the grain of Stó:lō historical practices to do that. So instead we used my daughter Kathryn [as a model]."

McHalsie's comment points to the particularity of Stó:lō historiography and the way in which it is deeply ingrained in practised community oral historians. In this sense, this Aboriginal practice closely parallels conventional historical methodology. But the Stó:lō historiographic sense is connected to specific spiritual sanctions in a way Western professional historical practice is not, and to an epistemology that is very demanding, perhaps more so than peer review in academic disciplines devoted to promoting new theses and to change itself, something like the point Wheeler was making in her expert report (2001). Perhaps it is an irony that a presentist culture, with a strong conviction that the future can and ought to be different and better than the past and present, disputes the ability to remember the past by members of what is often said to be a past-oriented people who find value in living as their ancestors have done. But I don't wish to create false dichotomies; Aboriginal people also want a better future, but they commonly say it comes from learning the practices of ancestors.

Contamination from Reading Academic Sources

"When I read Duff or Hill-Tout, I'm not reading what he wrote, but what the person who told him said. I'm not in Duff's mind, but that of the person who told him. I look at the filters" imposed by academics, said McHalsie. Wilson Duff was a professor of anthropology at the University of British Columbia and the author of a book about Stó:lō culture. His field notes from the middle of the twentieth century are a mine of information from what were then referred to as informants, by name. Charles Hill-Tout was an earlier semi-professional anthropologist whose texts were published long after his death. An interesting example of distortion of oral narratives by academics, a common problem as McHalsie notes, was Marius Barbeau's effort to strip Tsimshian Salmon-Eater stories of their "imagery or mysticism" to get at what he thought was their authentic meaning (Nurse 2006, 61-62).

The example of distortion by outsiders given by McHalsie was a book of poetry by Eloise Street, *Sepass Poems* (1963), which she translated through two languages into the rhythm of English poetry. McHalsie noted that Street claimed that it was given to her like that by Stó:lō people, even though the form is clearly distinct from Stó:lō aesthetics and language practices. It's unfortunate that the Crown report on oral traditions made reference to *Sepass Poems* without being aware of the problems with the work.

Commentaries by academics about the intrusion of academic publications into the thinking of Aboriginal people commonly fail to account for McHalsie's particularly insightful and trenchant comments. The academic and legal view appears to be circular: Aboriginal and other primitive peoples can't really remember, or they get it wrong, so they will invariably rely on academic sources, which itself demonstrates the failure of Aboriginal narratives. This view is a form of academic self-flattery and a disinclination to understand the role of Aboriginal intellectuals, who themselves have ways of evaluating texts, even those not from their own community. Duff and Hill-Tout can be evaluated to the extent that they reveal who their collaborators were. Duff's field notes, and to a lesser degree his publications, provide some contextual information about the people he worked with. These collaborators, now deceased, are well-known in the Stó:lō community, because Duff worked with some of the most noted oral historians whose practices continue to be discussed; they are, after all, among those referred to in contemporary oral footnoting. The genealogies of Duff's collaborators are well known to present-day oral historians.

The Floating Gap

A key issue in the literature on oral narratives in non-Western societies is the "floating gap," that inclination to focus clearly on the immediate past and the deep past, leaving the intermediate past hazy and possibly telescoped. Sonny McHalsie had a rather interesting comment on this issue, to which he seemed not to have given much previous thought. The academic term, at least, was new to him. He said:

> If there is a gap, as long as the main point of something ancient is what is emphasized [there is no problem]. As long as the protocols are followed. Ten generations ago they were doing the same thing. It's important for the present generation to know [about today] *and* a long time ago. The in-between time may not be emphasized ...
>
> Some can go back ten or twelve generations in their genealogy. Seven to eight is the usual. The Malloways, fourteen generations. They are *still* connecting way back there about important points way back then. There is an important teaching of thinking about seven generations. The word *tomiuk*, great-great-great-grandparent, is the same word as great-great-great-grandchild. The obligations run some seven generations backward and

> forwards. *The history is important in both directions to maintain the integrity of Indian names.* (emphasis mine)

McHalsie is here referring to the system of names commonly called "Indian" names, which are ancestral prerogatives given by senior family members to those they think have the same qualities as ancestors who held those names. It is a kind of spirit immortality, but the details are complex. An important point is that the Stó:lō have a specific motivation to recall details of the history of their family. Other families may make claims to the names, especially those that are highly esteemed and greatly prized, so historical knowledge remains important to be able to protect those names. And since the previous name-holders made their names great by their actions, the actions, too, are recalled. This sort of specific motivation to remember has not been understood by the Crown expert.

Chronology Is Essential to Western History and Place to Aboriginal Narrative

I explained the idea that, for some, history requires an implicit chronology and that Aboriginal narratives are thought to lack this in favour of emphasizing the landscape. McHalsie gave his own test for understanding chronology in a way that is culturally specific. There are three elements to this test: the existence of words in Halkomelem, the presence of a *sqwelqwel* story, and presence in cultural teachings. His approach supports the idea that expert interpretation is needed for Stó:lō narratives. This approach might be considered a historiographic method:

> I'm looking at things to see if things are *truly Stó:lō,* for example the Medicine Wheel and the Pow-Wow [come from the outside]. Is there a Halkomelem word for Pow-Wow costume? There's no word for it. The Pow-Wow came in 1976. There are words for *sx̱wó:yx̱wey* dances [masked dance], or Spirit Dances [sometimes referred to as Winter Dance]; there are Halkomelem words for parts of the costume. The *sx̱wó:yx̱wey* and Winter Dance was not supposed to use bright colours like Pow-Wow dancers. I look to whether there is a cultural teaching about something.

Lost Oral Narratives

Crown testimony, as I detail in Chapter 4, has featured the idea that communities have simply lost their oral traditions. In particular, they fail to have oral traditions about what seem to outsiders to be crucial events in the communities' history, casting doubt on the existence of any oral materials and on the veracity of those that are presented in court.

McHalsie noted, "It's more about important events ... An example is the rock walls [near Yale, BC]. The elders knew about it but never talked about it. Recently Chief Archie Charles told [BC Lieutenant Governor and Grand Chief] Steven Point, who told Ernie Crey, who told me and [historian] Keith Carlson. Archie Charles knew since the 1930s but didn't know its importance. It's extremely important."

McHalsie is referring to a set of rock walls on the Fraser River near Lady Franklin Rock that have since been studied carefully by archaeologists and Stó:lō people (see Schaepe 2006), and have been described as part of a system of fortification and communication in this region of intensive salmon fisheries and storage.

"Some refuse to tell about teachings tied to the Winter Dance. Something special shows itself to you – it's your power. If you tell it you can lose it or part of it," McHalsie said, telling of his feeling that when he gives tours of the cultural landscape and describes encounters in the myth period, he loses something of himself. He hesitates to tell these stories. "People with Spirit Power *can't* tell. Elders test them jokingly on it. Some don't get it. 'Look after what you have. Take care of it.'" That is, particular narratives aren't told because of the damage it can do. McHalsie refers to the need to be careful with knowledge and stories that have particular association with one's being – which includes spirit power. This reticence is different from the *loss* of oral narratives.

Variation in Stories Told by Individuals

McHalsie responded to the issue of variation in stories by noting the importance of proper training:

> Has a person been trained to tell stories? Tilly Guiterrez was brought overnight at puberty to the place where Xexá:ls stories were told. There were responsibilities to know. Then people came and told stories to her. Even people from Lytton [the home of other Indigenous groups]. Also, she practised to tell them. And, the teaching is that you have to be told three or four times before you can tell them.

Regarding tapes and transcripts of oral narratives, he asked: "Did the interviewer *ask* if they [the narrator] were a trained storyteller?"

Oral History as Documents

When asked if oral narratives might be regarded simply as historical documents, McHalsie responded, "But from the First Nations perspective there are different protocols to consider. There are connections to stories through *shxwelí*. That's still part of it." He added, "It [the documents] might still have *shxwelí*."

Moreover, movement and other aspects of an oral narrative are difficult to represent in a document: "Frank Malloway at the Chief's meeting said that stories in part are told with movements and actions to make the stories real." McHalsie noted that Chief Malloway brought to his attention that he was not using movements. "An important part was how it was told – the voice, expression." Amateur ethnographer "Oliver Wells got [elder] Dan Milo word-for-word." McHalsie noted, "Stories are in the voice and words."

Dancing and drumming are also part of storytelling. "Tilly [Guiterrez] says that oral tradition is songs. There are different categories of songs, travelling, spirit dance, and greeting."

For McHalsie, problems raised by the Crown regarding the nature of oral narratives are based on misunderstandings of Aboriginal practice.

Oral Narrative in Tribal Courts

Oral narratives appear in several jurisdictions other than mainstream Canadian courts, so it is useful to consider how they are treated there. These include US tribal courts and US courts handling cases under the *Native American Graves Protection and Repatriation Act* (NAGPRA; cases involving the repatriation of cultural materials to tribes). These tribal courts are the successors to earlier courts operated by the Bureau of Indian Affairs, and have limited jurisdiction over civil matters that arise between tribal members. In criminal cases, tribal jurisdiction exists but is limited by US legislation and constantly changing case law. Nevertheless, tribal courts exist all across the United States.

A small emergent literature deals with the specific workings of these tribal courts (e.g., Richland 2008, Nesper 2007, Miller 2001). (There is a larger literature regarding other issues in the tribal courts. See Pommersheim 1995, for example). In a study of the Hopi Appellate Court, Richland (2008, 9) noted that the Hopi court had been mandated by tribal legislation to consider Hopi traditions as binding sources of law, but had no formal way to introduce these into the court. In one particularly contentious case, the court heard the facts of the case before hearing the evidence regarding traditions of the community. Consequently, the court was left without traditional legal standards to evaluate the facts of the case. The court chose to remand the case for a re-hearing because of the procedural errors in the lower court, symptomatic of a growing procedural formalism. The case is also indicative of a tug-of-war between "competing legitimacy demands and of courtroom interactions which treat tradition discourses as either *statements of law* or as *testimonials of facts*" (10, emphasis mine).

The discourses in the Hopi courts engage a legitimizing strategy by linking to legal precedent in a manner similar to mainstream courtrooms. Interestingly, Richland observes that some Hopi themselves object to statements about Hopi law and governance "on the grounds that they *constitute hearsay statements* – that is, factual evidence of out-of-court statements typically treated in Anglo-adversarial litigation as illegitimate" (2008, 11, emphasis mine). Richland isn't writing directly of extended oral narratives, or narratives by community historians, but, rather, appeals to tribal practice couched in terms of tradition and traditional law. Yet the issue remains the same: the application of Aboriginal thinking, concepts of fact, and modes of expression to the courtroom.

My own study (Miller 2001) of the Northwest Intertribal Court System in western Washington State, established in 1979, indicates that no formal place is given to oral narratives in tribal litigation. Indeed, the chief justice of this intertribal system suggested in an interview with me that he thinks that he places little weight on traditional practice, but is unsure. Examination of the appeals court case law shows the opposite, however, and oral histories that embed in them statements of community values and legal practices are commonly presented in court. The opportunity to do this arises because for the tribes in this intertribal legal consortium, the sources of law are the tribal constitution and customary law. Given that each tribe has its own code, there are several ways in which prior practice, including that embedded in oral narratives, can enter into legal practice in this court system. One way is through the use of standing elders' councils that may offer advice to the court and may think through the situation in terms of oral narratives. In another variant, elders can be called as needed. In a third, elders are called upon in the sentencing phase. There does not appear to be the hesitation apparent in the Hopi system, although individuals entering into the system sometimes report concern that their civil rights be protected as in a mainstream court. The fourth way is through direct application of oral narratives available to the trial judge in the initial trial. Here, the language in the tribal codes allows for such appeals to "tradition."

One tribal youth code provides that "tribal law or custom shall be controlling, and where appropriate, may be based on the written or oral testimony of a qualified elder, historian, or other tribal representative." Another code allows that "if the course of the proceeding be not specifically pointed out by this code, any suitable process or mode of proceeding may be adopted which may appear most comfortable with the spirit of Tribal Law" (Miller 2001, 104). An example of the latter occurred in the intertribal appeals court, in which an appeal was lodged on the grounds of the failure to apply the exclusionary rule regarding pretrial testimony (formulated to prescribe police conduct) because it does not take into account Indian cultural background and community common knowledge (105). Further, one tribe's legal system includes the deployment of customary law, expressed through oral histories, at a stage of "sorting out" before the entry into the formal, adversarial courtroom, on mutual agreement between the parties.

Nesper (2007) looks at this question in more detail concerning an Ojibwe tribal court. He regards the tribal court as a vehicle for the creation of a tribal state and reflective of that process rather than what I refer to as "prior values," or what is often referred to as customary law. He describes the difficulties arising in the Lac Du Flambeau Ojibwe court with the tribe's indigenous discourse rules and the process of cross-examination. Further, he describes the entry of "customary law" into the court and the use of a cultural defence by defendants who "may be listened to and even engaged in their own terms. Their [sentences] may be reduced, but they rarely win" (692).

Other publications consider the role of oral traditions. Hutchins et al. (2008, 18) note,

> In the United States, certain American Indian nations' constitutions reflect the legislative and adjudicative roles of the nations' Elders (e.g., Bill Moore's Slough in Alaska, Wampanoag Tribe of Aquinnah in Massachusetts). For example, the Pueblo of Laguna's traditional governing officials, the *mayordomos,* are village Elders who participate in the resolution of village disputes referred to them by the elected Pueblo Council. *Mayordomos* rely on oral tradition to guide them in their dispute resolution. The Pueblo of Laguna have protected their oral traditions by never allowing their written codes to prevail over or displace their oral traditions or unwritten "customary or traditional law."

They further observe that in Canada the Labrador Inuit Constitution allows for customary law, which can be embodied in oral narratives, to be recognized before any established administrative or judicial authority. Further, the constitution enables two or more community members to give evidence as a group (Hutchins et al. 2008, 19-20). There are other developments of interest, but I wish to note that determining precisely *what* customary law might be is highly problematic. It is frequently contentious, and can be interpreted considerably differently, even in culturally related communities with overlapping kinship and ceremonial life (see Miller 2001).

Oral Narratives in Other Jurisdictions

Indigenous oral narratives have appeared in US courts for many decades, not always with a good reception. There does not appear to be a definitive decision, like *Delgamuukw III* in Canada, that opened the doors to these narratives. One scholar argues that the law marginalizes North American oral traditions despite their use as evidence in land claim cases (Stohr 1999, 7). A decision in a 1933 case, *Assiniboine Indian Tribe v. United States,* revealed that the court distrusted oral testimony. In *Coos Bay Indian Tribe v. United States* (1938), the testimony of twenty-one Indigenous people was disregarded because it conflicted with documents and because they may have been biased by a direct interest in the case (Stohr 1999, 7; Gover and Macaulay 1996, 9).

Later, the US Congress passed the *Indian Claims Commission Act* in 1946 to speed up the processing of Indigenous litigation. The Court of Claims that emerged from the act ceased operations in 1978 after hearing 617 separate dockets, many of which enacted the clash of orality and literacy (Stohr 1999, 7). In this legal venue, *Pueblo de Zia v. United States* (1962) deemed Aboriginal oral testimony entitled to some weight, but this was following corroboration by other forms of testimony. This approach to oral narrative as evidence was again applied in *Warm Springs Reservation v. United States* (1966), in which the judge ruled that oral evidence has some weight but needs corroboration. In addition, the judge believed that some informants may have described the wrong historical period in their testimony. Stohr (1999, 8) notes that the decision in *Warm Springs* implies that oral evidence is less important than documentary evidence and that the Indigenous testimony was limited to that which could be linked directly to the pre-contact period, leaving out more contemporary evidence.

Finally, in the highly significant case of *Mashpee Tribe v. New Seabury Corporation* (1978), the Mashpee Indians, among those who greeted the Pilgrims after their landing in the early seventeenth century, sought unsuccessfully to prove their existence as a tribe. Their oral testimony was said to be fluid and culturally based and therefore frustrating to the judge. Stohr notes that the judge could "only pick one version" of the truth and writes that the "shifting oral history of the Mashpee had to be set in documentary stone" (1999, 11; and see Clifford 1988; Miller 2004). The Mashpee were federally recognized several decades later.

An interesting feature of *Zuni Tribe of New Mexico v. United States* (considered in Chapter 1) is the use of anthropological informants as noted by Pandey, describing his own expert testimony:

> By the time we went to court in 1981 we had over eighty thousand "exhibits" in support of the Zuni case; we were a well-prepared team of historians, archaeologists, and anthropologists, but none of our evidence seemed to be getting through to the court. So when I took the stand I saw it as my task to *translate*, to interpret the Zuni vision of life.
>
> I started to treat the court like my classroom and asked whether I could use the blackboard. I then embarked on the telling of the Zuni myth of creation; and I began to plot on the blackboard the inclusive Zuni land area – all this on the basis of what I had learned about their traditions concerning habitation sites, hunting and gathering activities, agriculture and, most important, the sacred sites. Rather to my surprise, the judge started to take an interest in what I was saying – and he questioned me for several hours. So I became his informant ... I acted as mediator between tribal elders and the judge. (Pandey quoted in Paine 1985, 172, emphasis in original)

Pandey delivered Zuni oral histories second-hand and thereby included himself in the system of transmission. This raises the issue of outsiders as oral historians, which perhaps could be described as an inverse form of contamination. The more usual version is one in which an Indigenous person reads anthropology and bases his oral narrative on that; here, the anthropologist hears oral narratives and delivers them himself. But as Cruikshank (1944b) has pointed out, the concept that oral narratives are transmitted strictly along lineage lines and between each successive generation is a misreading of the reality and an unnecessarily ideal type.

Indigenous oral narratives were invited into the court for a new category of litigation following the US NAGPRA legislation, which enabled tribes to regain control of artifacts lodged in museums and other locations, following an adjudication of origins and ownership. NAGPRA proceedings have not yet produced a clear statement of the appropriate use of oral narratives as evidence.

4 Court and Crown

Shifts in the Canadian Court's Opinions

The historical predecessor to the Canadian court in Canadian territory, the British Crown, was once entirely familiar with oral tradition, which lies at the origin of concepts such as "time immemorial," and which is essential to the common law. But gradually oral tradition was supplanted by written statutes and case law. In the seventeenth and eighteenth centuries, treaties were negotiated with Indian nations according to the laws of these Indian societies that relied on oral narrative. By the 1820s, following the War of 1812, Aboriginal peoples and polities were no longer regarded as important allies, and the use of oral narratives in legal and diplomatic proceedings lost ground (see Williams 1996, 29). It is only later that our story returns to focus.

Legal decisions are always shadows of things gone before. There were rudimentary efforts at including Aboriginal perspectives even earlier than *R. v. Van der Peet,* as well as cases that apparently repudiated them. Gover and Macaulay (1996, 2) report, for example, that Mr. Justice Dickson in *R. v. Kruger* (1978) wrote that claims to Aboriginal title "are woven with history, legend, politics and moral obligations. If the claim of any Band in respect of any particular land is to be decided as a justiciable issue and not a political issue, it should be so considered on the facts pertinent to that Band and to that land, and not on any global basis." Chief Justice Lamer cited this decision on behalf of the majority in *Van der Peet.* In 1982 the Ontario Court of Appeal in *R. v. Taylor* (known as the *Bullfrog* case) ruled that oral traditions were relevant to interpreting treaties, creating an unspoken and unwritten exception to the hearsay rule (Williams 1996, 29).

In a more onerous decision in 1989 in the Supreme Court of Ontario, *Ontario (A.G.) v. Bear Island Foundation,* Mr. Justice Steele found that a chief, Gary Potts, could not give oral narrative evidence because he was not a proper carrier of the tradition on two grounds. He was not the son of a chief from whom he learned the traditions and he was not fluent in Ojibwe (Williams 1996, 29; Culhane 1998, 97-100). Regardless of the merits of the case, from an anthropological viewpoint this decision appears to make unwarranted assumptions about the nature of the transmission of oral histories. Further, the justice expressed disappointment that there was so little oral material entered as evidence, which he regarded as a weakness in the case (Simpkins 2000, 82). McLeod (1992, 1282) observes that in this case the "best evidence rule" caused the court to frown on the use of inferior evidence and to hold the position that factual records can be used to contradict oral history.

Newman (2005, 448n58) notes the opinion of the court regarding oral narratives at the time of the trial judgment in *Delgamuukw v. British Columbia,* as delivered by Chief Justice McEachern:

> The lengthy trial judgment of McEachern C.J.B.C. had examined general difficulties with oral history evidence, referring to the challenges in distinguishing the claimed factual content (at 243, 246, 247-48), the potential biases of oral history recounted by those involved in preparing a lawsuit (at 248), the potential that anthropologists might be required by their ethical codes to act in favour of the groups they studied (at 248-51), and the specific problems in the case that the oral histories had been subject to serious questioning under cross-examination (at 259), all of which, along with general issues around consistency and lack of detail (at 250-60), had led him to place little weight on the oral histories in the case: *Delgamuukw v. British Columbia* (1991), 79 D.L.R. (4th) 185 (B.C.S.C.) [Delgamuukw (Trial)]. This reasoning was not accepted in the context of the Supreme Court of Canada's expansive moves in favour of oral history evidence in *Delgamuukw,* though we shall later see similar factors returning.

As Newman suggests here, the Canadian court is not moving unambiguously toward an embrace of oral narratives. There appears to be a retreat since *Delgamuukw.* Val Napoleon, a leading Aboriginal legal scholar, certainly thinks so:

> The Court of Appeal's *Benoit* [*v. Canada*] decision denotes a regression from the promising principle set out by the S.C.C.[Supreme Court of Canada] in *Delgamuukw* to adapt the laws of evidence in order to accommodate Aboriginal oral histories. Indeed, while there is some optimism in the legal literature regarding a paradigm shift in the Western legal system's treatment of oral histories, and certainly, decisions such as *R. v. Marshall* could be seen to support such optimism, the court decisions on the whole appear to be increasingly restrictive. (2005, 137)

Hutchins et al. (2008, 11), however, don't see *Mitchell v. M.N.R.* as a retreat, as I explain below.

Chief Justice Beverley McLachlin, writing in *Mitchell* in 2001, articulates a sense that a wholesale abandonment of evidence rules is out of bounds:

> Again, however, it must be emphasized that a consciousness of the special nature of aboriginal claims does not negate the operation of general evidentiary principles. While evidence adduced in support of aboriginal claims must not be undervalued, neither should it be interpreted or weighed in a manner that fundamentally contravenes the principles of evidence law, which, as they relate to the valuing of evidence, are often synonymous with the "general principles of common sense" (Sopinka and Lederman, *supra,* at p. 524). As Lamer C.J. emphasized in *Delgamuukw, supra,* at para. 82 [*Delgamuukw III*]:
>
> > *... accommodation must be done in a manner which does not strain "the Canadian legal and constitutional structure"* [*Van der Peet* at para. 49]. Both the principles laid down in *Van der Peet* – first, that trial courts must approach the rules of evidence in light of the evidentiary difficulties inherent in adjudicating aboriginal claims, and second, that trial courts must interpret that evidence in the same spirit – must be understood against this background.[Emphasis added]
>
> There is a boundary that must not be crossed between a sensitive application and a complete abandonment of the rules of evidence. As Binnie J. observed in the context of treaty rights, "[g]enerous rules of interpretation should not be confused with a vague sense of after-the-fact largesse" (*R. v. Marshall,* [1999] 3 S.C.R. 456, at para. 14). In particular, the *Van der Peet* approach does not operate to amplify the cogency of evidence adduced in

> support of an aboriginal claim. Evidence advanced in support of aboriginal claims, like the evidence offered in any case, can run the gamut of cogency from the highly compelling to the highly dubious. Claims must still be established on the basis of persuasive evidence demonstrating their validity on the balance of probabilities. Placing "due weight" on the aboriginal perspective, or ensuring its supporting evidence an "equal footing" with more familiar forms of evidence, means precisely what these phrases suggest: *equal* and *due* treatment. While the evidence presented by aboriginal claimants should not be undervalued "simply because that evidence does not conform precisely with the evidentiary standards that would be applied in, for example, a private law torts case" (*Van der Peet, supra,* at para. 68), neither should it be artificially strained to carry more weight than it can reasonably support. If this is an obvious proposition, it must nonetheless be stated. (*Mitchell,* para. 38-39)

There is no mistaking the chief justice's aggrieved tone. She mentions the possibility of a "complete abandonment of the rules of evidence," and the existence of "highly dubious evidence" presented in support of Aboriginal claims. She fears a lack of credibility because of "a vague sense of after-the-fact largesse." She spends significant energy clarifying the positions emerging from the *Delgamuukw* and *Van der Peet* cases. There is a palpable sense that she feels things are getting out of hand, such that she has to make her position clear even though she feels it ought to be obvious; she senses confusion. Newman's view (2005, 239) of *Mitchell* is that it reinvokes the general principles related to hearsay evidence and the principles approach to exceptions.

In the euphoria in some quarters immediately after *Delgamuukw,* and before additional judicial commentary began to clarify, there were, perhaps, some ill-thought-out positions. One historian reports that some Aboriginal elders believed that only elder testimony should be accepted by the court and expert testimony excluded (Keith Carlson, personal communication, 2007).

The judgment in *R. v. Haines* provoked further controversy. A British Columbia judge dealt with the endlessly complicated and provocative issue of fisheries (in a resource extraction province) by undertaking a lengthy analysis of the background of the witnesses and their reliability. Meanwhile, the same year as *Mitchell,* in *Hwiltsum First Nation v. Canada (Minister of Fisheries and Oceans),* a federal judge determined a minimal threshold for reliability and found inconsistency between affidavit evidence and direct testimony, and therefore held the oral testimony inadmissible (Newman 2005, 239). Newman finds this to be a "tonic" to the controversy over evidence, but I believe the issue is more akin to the one that arose in the UK with the Chagossians, reported by Jeffrey (2006), who found confusion in the production and comprehension of evidence. This may reflect a disciplinary difference between anthropology and law.

A 2003 appeals court decision, *Benoit v. Canada,* developed the idea that there should be a boundary on oral historical evidence. Further, the trial judge wrote that there should be a *mandatory,* instead of possible, inquiry process concerning witnesses' ability to know about traditions and oral history. (Compare this to the later "may" provision in *Tsilhqot'in Nation v. British Columbia*.) Even Newman (2005, 240), who seems to me to lean more toward legal formalisms than toward viewing oral traditions from an Aboriginal perspective, calls these "a rough test to oral history." Napoleon (2005, 133) was blunter; to her, *Benoit* was a "chilling example of the continuing problems encountered by aboriginal claimants when tendering oral history as evidence." But Hutchins et al. (2008, 7) take a different view in a discussion paper, noting, "In actual fact, the Federal Court of Appeal in *Benoit* does not reject a reliance on the community standard for designating a community member as 'expert' or reliable in relation to a given oral tradition; the Court simply required more information on the standards applied by the community when qualifying an oral narrative as reliable."

In *Benoit,* the idea arose that corroboration might be necessary to render oral histories reliable and hence acceptable to the court, as well as the notion that oral history is different from more formally transmitted history and therefore suspect. To the extent that the latter is believed to be true, it doesn't seem that much progress has been made. And, if the Crown's argument is that oral histories are rendered documents amenable to standard historiographic methods, how is difference established? Overall, Newman (2005) saw a powerful reconciliation of principles, with particular features including reluctance to set out rules, flexibility, and the preference for government. First Nations, meanwhile, made clear that negotiations with government were made possible by the leverage provided by victories in the courts. And *Benoit* relied on Crown expert testimony that was highly suspect to anthropologists and Aboriginal scholars alike (Napoleon 2005, 135-36). Napoleon's view was that "there are several other very troublesome parts to the Court of Appeal's judgment. The Court relied on the evidence of von Gernet, quoting him at great length about weighting oral history evidence" (136). It's possible that *Benoit* was the high-water mark of this restrictive approach to oral narratives.

The 2008 judgment in *Lax Kw'alaams Indian Band v. Canada (A.G.),* another fishing rights case, employs another argument that appears to diminish the relative significance of oral narratives. In this case, the trial judge, Madam Justice Satanove, distinguished among primary, secondary, and tertiary sources, giving the greatest weight to primary sources, which are "the most immediate," including artifacts and observations of persons present at the relevant time and place. She writes, "Examples of primary evidence in the context of this case are artefacts and impressions from archaeological sites, ships' logs, journals and charts of fur traders, and later accounts of missionaries" (para. 4). Significantly, "There is no actual primary oral evidence available to me because no eye witnesses to the events of the 18th and 19th centuries are still alive." This perspective ranks oral narratives below written documents as a category of evidence; the proposition in *Delgamuukw* that oral narratives be given the status of history is thus long gone. Sadly, even the highly valuable but highly interpretive practice of archaeology is given more weight as a category. Many archaeologists themselves might dispute this relative ranking of evidence (University of British Columbia archaeologist Michael Blake, personal communication, 2008).

But Justice Satanove observes that the directions from the Supreme Court concerning the treatment of oral narratives usually pertain to true *adaawx,* or at least to testimonies of declarations made by a now-deceased member of a band as to land use and traditions. Here she is referring to formal chiefly oratories that recount clan histories. She clarifies that these deserve distinctive treatment because they are recounted in formal settings that provide opportunities for witnesses to confirm or object regarding accuracy. This is important, because the Crown had long argued against the position that accuracy could be ensured by these social processes. However, the justice's treatment of *adaawx* diminishes the value of other forms of oral narrative, which she largely discredits in her reasons for judgment. Because many communities do not have something equivalent to *adaawx,* this ruling appears to put the use of oral narratives in jeopardy.

Having noted that evidence can vary in cogency, the justice agreed with the defendant, the Crown, regarding how to evaluate the oral narrative evidence in this case, providing six factors:

> Therefore, the rules of evidence must be adapted to accommodate oral histories, but the admissibility and weight of such evidence must be determined

on a case-by-case basis. I agree with the list of factors that the defendant submits may affect the admissibility and weight to be given to oral history evidence:

a) the date and context in which the data was collected including the instructions under which the fieldworker was operating;
b) the identity of the informants, their age, tribal affiliation and connection to the Aboriginal culture;
c) whether a narrative is an *adaawx,* and, if so, whether or not it was recorded within the context of a feast;
d) whether the information that is to be relied upon is part of the "core" of the narrative;
e) the source and nature of the data upon which any conclusions are based from ethnographic summaries prepared by ethnographers; and
f) a comparison of alternative versions of oral narratives, historical or archaeological data. (*Lax Kw'alaams,* para. 41)

These six factors strike me as useful yet too literal. Why, for example, is it necessary that information that might be valuable be the "core" of a narrative, and how is the core to be determined (an old and intractable problem in anthropological theorizing)? Evidence elsewhere shows that apparently minor details of an oral narrative might be the most relevant for a particular case. Does factor (f) refer to comparing oral narratives and archaeological interpretations? Or is it about looking for various versions within each category?

In the 2005 decision in *Samson Indian Nation and Band v. Canada,* in which the court sat for three weeks on the Samson Cree reserve to hear the testimony of five elders, Mr. Justice Teitelbaum rejected the protocols used in gathering and transmitting oral history materials as guarantees of validation. Instead, he accepted the testimony of the Crown's expert, even though the expert had no knowledge specific to the plaintiff First Nation. Hutchins et al. (2008, 12) believe that this illustrates the opposition in the Canadian judiciary to the application of Aboriginal standards of reliability to oral traditions, even when they are formal and regimented. One critic observed that *Samson* discounted the reliability of oral narratives based on distinctions of the relative weight given to sacred and official oral histories, thereby treating oral histories as hearsay evidence (Davey 2007, 33).

The *Tsilhqot'in* case, in 2007, provided more court responses to the question of oral narratives. Hutchins, a prominent trial lawyer, found cause for optimism in Mr. Justice Vickers' approach, writing:

> Justice Vickers also asked plaintiffs' counsel to "outline the traditions of the people they represent," including how their oral history and traditions are preserved, who has authority to transmit such traditions, the community practices to ensure the integrity of these traditions and why the particular witnesses presenting evidence of such traditions were being called. He also considered how the Tsilhqot'in people assess the reliability of oral history and traditions as a preliminary guide for the Court. Thus, Justice Vickers looked largely to the Tsilhqot'in Nation to set the appropriate evidentiary standards for the admissibility of oral history evidence, thereby implicitly acknowledging the legal authority of the oral traditions and practices of the Tsilhqot'in Nation. (Hutchins et al. 2008, 14, citing *Tsilhqot'in,* para. 24; and see Mildon 2008, 92-93)

Further, Milward (2009) also found cause for limited optimism in those cases where oral historical evidence has helped prove Aboriginal rights claims. These cases include "*R. v. Jacobs,* where Justice McAulay found the oral evidence of the Stó:lō persuasive as to pre-contact use of tobacco despite the insistence of the Crown expert witness that there was a lack of support in historical and documentary evidence for such a conclusion." In addition, Milward (2009) noted oral evidence has been persuasive and has helped prove Aboriginal rights claims in *R. v. Willison, R. v. Morris, R. v. Breaker, Klahoose First Nation v. Sunshine Coast Forest District (District Manager), R. v. Goodon,* and *R. v. Catarat* (9).

"Sui Generis" Conference, February 2007

The court is not the only Canadian institution that has taken up the oral narrative question. The Canadian Department of Justice (DOJ) has also engaged the issue, sponsoring the *"Sui Generis"* conference in Vancouver in 2007. This conference was held to address some of the questions this book raises and to enhance the relationship between Indigenous litigants and the department. The title of the conference, *Sui Generis,* references the fact that the position of Aboriginal people of Canada is unique, and Aboriginal litigation is therefore distinct. Feelings have been ruffled for a long time in Canada, particularly following the 1980 decision in *Hamlet of Baker Lake v. Canada (Minister of Indian Affairs and Northern Development),* the Inuit land claim case in federal court that required the litigants to prove "that they and their ancestors were members of an organized society," as part of a four-part test set out by Mr. Justice Mahoney to establish Aboriginal title in common law (Culhane 1998, 92). This struck many people as tantamount to having to prove that they exist and are human, a comment I hear frequently from Aboriginal people of British Columbia. It also appeared to be a waste of courtroom and Aboriginal peoples' time and money, a delaying tactic meant to impoverish the communities until they simply gave up on their litigation. It has long seemed like foul play, insulting and humiliating. (The Liberal government of British Columbia in 2008-09 floated a proposal for legislation, which, among other things, might have eliminated this tactic by recognizing Aboriginal title. Political pressure from a variety of parties forced this measure to be dropped in 2009.)

The Department of Justice believes that conferences such as *"Sui Generis"* could help ease the antagonism (*Sui Generis* 2007). But others, including myself, believe that although people working for the Crown operate professionally and within professional ethics, current legal strategies make the antagonism unavoidable in an adversarial justice system. As I have shown in the section on oral narratives in the hands of the Crown researchers (Chapter 2), legal teams concoct legal strategies that strike them as winnable without necessarily considering the social costs. They carefully calculate the probabilities of legal success, as my collaborators pointed out, but it is less apparent that other costs are factored in. They have huge resources available to them in the form of money and researchers, and the Crown appears to employ the strategy of winning by attrition – simply wearing tribes out and running them out of money. Legal teams, after all, are focused on legal strategies to meet the objective. Making communities prove that they are "organized" must have seemed like a good idea, and it has been treated as an important precedent.

My thoughts, after attending two such DOJ meetings and speaking at one, are that the Crown lawyers and Aboriginal litigants are two solitudes largely unable to hear each other, even though groups such as the Indigenous Bar Association schedules meetings with judges' associations and others. While I applaud the Department of Justice for hosting such meetings as *"Sui Generis,"* and realize that they regard them as important and healing, I don't believe they have served this purpose. If you think someone else believes you are less than human, as I heard several Aboriginal people say at the *"Sui Generis"* conference, then coffee, muffins, and some talks will not heal the wounds.

At the 2007 conference, two very distinguished academics and eminent expert witnesses in Aboriginal litigation, Jim Miller (no relation), a historian at the University of Saskatchewan, and Arthur (Skip) Ray, a historian from the University of British Columbia, spoke bluntly about the Crown's employment of an unqualified and biased expert witness for oral materials (and see Ray 2008, 291). They plainly warned the Crown of the costs of hardball litigation practices.

In my own talk, I pointed out ways in which people gain expertise in Aboriginal affairs and how one might properly serve as an expert witness. My intention was to highlight the problem of deploying people without direct experience of Aboriginal communities, such as the Crown witness of that period. The notion of scientific neutrality denies the very messy process of anthropological (including archaeological) fieldwork. Scientific neutrality, one might note, appears possible if you haven't engaged in the sort of work that provides the insights necessary. The critique of the Crown position articulated by community intellectuals such as McHalsie, for example, would be unknown to those without fieldwork experience.

In recounting my talk here, I move from notes to an oral narrative, back to notes. I'm recreating what I might have said at the conference from a skeleton of notes. Unlike trained oral historians, I'm not using verbal cues or a memorized text to make a presentation. I'm just speculating. But, as I argue here, what is important in evaluating the reliability of oral narratives is that the message remain intact. That I can promise, in this case anyhow.

My Recreated Talk at the *Sui Generis* Conference

I start with this question: what can social scientists do for legal systems? Generally, we can provide specific knowledge directly relevant to a legal question. In that sense, we can help the court. And, since knowledges (including histories) are cultural products and are by their very nature interpretations, I will argue that there are both *authority* and *relational* qualities to knowledge and its production. I note that service as an expert witness requires a period of tutelage, of learning. It therefore requires an approach to knowledge. These facts generate these questions:

1 How do scholars learn about Aboriginal lives? How do they learn about Aboriginal histories and narratives?
2 How do they (we) apply this knowledge to particular legal questions?
3 What forms does this knowledge take? What epistemologies underwrite it? What rhetorical strategies are deployed?
4 What are the knowledge claims? Are there disjoints between what is claimed and the extent of one's knowledge?

Academic systems of tutelage (including university training) have properties that can be considered systems of authority and systems of relationship. By authority I mean subordination to mentors and supervisors. Students submit themselves to courses and to exams and other forms of evaluation. Within this system of tutelage there are titles of authority (such as the ranks of the professorate), there are boards of authority (such as councils of deans and university senates), and there are practices of authority (such as promotion and tenure exercises).

This system of authority has *adversarial* properties. Learners can claim something in course papers or in academic publications and be contested or refuted by authorities, such as professors and academics writing in journals. They can then counterclaim through revised papers and subsequent publications. Others, such as professors and editors, may serve as referees or even judges in this process. Within anthropological exchange theory (Boissevain 1974) all of these are regarded as *transactional* exchanges, which means they are contests of power, resources, and knowledge. Often particular people hope to win the day, just as a merchant hopes to sell his goods for the maximum price possible and the consumer hopes for the best deal.

By *relational* qualities in social sciences I mean that within scholarly communities there are processes of accommodation, interpenetration, response, reflection, listening, adaptation. People share ideas over coffee. People listen and reflect on what they encounter and turn it into something new, a new idea or approach. Concerning the body of knowledge, people understand, reject, revise, contribute. The modes of learning concern not just the familiar abstract and linear modes associated with seeing and hearing: reading, studying, and exam taking. There are also experiential, embodied modes of learning. People learn through other bodily senses; sound, music, smells, tastes. People learn through dreaming and through intuition.

Goulet and Miller (2007, 1) write, following Fabian:

> We know firsthand that in our own research activities we gained significant insights and knowledge precisely when we found ourselves, inadvertently, beyond the boundaries of our initial research intentions and proposals ... Our fieldwork was [enhanced] when the single-minded pursuit of data within a clearly defined research agenda was momentarily set aside, and the opportunity to enter deeply into the world of our hosts was embraced. To our surprise, this led to insights and knowledge that redefined our relationship with our hosts, deepened our ability to interpret them in more

meaningful ways, and opened the door to epistemological and ontological questions that begged to be addressed.

The exchanges Goulet and I describe here are *interactional* exchanges. They are not aimed at winning an exchange but rather at establishing and reproducing the exchange and the associated relationships, and using these to convey information.

Relational and authority systems overlap; they are not wholly distinct. For example, peer review of scholarly work has both properties: there is give and take, adjustment, revision, and also judgment and condemnation. My argument so far is that knowledge and our process of learning have relational and authority properties. Knowledge is not monotone (in one tone only); it is not simply monotonous. We don't learn only via text. Geertz wrote of culture as text, but read *in situ,* not primarily in a book. We learn with a greater inventory of senses; to learn only textually is impoverished.

Knowledge is not independent of our processes of learning. As social scientists and historians, we can't represent our knowledge as existing outside of these processes. That would misrepresent our knowledge. Knowledge is developed in several modes. One, as I mentioned, is embodiment. We learn via sensory perceptions. We might smell decay or wealth; we hear music that depresses, elevates, or mystifies. We sense others being moved by the music. [Medieval law had similar notions of the role of our senses in acquiring knowledge and owning property, as I noted in the Introduction]. We see images and feel the power of symbols. This is part of the relational mode. It is not incompatible with empiricism and positive science. Rather, these modes can be additive and interactively creative. Embodied knowledge can lead us to challenge and test empirical knowledge and to both see and expand the limits of authority.

Knowledge received only via disembodied and linear abstractions fails to be tested in particular ways. It's too flimsy and shallow. It's not adequate for our job with the legal system. We risk letting the legal system down. We don't know enough.

Now I can advance my claim: We want approaches to knowledge that (more) adequately reflect our modes of learning – that are broader, more embracing, offer more insight, and hence are more powerful, truer. Such an approach can connect to the way we learn in Aboriginal communities that offer their own practices of learning and their own epistemologies. Broader approaches to knowledge overcome false, misleading binary logics of useless postmodernism versus good positivism. As an example, I think of the application of binary logic to the comprehension of oral traditions, in which oral traditions are regarded as something like jukeboxes: you put in a coin and a particular tune plays. It has to be always the same; it can't reflect processes of interrogation and reflection. People, in this view, are from cookie-cutter societies without histories. They simply do what predecessors have done. Deviation from this is bad; conformity is good. Eric Wolf took on this problem thirty-five years ago in his book *People without History*. He demolished the idea of frozen non-European societies that experience no change, which are merely oral and mythological in contrast to the historical and dynamic societies of the European peoples and their diaspora.

We can dump these shallow debates, which emerge too often in academic and legal settings. The academics can persist in these debates at home, but when we dress up and go to courts, officials there want breadth, experience, and informed judgment from us. They want us to assist the court. [One of the four criteria for being accepted by the court as an expert under the *Mohan* test is "necessity in assisting the trier of fact" *(R. v. Mohan)*.]

Judgment is derived from broad experience and multiple modes of learning, not simply from systems of authority. Judgment derives from relational knowledge as well as systems of authority. My argument is that we need to tie our knowledge claims specifically to our modes of learning, instead of hiding them. Authority need not be at the expense of judgment. And authority claims without relational properties – without relating to the larger academic community, to the process of querying and peer review, in the give-and-take process of learning by adjustment, adaptation, innovation – is too limited.

I end with this question: Why should courts engage anyone's expert claims to knowledge that misrepresent or obscure their epistemological status or that limit their breadth, scope, and ability to offer judgment and merely offer authority? These comments frame my approach to the history of expert testimony on oral narratives in Canadian courts, which I narrate next.

Critique of Crown Theory and Practice

A Brief History of Crown Testimony

Following the decision in *Delgamuukw,* the Crown (more specifically, the Department of Indian Affairs and Northern Development, or DIAND) in 1996 commissioned an anthropologist, Alexander von Gernet, with a 1989

PhD from McGill, to prepare a study of oral history. Von Gernet's curriculum vitae, filed in 2006 in the *Tsilhqot'in* case with his expert report on behalf of the British Columbia branch of the Department of Justice, lists a string of federal agencies as his clients, including DIAND, the RCMP, and the Department of Fisheries and Oceans. His list of service as an expert witness includes nineteen entries, starting in 1993. Notably, his work as an expert includes such major cases as *Samson* (2005), *Tsilhqot'in* (2007), and *Benoit* (2003). Since the Crown repeatedly and frequently called on von Gernet to act as expert in landmark cases of Aboriginal litigation, the qualifications the Crown sought for their expert are significant.

He claims expertise, as noted by his submission of expert reports, for groups including the Plains Cree, Woods Cree, Sarcee, Blackfoot, Mohawk, Blood, Mi'kmaq, Cayuga, Chipewyan, Dene, Ojibwe, Oneida, Tsilhqot'in, and Tsimshian. These groups are located across the entirety of Canada from the Atlantic to the Pacific, and include coastal peoples as well as prairie groups.

The Crown's reliance on a sole anthropologist for cases involving distinct peoples from widely ranging local cultures seems to follow the aforementioned logic that Aboriginal peoples are a "people without history." While some anthropologists do cross-cultural work (producing insights into human culture and society generally), they ordinarily work with specific communities, often for many years. Some work with several communities, but few, I believe, would claim expertise about a large number of distinct Aboriginal nations.

The Crown, I would argue, has a duty to identify and retain academically prepared experts with the appropriate training and ability to deal with the complex issues concerning Aboriginal history and oral narratives. I would argue further that the task for such an expert requires detailed knowledge of the culture and history of the group entered into litigation.

Specifically, I suggest that the Crown retain anthropologists and scholars from other disciplines who have active programs of field research in the community (Mills and Daly come to mind for their work) and who have been able to develop their insights over time. The Crown expert should be able to understand local notions of fact, as I discussed in Chapter 3, or put more broadly, the epistemological system. Vansina (1985) and Wheeler (2001), for example, discuss the importance of immersion in a society to understanding its sense of time and chronology, points that McHalsie also raised in Chapter 2. The work of those employed by the Crown should have been exposed to critique by professional peers, and, I suggest, by knowledgeable Aboriginal community members, as Winona Wheeler and others have suggested. In fact, Wheeler talks of scholars being educated by the Aboriginal community in epistemology and modes of thought. I described this above as participation in systems of tutelage; Goulet and I noted the importance of openness to ideas and insights outside of a formal research agenda. Knowledge in this sense is embodied as well as rational. Further, Cruikshank's work (1998), for example, demonstrates the value of long-term fieldwork for gaining access to community views, stories, and perspectives. Wiget (1995) describes the importance for litigation of the ability to properly "decode" the local community, which comes from fieldwork. The Crown has had difficulties recruiting experts with the qualifications I describe here, but, nevertheless, the Crown's engagement in vastly expensive litigation on behalf of Canadian citizens demands that they recruit qualified people.

The Crown has made extensive use of an expert whose academic training is considerably different than what I propose here. This expert is trained in archaeology and ethnohistory, but not ethnography or ethnology, and does not use field-based ethnographic methods to understand the culture, oral narratives, and history of the community in question. However, the Crown expert has frequently, but not uniformly, found favour in the courts, and the Crown's history of deploying this expert in a series of cases follows from these successes. For example, Mr. Justice Nadon, of the Federal Court of Appeal, in the reasons for judgment in the *Benoit* case (para. 112), writes, "In my view, the approach suggested by Dr. von Gernet to oral history evidence is undeniably a proper approach and is entirely in line with the remarks made by McLachlin C.J. at paragraph 38 of *Mitchell, supra,* where she indicated that evidence adduced to support Aboriginal claims should not be weighed in a manner that 'fundamentally contravenes the principles of evidence law.'"

Other judges have noted difficulties with the Crown testimony and its theory of oral narratives. Justice Vickers writes,

> Despite what Canada has argued, I was left with the impression that Dr. von Gernet would be inclined to give no weight to oral tradition evidence in the absence of some corroboration. His preferred approach, following Vansina, involves the testing of oral tradition evidence produced in court by reference to external sources such as archaeology and documentary history ... Trial judges have received specific directions that oral tradition evidence, where appropriate, can be given independent weight. If a court were

> to follow the path suggested by Dr. von Gernet, it would fall into legal error on the strength of the current jurisprudence. (*Tsilhqot'in*, para. 154)

All of this takes on additional significance because, as Ray (2008, 290) observes, the burden of proof in civil matters such as land claims cases requires the Crown merely to raise reasonable doubts about the evidence brought by the Aboriginal claimants.

The Department of Justice asked their expert to create a baseline study of oral materials prior to conducting legal defences of the Crown position in opposition to Aboriginal claims of various sorts, but particularly land claims. In effect, this report (von Gernet 1996) constitutes the Crown theory of oral narratives. In the words of the Crown expert:

> The Department of Indian Affairs and Northern Development requested that I undertake research to answer the following questions:
>
> 1 How are oral tradition and oral history defined in the literature? Does the literature distinguish between these and modern oral accounts?
> 2 Based on a secondary source review, what are the issues which surround the use of North American oral tradition in mainstream history [and anthropology, as well as related disciplines]?
> 3 Based on a review of contemporary and modern oral accounts of historical events, how consistent do oral traditions remain over time? What factors contribute to the changing expressions of oral tradition?
> 4 What research (or secondary source material) has dealt with oral tradition in a legal perspective?
> 5 Based on a list of summarized court cases which deal with the issue of oral tradition and on a secondary source review, what are the factors that limit, and/or enhance, the utility of oral tradition in the Canadian legal system?

The responses to these questions constitute a framework for the Crown's effort to respond to Aboriginal oral narratives entered as evidence in court. But, in my reading, there are several significant problems with the Crown's position.

Crown Written Testimony

After the Crown researchers and lawyers have prepared a position regarding litigation with Aboriginal communities, experts are commonly brought into the proceedings to answer particular questions of interest to the court. The Crown has an obligation to Aboriginal peoples sometimes subsumed under the phrase "the honour of the Crown." This obligation, I argue, includes the need to develop appropriate theories of evidence regarding oral narratives, and to ensure that evidence is carefully prepared. To get at these issues, and to represent Crown practice, I give a textual interpretation of a Crown report presented in *Sawridge Band v. The Queen* and *Tsuu T'ina First Nation v. The Queen* (von Gernet 2006a). This report relies on the same approach used by the Crown in other cases. My reading of the sources relied on by the Crown has led me to draw different conclusions.

Definitions

At the heart of developing an adequate theory of oral materials is determining how they might be defined and understood. The Crown established its position through the work of their expert, but the sources do not adequately support the Crown's proposition. The Crown report (von Gernet 2006a, 20) addresses the issue of definitions and advances the position that the field of oral materials can be divided into oral histories and oral traditions. Here the Crown expert acknowledges that definitions vary by disciplinary affiliation and problem orientation, and that some scholars differentiate between the ideas of oral materials as processes or products. There are important implications for the Crown theory of oral narratives.

The Crown cites Henige (1974, 2) on page 20, footnote 60. Henige says oral traditions span more than three generations, not one, as in the Crown formulation:

> For the purposes of this study the term "oral tradition," unless specifically qualified, refers to that corpus of orally transmitted material which addresses itself to specifically recounting the past. This implies in most instances some attempt at assigning some form of duration and sequence to events *over a period of time exceeding three generations,* that is, a length of time beyond the maximum limits of personal testimony and experience. (emphasis mine)

Notably, Henige does not give a definition of *oral history* at that point. However, in a later work, Henige (1982) defines both *oral history* and *oral tradition.* These also differ from those of the Crown expert and cast doubt on his claim that his definitions have "widespread usage," as the following passage reveals:

> "Oral history" and "oral tradition." Though quite different – one an activity, the other a genre of source, these terms have frequently been used interchangeably. As normally used nowadays, "oral history" refers to the study of the recent past by means of life histories or personal recollections, where informants speak about their own experiences ... Tradition – as in "oral tradition" – also has, or should have, a connotation of its own. In order for anything to be regarded as a tradition, it should be widely practiced or understood in a society and it must have been handed down for at least a few generations. The term, however, is all too often misapplied to represent just about anything to which anyone wishes to give legitimacy or added luster. *Strictly speaking, oral traditions are those recollections of the past that are commonly or universally known in a given culture.* (Henige 1982, 2, emphasis mine)

This last point is considerably different from the Crown view that oral traditions are "documents about past events transmitted by word of mouth over at least a generation" (von Gernet 2006a, 21). Further, Henige (1982, 106) writes, "This practice of interviewing people about their own experiences is generally called oral history, or sometimes life history." To Henige oral history is a *practice* rather than a body of material.

I also draw different conclusions regarding Vansina's views of the topic than does the Crown. Vansina (1985, 19), cited frequently by the Crown, writes,

> *Group accounts are the typical "oral traditions"* of many authors. They are oral memories of groups such as villages, chiefdoms, kingdoms, associations, and various kinship groups. I have called them "groups" because they embody something which expresses the identity of the group in which they are told or substantiates rights over land, resources, women, office, and herds. They are all institutionalized to some extent. They are told officially on formal occasions. They are often property of a group. (emphasis mine)

This definition of "oral traditions" differs from that of the Crown, which defines oral traditions as recollections of *individuals*. The Crown doesn't clearly specify whether oral traditions are group activities. Another issue is that, to Vansina, oral traditions are very significant features of the life of a group. As indicated in the quotation above, oral traditions embody the identity of the group, substantiate rights, and are institutionalized. The Crown definition tends to trivialize oral traditions by omitting these features, and consequently the Crown theory is thin regarding a significant issue.

Next, Vansina (1985, 27) writes, "We are now ready to define oral traditions as *verbal messages* which are reported statements from the past beyond the present generation. This definition specifies that the message must be oral statements spoken, sung, or called out on musical instruments only." The point here is that, to Vansina, oral traditions are not documents but rather *verbal messages.* However, oral traditions are transmitted in ways other than speech, including music and dance. The definition advanced by the Crown doesn't take any of this into account.

The Crown report also cites Finnegan (1992, 7-8) who provides a two-page explanation of the terms *tradition* and *oral tradition,* and points to the complexities of these ideas, noting that they conceal ambiguities. My reading of Finnegan leads me to conclude that her views are contrary to those of the Crown.

Cohen (1989) is yet another scholar whose work is cited by the Crown. Here, too, I draw different conclusions from the texts. Cohen summarizes the changing definitions, beginning with Henige's definition (1980) of *oral tradition.* Cohen also uses the term *oral testimony:* "Versions that are not widely known should rightfully be considered as 'testimony' and if they relate to recent events they belong to the realm of oral history" (Henige 1980, cited in Cohen 1989, 9-10). Then Cohen discusses Vansina's "far more complex definition" (including specific and distinctive types), and notes that Joseph Miller does not include "universality" within a culture as a requirement and defines oral tradition as "a narrative describing, or purporting to describe, eras before the time of the person who relates it" (Miller (1980), quoted in Cohen 1989, 10).

Cohen (1989, 9-10) also discusses Sahlins's definition (1983), which highlights the "heroic" and the "collective" traditions, which can be seen as elite and commoner traditions. Cohen notes the problems in these formalist definitions. In sum, Cohen is doing what his title says, which is "The Undefining of Oral Tradition" to avoid the rigidity of these formal definitions. He does not provide his own definitions in these two pages cited by the Crown expert, but shows how existing definitions are problematic. A reading of Cohen's work therefore does not support the Crown position regarding definitions of oral materials.

Julie Cruikshank is a major authority on oral materials. She is the winner of the Victor Turner Prize from the American Anthropology Association for her 2005 book *Do Glaciers Listen?,* the John A. Macdonald Prize from the Canadian Historical Association for her 1990 work on oral history, *Life Lived Like a Story,* and the Robert F. Heizer Prize, awarded by the American Society for Ethnohistory, for paper judged to be the best paper in ethnohistory published in 1994, for "Claiming Legitimacy: Prophecy Narratives from Northern Aboriginal Women" (1994a). She summarizes several of these issues about the Crown's use of Vansina and draws different conclusions than does the Crown. She notes that the Crown definition ignores key points that Vansina makes in response to criticisms of *his* definition by anthropologists:

> Further, this definition originates with Vansina, a source frequently cited by Dr. von Gernet, who [Vansina] does distinguish between oral tradition and oral history, but also says (1985, 28), "Obviously, our definition is a working definition for the use of historians" and notes that other disciplines, including social sciences, will have their own definitions that meet their own needs.
>
> a) Vansina concurs that most specialists in this area *reject* this sharp distinction between oral tradition and oral history: "in practice they fuse oral history and oral tradition" (page 29).
> b) Vansina makes the distinction between product (the message) and process (transmission) (page 1, pages 27-29).
> c) Vansina says that there is a distinction between "news"/information and "interpretation" (what we would call historiography).
> d) *Vansina* (p. 30-31) concurs with his critics that the idea of a single chain of transmission is probably idealized; that as traditions are discussed and debated there are probably no neat lines of transmission; *that redundancy and incorporation of written documents is common and does not necessarily result in distortion: "Multiple flow does not necessarily imply multiple distortion only, rather perhaps the reverse" (p. 31). He cites examples where written documents are incorporated into oral tradition and "serve as a fountainhead for oral tradition" (page 31).* In other words, even Vansina is more nuanced than von Gernet. (Cruikshank, personal communication, 2006, citing Vansina 1985, emphasis mine)

Responding to a different expert report filed by von Gernet (2006b), Cruikshank (personal communication, 2006) noted that the Crown use of her own materials was not supported by her work: "My objection to this definition (von Gernet's distinguishing oral history/oral tradition) [is] *it doesn't represent Aboriginal definitions – they don't make this distinction*" (emphasis mine). She also notes several errors in his citations of her publications.

The Claim of Lost Oral Traditions

Another theoretical issue of importance is what the Crown refers to as "lost oral traditions." Von Gernet (2006a, 24) writes, "An oral tradition, on the other hand, is irrecoverable once lost." This is an important point, but not supported by the references cited, some of which point to the importance of conducting fieldwork to find whether oral materials are present. Even then, my years of fieldwork have shown me that one cannot ever be sure that particular sorts of oral materials are not present in a community, since any researcher knows only a limited number of community members and since some simply don't wish to share their knowledge for many reasons, a position supported by the sources cited by the Crown. Further, oral traditions can be retrieved in pieces with mnemonics and through the use of related oral materials, or oral materials from surrounding communities, another point identified in the Crown sources.

Von Gernet (2006a, 26-27) makes the claim that the Assiniboine could not remember acquiring horses, believing mistakenly that they had horses since time immemorial. The Crown argues that the Assiniboine don't remember their own history because they "had no idea that they [horses] would become such an integral part of their life and *saw no need to take special note of the circumstances*" (27, emphasis mine). Von Gernet cites a secondary source written by a historian of Africa (Vansina 1985, 115-16) regarding this topic, but Vansina does not support the Crown proposition. Vansina's point is not that the Assiniboine lacked an account of the acquisition of horses, but that the account is contained within a creation myth rather than other forms of oral narrative. The problems here are that secondary materials like this aren't sufficient and that there are questions about the idiom of expression. Vansina noted that Lowie misunderstood the same point:

> Lowie, however, did not realize that the first horse may not have ranked as an important event, because the people then could not know how it was about to change their lives. Some three generations later when the horse had become central to the Assiniboine, it could no longer be imagined that such an important acquisition had ever been absent, just as one could no longer imagine that life had ever been fundamentally different from what it was then. So significant had the horse become that it "always had been

> there" and hence belongs to creation myths ... The Assiniboine situation resulted because *they overestimated the importance of what happened, not because they had no sense of that importance.* (Vansina 1985, 115-16, emphasis mine)

The report (von Gernet 2006a) also cites "Oral Tradition as Complement," by Gordon M. Day (1972). Day notes, "But I am more interested in a programmatic deduction which can be made, namely, that if so much really old oral tradition can be obtained from a superficially extinct culture such as the Abenaki, how much more there must be lying about in North America waiting to be collected" (107). Day's observations do not support the Crown's theory that an expert is able to determine that a particular community has no oral traditions about a particular event. Australian courts have apparently found it unnecessary to treat an absence of evidence, including oral narratives, as proof of an absence of historical Aboriginal use of a particular location (French 2004, 89; Asche 2004, 57).

Invented Tradition/History

The Crown has relied on a theory of invented tradition/history, a theoretical issue that has drawn considerable attention since the 1980s, in arguing that some oral narratives might not be legitimate. Here again, a reading of the cited sources leads to a different conclusion. Von Gernet's idea (2006a, 31) that "when there is no apparent history it inevitably is created" cites Hanson (1997), among others. Hanson's essay, titled "Empirical Anthropology, Postmodernism, and the Invention of Tradition," was written to *refute* claims that "invented traditions" are created from nothing. The article addresses the "radical misunderstanding" (200) of his views, particularly the idea that the phrase "the invention of tradition" means that such traditions are false. Hanson writes, "I was sufficiently persuaded by the theoretical position that *all* culture is invented, and is rendered in no way inauthentic for that fact" (199, emphasis mine). Further, he notes, "But the danger, of course, is that the inattentive reader, or someone who learns about it through newspapers or hearsay, may not follow the argument and, never getting beyond the initial impression, end up with the radical misunderstanding of it." Hanson writes that in hindsight he wished he had used the term "reformulation" of tradition to avoid any connotations of being invented from thin air or false (200).

Another citation in support of the Crown's view that "when there is no apparent history it inevitably is created" is Harkin (1997). I draw a different conclusion from Harkin's work. Like Hanson (1997), Harkin (1997, 98) writes, "We must thus contest the use of the term 'invention,' implying as it does creation ex nihilo. It seems clear rather that this phenomenon involves the selection and ritual framing of latent symbols, which are already present within the culture." The work of Harald Prins (1994, 385), also cited in the Crown expert report, helps here. Prins writes that Hobsbawm and Ranger (1983) need to be qualified, and Prins breaks down "invented tradition" into three subcategories, namely, invented tradition itself, retrieved tradition (or revivals), and adaptive tradition (those borrowed and inserted into local culture).

A third source cited by the Crown for the assertion "where there is no apparent history it inevitably is created" is Thompson (1988, 1), and here, too, I draw different conclusions. On that page, there is no reference to history being "created." Thompson's main point there is his first sentence, which serves to introduce his book: "All history depends ultimately upon its social purpose." Thompson follows with a demonstration of two poles of historical interest: one being that of a researcher paid by public dollars who cares for nothing but being able to maintain his job and do his research (ivory tower history that has no effect on society); the other ("at the other extreme") being that of history used in an Orwellian manner to serve political ends (wars, revolution, justification for exploitation, expulsion, etc.). In any case, Thompson *is not writing about oral material but about history.* He is suggesting that only in extreme cases will history be created.

Crown theory also builds on interpretations of Sider and Keesing. The Crown report (von Gernet 2006a, 32) notes, "Some groups antagonistically confront other people's version of their history [note 98] and in the process replace their own earlier traditions with new ones.[note 99]" Note 98 cites the 1993 work of Gerald Sider, an anthropologist, pages 6-7. There is no 1993 work by Sider in the report's bibliography, so I will assume the reference is to his key work on this topic, *Lumbee Indian Histories: Race, Ethnicity, and Indian Identity in the Southern United States,* an important book by a leading scholar. Page 6 in Sider's book critiques the idea that Aboriginal people invent history to legitimate their group interests and group claims:

> Superficially, what seems to happen when different historical claims become interwoven with different strategies for coping with domination is what anthropologists following the lead of Malinowski have called "history

> as charter." In this analytic perspective, people invent histories, either "mythic" (supernatural) or presumably "real" (secular), to justify or legitimate their group interests and group claims. This is *a drastic simplification of how histories actually develop and get used – for two major reasons.* 1. It makes history too much of an intellectual phenomenon, a matter of ideas and words, slighting the direct material expression of history – the multiple ways people's history becomes carved into their bodies and lives. 2. It makes the connection between history and the interests of the groups appear seamless and smooth, *when actually a people often must antagonistically confront not only other people's versions of their own history but their own.* (emphasis mine)

By my reckoning, Sider is making precisely the opposite points to those suggested in the report, saying that (1) it is in error to simply connect oral materials and their uses with instrumental ends, (2) members of a group must deal with their own circumstances and not simply what is said about them, and (3) histories are embedded in their lands, tools, hands and faces, the conditions of their houses and villages, and other features of the landscape. Sider is making the point, so often expressed by experts in oral traditions, that they are engaged and retained in more than just verbal performances (see, for example, Gordillo 2004, Berman 2004, Cruikshank 2005).

The second note in the quoted sentence on page 32 (von Gernet 2006a) cites Roger Keesing, a deceased anthropologist of international reputation and a former member of the Canadian Anthropological Society. Although the Crown report cites a 1986 journal article by Keesing, I believe his major work on this issue, *Custom and Confrontation: The Kwaio Struggle for Cultural Autonomy* (1992), should be considered. Keesing's point in this book is not that traditions are replaced wholesale, but rather that the Kwaio struggle to retain their traditions, their *Kustom,* as the Kwaio say it, in the face of colonization. The Kwaio, in fact, asked Keesing to help them do this by mirroring the colonial categories used to dominate them (196) while simultaneously encapsulating, insulating, and thereby protecting traditional practices to the extent that they could. Both Sider (1992) and Keesing (1992) are *not* making the point simply that people manipulate, but rather that they resist domination by colonizers. It seems reasonable and scholarly to me that the larger message of these two books be considered in selecting quotations from them in order to avoid drawing the wrong conclusions from their work. The abstract for the 1986 journal article by Keesing cited in the Crown report, in any case, emphasizes the richness and accuracy of Kwaio oral tradition, rather than inaccuracy:

> Abstract. A hundred years ago (1896) a Queensland schooner recruiting indentured laborers in the Solomon Islands was attacked by Kwaio warriors (Malatia) seeking plunder, vengeance, and glory. The attack, repulsed with loss of life on both sides, was recounted by survivors in an 1886 inquiry and their testimony is compared to accounts passed down in Kwaio oral tradition, including an epic chant. *The Kwaio accounts are surprisingly rich and accurate, and show the value of indigenous oral tradition in ethnohistorical analysis.* (1986, 169, emphasis mine)

The Crown report (von Gernet 2006a, 33) states that "anthropology has enlightened others about the range of human possibilities, examined assumptions about other cultures and offered a valuable critique of Western Society.[note 101] Similarly, historians have gone beyond what 'really happened' and developed an interest in what people believe." The work cited in the footnote 101 (Cruikshank 1990, 1992, 1996), isn't similar and must be understood differently because she doesn't claim First Nations *go beyond* what really happened. She has argued that the study of Aboriginal oral materials isn't simply about what happened, but that's a different claim than saying scholars "go beyond," which carries a connotation of falseness. She's talking about the direction of academic research, not about patterns of distortion or lying.

There is a useful observation on page 33. Von Gernet (2006a) writes, "Since people usually act in accordance with what they believe, scholars must try to understand each culture on its own terms." This is important and establishes a scholarly standard, but one that is inconsistent with the repeated Crown insistence that Aboriginal people are attempting to present biased or invented materials to the court.

The Crown, in building its theory of oral narratives, relies heavily on several sources, in addition to major theorists such as Vansina and Henige. The report cites Moss and Mazikana 1986 repeatedly (von Gernet 2006a, 7, 16, 17, 21, 25, 26, 33, 43, and twice on 51), as well as five other works by Moss (8, 22, 31, and 51). I presume from this that the Crown places some weight on the ninety-six-page pamphlet by Moss and Mazikana (1986), which the authors aimed at record management and archival practice, rather than the concepts of oral traditions. However, I have looked carefully at how the Crown addresses the ideas in this work and have drawn quite different conclusions. The report notes:

> Oral tradition is part of a continuous process of text-making and is at least partly transformed and reinterpreted by both tellers and listeners every time it is repeated. Each retelling is a separate composition-in-performance recreated around a skeleton. When taped or written down, a dynamic speech becomes, for better or worse, frozen at an *arbitrary point in time* and can be stored independently of human memory. As such, it is no longer able to readjust to changing circumstances and *may become disembodied from its original context.* (von Gernet 2006a, 7, emphasis mine)

In this instance, the footnote cites, among others, Moss and Mazikana (1986, 2). But these authors make different claims. They note that oral traditions make inherent and valuable contributions to social cohesion, dynamic evolution, and the durability of the culture they represent: "Oral traditions are therefore changed in the very act of recording from dynamic and developing or evolving self-consciousness into fixed and static 'snapshots' of the culture at one point in its development. They become *abstracted* from the process that creates and nurtures them and in this they necessarily become dated very rapidly."

Moss and Mazikana are not claiming anything about arbitrariness, as the Crown suggests. Nor do they use the language of disembodiment. Rather, they are suggesting that as cultures develop and circumstances change, so too do aspects of the oral traditions. They don't say that they become inaccurate or useless; indeed they state otherwise in this piece. They appear to be implying a shift rather than a disembodiment. Oral traditions may become outdated, say Moss and Mazikana, but this is far different from disembodied, surely a metaphor that suggests death. They use a different concept, that of abstraction. It doesn't appear to me that Moss and Mazikana argue, as the Crown does, that oral traditions become disembodied through their transcription for legal proceedings.

Moss and Mazikana 1986 (4-6) is cited again in the Crown report (von Gernet 2006a, 25n71) to support a paragraph that reads,

> An oral tradition, on the other hand, is irrecoverable once lost. In fact, today there are no oral traditions about the Albany "Deed" of 1701. Moreover, an oral tradition may have many additional encoding and decoding

> interpretations as it moves through time, for it must be recreated at least once every generation in a continuous transmission or it is lost to posterity. This does not automatically render it less reliable, but it certainly makes it *fundamentally* different from a primary record prepared at the time of the historical event and deposited in an archive. (emphasis mine)

But Moss and Mazikana don't write of any fundamental differences on the pages cited. Instead, they write about selective records and transactional records. Moss and Mazikana write that constitutions, laws, contracts, deeds, treaties, diplomas and other similar documents are all transactional records and primary documents. Selective records are attempts to preserve and communicate to others what is happening at a certain time. Recordings of oral history interviews and oral traditional narratives, they write, are selective records, as are audio and video or cinematic recordings, and stenographic notes. Some items, such as letters, are not clearly a member of either category. They conclude,

> Selective records are highly valued as historical evidence for their contemporary character, but their evidential value must always be somewhat less than that of transactional records. The very interpretive nature of the selective class of records, however, produces commensurate abstract value for the historian. Selective records, are, after all, primary evidence of what someone decided to record or was capable of recording. (Moss and Mazikana 1986, 6)

The issue at stake here, in my reading, is that Moss and Mazikana are not dividing materials strictly into fundamentally different classes with implied distinct and fundamentally different properties. Indeed, some materials are not easily classified. And, what they call selective records have the quality of being "primary," in this case evidence, just as transactional records are "primary" documents. As to their evidential value, Moss and Mazikana write that selective records have a value that is "somewhat less," not fundamentally less. They further note that if selective records are "generally more deliberate and purposeful than whimsical or random, then we may infer some contemporary value to the interpretations or selection" (7). This is far different from arbitrariness in the recording of oral traditions proposed by von Gernet (2006a, 7).

Von Gernet (2006a, 16) also quotes Moss and Mazikana (1986, 12):

> Oral traditions are similar to other sources of historical evidence insofar as they exist and therefore have to be consulted. Like all other sources of historical evidence, this consultation does not imply usage, merely that they be taken into account ... They are, however, sources that are not very easy to use, and they require much skill for reliable use. They also require a knowledge of the society in which they were created, the purpose of their existence, the manner of transmission and preservation and the circumstances of their narration or recitation.

These comments themselves require context, just as Moss and Mazikana argue for understanding the context of oral traditions. Their report is aimed at archivists and record managers without specialized knowledge of oral materials. It is not intended as a definitive scholarly study of oral materials. Moss and Mazikana, in their brief history of oral history and oral tradition, reveal that they are, in 1986, responding to the rapid rise of interest in oral histories in the United States following the success of the *Roots* television show about slavery and Studs Terkel's best-selling book of biographies of working people. This developing public interest in old-timer's tales, recordings of the lives of ordinary people, and folk traditions leads them to note that "some efforts have been made to bring traditional reins of discipline to the unruly practice of oral history" (18). They write of their concern for the "radicalization of history" in the 1960s. Their manuscript has the aim of imposing order on the masses of people engaged in the production of oral materials.

But, critically, *I can find no reference in the document to the oral materials (or practices regarding them) of the Aboriginal peoples of North America.* Moss and Mazikana 1986 is a primer for those who do not engage in the production or use of oral materials, the archivists and record managers, who were themselves facing masses of ordinary people, untutored in professional methods, coming to use their facilities. I witnessed this phenomenon myself while using federal archives in the United States during this period. The majority of people entering the archives, such as that at Sandpoint, in Seattle, Washington, were amateur historians hoping to find information about their genealogy and other recorded information about their pioneer ancestors. This posed significant problems for staff.

The Moss and Mazikana work, which is now twenty years old and not up to date, was never intended as a definitive characterization of the academic field. The section on oral history is only three pages long and addresses the oral traditions and histories of ordinary people and those other than Aboriginals of North America. The report (von Gernet 2006a, 50) later observes, "In this way, remembered facts are supplemented with constructed facts to produce a version of the past." The footnote at this point (n177) lists several sources, including Moss (1974, 9). Moss is indeed dealing here with the production of versions of the past, but this is part of a larger discussion of what is properly oral tradition, and the possibility of including barroom debates, telephone conversations, and electronic communications (7). He's interested in this section in the new use (in 1974) of magnetic tape recorders and stenography techniques. In particular, he is interested in a newer category of oral history, namely the "reflections and opinions of those whose lives are *still engaged in public activities. This kind* of oral history deals with a dynamic and ever changing source of data, the minds and memories of interviewees" (9). In contrast with the reading put forward in the Crown report, I suggest that the page referenced has nothing whatsoever to do with Aboriginal uses of oral histories. Rather, Moss is writing about the processes whereby interviewees think through their own experiences aloud with an interviewer. This might refer to, for example, a politician discussing the creation of legislation.

Another instance where the Crown's report can be seen to lack rigour is regarding the work of Goody and Watt. The Crown report maintains, "As such, it [oral tradition when written down] is no longer able to readjust to changing circumstances and may become disembodied from its original context" (von Gernet 2006a, 7, citing Goody and Watt 1968, 32-34, 67). Goody and Watt's essay, "The Consequences of Literacy," does discuss the implications of the conversion to oral tradition; however, its conclusions are about the limitations of static writing overall, not just oral traditions written down. In fact, the page cited in the report explicitly discusses how oral traditions are adaptable whereas written traditions present inflexibilities. Thus, the Crown uses what Goody and Watt argue is a limitation of written material in general as an indictment of written-down oral traditions. In my reading, *the Goody and Watt essay is more about the consequences of literacy, not the consequences of documented oral traditions.*

Similarly, I understand Morantz's work differently than the Crown. The Crown report notes that documents in archives are routinely subjected to critical analysis by historians and anthropologists: "Questions are asked, such as, 'Who wrote this? Why? For what audience was it intended? What was it meant to achieve? Can I trust it? Is it contradicted or confirmed by other sources, and are those other sources more reliable?' Oral traditions reduced to writing must undergo corresponding enquiries" (von Gernet 2006a, 16). The report here cites Morantz (1984, 186), among others. But Morantz provides no support for this interpretation. Instead, Morantz writes on page 186, "we have reached the point where oral tradition ought to be considered in itself trustworthy historical material, *subject only to the same tests of internal consistency and credibility* we use for all historical accounts" (emphasis mine). Outside sources are not mentioned. Morantz continues, "We have been using all these written materials uncritically while at the same time subjecting Indian folk history to extraordinarily rigorous testing or in most cases simply ignoring it." Morantz takes a very different stance than that of the Crown; she doesn't call for confirmation or contradiction of oral traditions by historical and anthropological sources but, rather, advocates the use of *internal* tests.

In a 1992 publication included in the Crown report bibliography, Morantz points out that anthropological and historical interpretations of Aboriginal involvement in the fur trade have been based on assumptions that must be examined more carefully: "We have much more to know about the early native involvement in the fur trade, and every scrap of information contributes to expanding our understanding. The representation of the history of native people requires ongoing surveillance" (187). Morantz, in short, is talking about surveillance of scholarly writings, not of the oral traditions of Aboriginal peoples, and is advocating for the use of information coming from the Aboriginal communities.

Contamination and Feedback

The Crown theory of oral evidence (von Gernet 2006a, 35) builds on the issue of "feedback," (or "contamination" in Henige's terminology), which is thought to infect oral narratives and make them suspect as evidence at trial. The sources cited do not support the Crown propositions, however. A standard scholarly position is to recognize feedback, in which Aboriginal people make use of non-Aboriginal resources (in this case narratives), as a regular feature of the contact process between different societies. Concepts such as syncretism or hybridity are sometimes used. Feedback is seen as a feature of life rather than a form of contamination or illegitimacy, as Cruikshank (1944b) points out. Scholars long ago abandoned the romantic search for "noble savages," who are members of "pure" and untouched societies. Von Gernet doesn't let on directly what he intends by the long discussion of the "feedback effect," but his examples about Tlingit fairy tales,

Sarcee confessions of borrowing from published sources (from which he presumably borrowed ideas), and Mi'kmaq borrowing from archaeological sources can reasonably be understood to indicate that those people can talk to new arrivals to their areas, and some can read, rather than simply implying inaccuracy or inauthenticity.

It's not clear why the Crown concludes that borrowing from other sources constitutes evidence of inaccuracy; perhaps it would be the other way around. All of this discussion, in brief, is built on a dated anthropological notion of authenticity as deriving from isolation. It's useful to consider that even with borrowing of ideas, the sources show that important Aboriginal ideas, the structure of logic, and the underlying storyline can be retained. Recognizing this requires experience with the language, culture, and history of a particular society.

It's notable that the work of Judith Berman, an important expert on the oral literature and ethnohistory of the North Pacific Coast, and a scholar with considerable fieldwork experience, is not consulted by the Crown report. She's taken up these issues directly in an essay that "considers the oral histories both as a form of history and as form of traditional literature" (Berman 2004, 129). She observes that "the narratives often contain a great deal of what would, from the Western standpoint, be considered accurate historical information" (130). She points to the agreement about detail from community to community and between groups, even when stories vary (130-31). What is important here is that, although the Kwakwaka'wakw stories Berman writes about are contained within conventionalized, thematic structures that are shared between communities, they still contain accurate historical information because details are specific to communities.

One of the most important scholars of oral traditions, Dell Hymes (1981, 274-308), observes that although stories with particular motifs have diffused from one community to another, they nonetheless can be understood by local people as having surface structure and underlying features that are appropriate or inappropriate to their location. The stories, in brief, are *reworked* for their community, in Hymes's terminology. Consequently, the existence of similar story motifs in various communities is neither contamination nor a reason to dismiss the value of such a story. Boas himself observed that widely diffused mythic elements were disengaged from narratives and plots (in Voget 1975, 324). Consequently, the Crown conclusion (von Gernet 2006a, 72) that "the feedback effect not only undermines the distinctions between oral and literate traditions but affects the assessment of traditions as independent or dependent evidence" may be true, but it is misleading, irrelevant, and not supported by the literature cited. Oral and written materials do not need to be treated as wholly separate, nor do the oral materials of different communities.

Further, concerning contamination, the report concludes, "An aversion to oral data is, as Shepard Krech notes, 'prompted in some instances by reflections on the contaminating presentisms that infect some oral testimony'" (von Gernet 2006a, 35n113, citing Krech 1991, 358). A close examination of Krech leads me to a different conclusion. Krech's passage reads as follows: "There is no consensus in the works discussed in this section on the usefulness of informant or consultant testimony. *In rare instances,* neither ethnographic work nor oral data are considered salient, an aversion prompted in some instances by the contaminating presentisms that infect some oral testimony" (emphasis mine). That is, Krech is talking about *"rare instances"* where *"neither ethnographic work nor oral data* are considered salient." This is a far different position from that of the Crown, which features the drawbacks of feedback.

A journal article by Anna Christine Hornborg cited in the Crown text, "'Readbacks' or Tradition? The Kluskap Stories among Modern Canadian Mi'kmaq" (2002, 9), discusses the issues surrounding Mi'kmaq oral materials. In the 1960s, anthropologist Philip Bock was pessimistic about the survival of Mi'kmaq oral traditions and considered the effects of TV shows about myth figure Kluskap and writing by whites about the oral traditions. Hornborg focuses on whether Mi'kmaq opposition to a proposed mining site that was said to be Kluskap's home was due to a cultural revival that relied on TV and published sources. Hornborg concludes that the Mi'kmaq had their own views of how to evaluate the white story of Kluskap and how to look for evidence of their own traditional beliefs (views similarly articulated by Sonny McHalsie): "When the Mi'kmaq spoke about their traditions they sometimes used scholars' texts (readback), but it was equally common and important to refer to memories of the elders. To strengthen the credibility of their memories, the Mi'kmaq stressed that they are told by reliable sources," based on protocols of respect and connection to persons of authority in Mi'kmaq society (9). White versions of their stories were thought to grasp only the surface or to be reshaped to fit European models. The Mi'kmaq thus differentiated between white versions of their stories and their own.

A last note about feedback or contamination concerns the use of sources. The Crown report states,

> In 1944 the anthropologist John Honigmann did fieldwork at the Sarcee Reserve near Calgary, Alberta, where he hoped to gather oral traditions relating to the culture of this First Nation as it existed at about the time of first European contact. One of his Sarcee informants, however, "confessed to having borrowed from the Calgary Library many books dealing with the Plains Indians." Such experiences have become increasingly common in the second half of the twentieth century as more First Nations people consult the corpus of written research in the public domain, while at the same time drawing on their rich inventory of non-recorded oral traditions. Interestingly, a few of these traditions are derived in whole or in part from non-Aboriginal traditions. A good example is the case of Russian fairy tales in the Tlingit tradition. (von Gernet 2006a, 40-41, citing, at the end of this passage, Dauenhauer and Dauenhauer 1998)

A careful reading of this Dauenhauer and Dauenhauer article (1998) shows that it is emphatically not a good example of the Crown claim. The authors specify that Russian stories have had negligible impact on Tlingit stories, likely because the social structures of the societies are different and reciprocity is thereby limited. The story discussed by the authors had limited circulation and was recognized by Tlingit community members as Russian:

> Such a story is the tale of "Yuwaan Gagéets," which we analyze here to study the process of borrowing in Tlingit oral tradition and to contrast the minimal European influence in the repertoire of Tlingit oral tradition with the widespread exchange of songs, stories, and motifs among the Indians of the Northwest Coast. (58)

> The story of "Yuwaan Gagéets," however, is clearly of Russian origin, and remains one of the very few clearly non-Indian borrowings taken directly into Tlingit oral tradition and kept by storytellers as a Russian story. But its influence was marginal and its position precarious at best. (76)

The Dauenhauer and Dauenhauer article (1998), in brief, does not give an example of First Nations people consulting a library or of consulting a rich inventory of European oral traditions. A "good example" of the use of non-Aboriginal oral traditions by First Nations would be one that was well circulated and not simply identified as foreign. The disinclination by Tlingit to draw on European sources or oral traditions was the major conclusion of the article, which therefore does not support the Crown view of feedback, a major theme of the report.

Possibly a better example might have been another piece cited in the Crown report, a book chapter by Patricia Partnow (1995). In this rather exciting and provocative piece, the author argues that a sort of categorical confusion arose in Alaskan Indigenous communities following a volcanic eruption in 1912 that forced the evacuation of two communities and their eventual amalgamation. This led to the merging of two emic categories of stories, one type roughly corresponding to etiological stories with generalized locations, and the other to events after the current world was established. But, Partnow writes, since all "old" stories are essentially alike and are part of the same genre, stories from pre-eruption merged with myth period accounts. Meanwhile, the etiological stories fell out of use. Hence, the myth time occurred not with Raven and other spiritual beings but with the twentieth-century eruption (175). Stories here meld Christian and Eskimo themes, and accounts of the murder of a Russian trader are transformed and incorporated into accounts of Eskimo self-definition (170). These Indigenous people may have blended Russian, American, and Indigenous portions but they are not blurred. Wiget (1982, 96) may offer a better explanation for these changes, or perhaps a supplementary one, in his notion that what Western historians perceive as a shift from history to myth may be a communal attempt to make personal events culturally meaningful and place them in the public domain.

Memory Research Issues

The Crown theory of oral materials builds on possible failures as a result of particular problems of memory. The sources cited in this respect do not support many of the Crown propositions, however. The Crown report (von Gernet 2006a, 49n171) cites Henige (1982, 11) and others to the effect that "the common sense assumption that eyewitness testimony is by nature reliable has been *vitiated* by ample research that suggests people are frequently inaccurate when recalling events they themselves have witnessed in the very recent past" (emphasis mine). But a careful reading does not support this conclusion. What Henige writes is "Since no two people have had the same blend of training and experience, no two people will ever see a complex event – and all events are ultimately complex – in quite the same way." This statement hardly "vitiates eyewitness testimony." Rather, it implies that people are attuned to different aspects of the same event.

Considering the question of eyewitness accounts, the Crown claims, "On the whole, however, anecdotal accounts of the prodigious or phenomenally-accurate memories of elderly individuals have not been substantiated by rigorous testing" (von Gernet 2006a, 50n175, citing Henige 1982, 67). Here again, a close reading doesn't support this view. Henige says something quite different: "There is sometimes talk of 'prodigious' or 'phenomenal' memory among some members of oral societies but before accepting this argument it must be understood that, however attractive it may be, *it is largely untested and untestable*" (emphasis mine). Henige doesn't say anything about elderly people here; rather, he's talking about "some members" of oral societies. Nor does Henige say that the prodigious memory of members of oral societies has been unsubstantiated. Rather, Henige says the issue of prodigious memory is untested and untestable in oral societies. Although the Crown report mentions "elderly individuals," the issue in court isn't the capacity of elderly individuals only, but, rather, a particular set of people, some of whom are not elderly. Finally, there is counter-evidence, such as Berman's observation of material regarding cross-checked genealogies of great depth and other information (2004, 130; see also Bringhurst 2004, 164).

The Crown report also notes, "It was once thought that the memories of non-Western, traditional, or 'oral' cultures are vastly better than those of literate peoples, but this has turned out to be unfounded" (von Gernet 2006a, 51, citing Finnegan 1992, 114). This conclusion is not borne out by the material cited, which says:

> This approach also sometimes drew on assumptions about the "traditional" or "past-bound" nature of non-western societies, with the conclusion that people's memories in this "primitive" state must necessarily – and naturally – have been vastly better than in literate societies. Recent thinking has made some notions more controversial ... The newer theoretical approaches to memory form a useful background, *but the issues they point to also need to be explored ethnographically.* (emphasis mine)

Finnegan lists various research questions that could address this issue. She does *not* conclude what the Crown concludes, that these assumptions are unfounded; rather, she proposes to investigate and test such ideas.

Further to this issue, the report quotes a historian, Hagan (1978), to the effect that "Indian memory can be as fallible as that of non-Indians. Indians too fall prey to senility" and are influenced by factional loyalties. But a different conclusion must be drawn from Hagan. The issue is not whether *senile* people can remember. (In any case, in some instances even senile people can have very specific and accurate memories of oral narratives, as I found out in preparing evidence regarding a sacred site for a Washington State court [Miller 1996]). Further, Hagan's discussion of the fallibility of Indian memory is misleading because it switches topics from memory to factionalism.

The Crown report discusses "memories of memories" (von Gernet 2006a, 55). There is a discussion of an experiment regarding the game of Chinese Whispers by Frederick Bartlett (1932). Bartlett concluded that the process of recalling an event or episode was one of construction or recreation rather than reproduction. The Crown report observes that Bartlett's work on memory has been corroborated, but a careful reading of Bartlett and other sources leads me to a different conclusion. While Bartlett demonstrated change in a message from one individual to another, University of Toronto anthropologist Tom McFeat, in *Small-Group Cultures* (1974), shows that a message is retained if it is part of group activity and if it fits a cultural schema. For Bartlett, the important point is not that there is reconstruction of a message but that there is an underlying structure (or schema in Bartlett's terminology) as a basis for influences on which memory is built, making it possible to retain the underlying message even though particular accounts vary. The value then depends on what the stories are about. In fact, oral materials can retain the original intention of a message, whereas documents can lose the original intention.

In addition, Chafe (1992) points out that in ritual speech in Seneca, a northern Iroquoian language, authority to speak is "located." These linguistic qualities in Seneca are absent in English, and experimental studies of English language use are not necessarily applicable to languages with these different conventions. In this sense, too, *the Bartlett experiment isn't applicable here.* Myth arises out of ritual, and the important thing is not only what one says but what one does ritually. Something left out of the verbal performance can be inferred because it is part of the performative context, a point similar to that made by Sider (1993). Bartlett is irrelevant to the discussion of oral materials among Aboriginals of North America, contrary to the conclusions drawn by the Crown.

The Crown treatment of the topic of "memories of memories" relies on a reading of Hallowell, Wylie, Hickerson, and others. But there are some problems regarding this reading of their work. The Crown report states,

> Oral traditions have been described as memories of memories. As such, they compound the problems inherent in eyewitness testimony. There are

> varying opinions on how long memories can sustain relatively accurate information. Some scholars have suggested a temporal span of many centuries or even millennia, while others encourage skepticism about "historical" memories reaching back beyond the present generation. (von Gernet 2006a, 54)

Here, too, I suggest that sources don't support these propositions. Hallowell (1937, 666-67), one of the sources cited, doesn't "encourage skepticism," as the Crown suggests. Rather, Hallowell writes, "The collection of extensive genealogical information has *convinced me of the accuracy* of the knowledge that is the basis of this human frame of reference" (666). Hallowell goes on:

> But, in quantitative temporal terms retrospective genealogical information of this sort completely fades out in less than two centuries. One hundred and fifty years is the outside limit of any genuine historic past so far as the Berens River Indians are concerned. Events attributed to so distant a past that they cannot be connected with any known generation of human individuals are simply described as having taken place "long ago." Consequently we are plunged into a bottomless mythological epoch that lacks temporal guide posts of any conventional sort. As a matter of fact, it would be more accurate to assert that once we enter the mythological world of Saulteaux belief, temporal concepts actually lose most, if not all, chronological significance. (666-67)

First, Hallowell emphasizes the impressive accuracy of their genealogical memory. Second, their memory of historical events is also solid as long as those are connected to the lives of those in their genealogical memories up to about 150 years (much longer than the "generation" that the Crown cites him for). Third, and most important, Hallowell doesn't question the accuracy of the older information conveyed, but rather notes its vague temporal positioning as simply "long ago." Even then, Hallowell later states, "It is true, nevertheless, that certain episodes in the mythological narrative [as "long ago" tends to convert to mythological age] provide a basis for certain broad temporal inferences. And independently of immediate mythological references, I found that the Indians entertain similar chronological notions [to Westerners]" (667).

The Crown also cites Wylie (1973, 709-10) on this point of scholars purportedly encouraging skepticism about oral materials, and this too is worth a second look. On those pages, Wylie summarizes some of the "relevant 'schools' of thought" regarding ethnohistory, not his own point of view, except as commentary upon those summarized. In so doing, he discusses Raglan's views (1956), writing, "Raglan was certain that nonliterate cultures could not keep the oral record of any event more than a century and a half, which, though not a surprising conclusion, is wrong." The Crown in this instance should be citing Raglan, not Wylie, for skepticism about those oral histories dating back more than a century and a half. Wylie himself is clear that Raglan is "wrong." In fact, Wylie later writes that "oral traditions or other nonwritten sources [should] be given emphasis at least equal to written sources, with the actual weight given to each determined in direct proportion to their abundance and applicability" (711).

Conclusion

The foregoing textual analysis of materials submitted on behalf of the Crown concerning oral narratives found that the Crown has primarily entered evidence around ways in which oral materials are said to fail in providing information useful in presenting the Aboriginal perspective in litigation. I've emphasized that in many cases the sources do not support the Crown's propositions. Most notably, there are problems regarding the propositions drawn from the work of major scholars, including Vansina, Henige, and Cruikshank. I've also pointed to other materials used in support of an inadequate Crown theory of oral narratives. Although the Canadian Supreme Court has called for the use of oral materials, these Crown materials haven't helped in the effort.

I have presented this account of the Crown report in order to critique, specifically, some of the arguments and approaches to oral history used by the Crown, which presumably might continue to be used in the future. In addition, this report shows something of Crown practice in litigation. In the next chapter I move from Crown practice to an examination of the current state of evidence rules from an anthropological perspective.

5 The Way Forward? An Anthropological View

An Anthropological Look at Rules of Evidence and the Evaluation of Evidence

If the court holds that oral historical evidence has the same weight as historical evidence, there still remains the question of how this squares with rules of evidence more generally. Chief Justice Beverley McLachlin, writing in *Mitchell v. M.N.R.*, gave a good look at the issue:

> The flexible adaptation of traditional rules of evidence to the challenge of doing justice in aboriginal claims is but an application of the time-honoured principle that the rules of evidence are not "cast in stone, nor are they enacted in a vacuum" (*R. v. Levogiannis,* [1993] 4 S.C.R. 475, at p. 487). Rather, they are animated by broad, flexible principles, applied purposively to promote truth-finding and fairness. The rules of evidence should facilitate justice, not stand in its way. Underlying the diverse rules on the admissibility of evidence are three simple ideas. First, the evidence must be useful in the sense of tending to prove a fact relevant to the issues in the case. Second, the evidence must be reasonably reliable; unreliable evidence may hinder the search for the truth more than help it. Third, even useful and reasonably reliable evidence may be excluded in the discretion of the trial judge if its probative value is overshadowed by its potential for prejudice. (para. 30)

But there remain difficulties other than finding utility and reliability. Chief Justice Antonio Lamer, writing the reasons for judgment in *Delgamuukw v.*

British Columbia [*Delgamuukw III*] in 1997, pointed to some of the problems, particularly the multiple purposes of oral narratives.

> Many features of oral histories would count against both their admissibility and their weight as evidence of prior events in a court that took a traditional approach to the rules of evidence. The most fundamental of these is their broad social role not only "as a repository of historical knowledge for a culture" but also as an expression of "the values and mores of [that] culture": Clay McLeod, "The Oral Histories of Canada's Northern People, Anglo-Canadian Evidence Law, and Canada's Fiduciary Duty to First Nations: Breaking Down the Barriers of the Past" (1992), 30 *Alta. L. Rev.* 1276, at p. 1279. Dickson J. (as he then was) recognized as much when he stated in [*R. v. Kruger*], [1978] 1 S.C.R. 104, at p. 109, that "[c]laims to aboriginal title are woven with history, legend, politics and moral obligations." *The difficulty with these features of oral histories is that they are tangential to the ultimate purpose of the fact-finding process at trial – the determination of the historical truth.* (para. 86, emphasis mine)

Rules of evidence are not entirely the same in all jurisdictions within the common-law tradition, although there are important commonalities. In Canada, there are a number of lingering problems regarding oral historical testimony. The first concerns how and when to enter such evidence and what evidence is allowable. This problem is exacerbated because in the Canadian system a trial judge has to "decide in a nanosecond between question and answer if evidence is allowable. Then the appeals court has the time to point out the stupidity of the trial judge" (former justice John Bouck, interview, 2008). Canadian jurisprudence to date has relied on the tests of whether oral traditions are useful to the court and reasonably reliable (*Mitchell* 2001). But this just begins to address the situation, even though rules of evidence in general provide latitude for judicial reasoning, as pointed out by Chief Justice McLachlin in *Mitchell*. "For the most part, the rules of evidence are concerned with issues of admissibility and the means by which facts may be proved. As Sopinka and Lederman (1974, 524) observe, 'the value to be given to such facts does not ... lend itself as readily to precise rules. Accordingly, there are no absolute principles which govern the assessment of evidence by the trial judge'" (para. 36).

One category of problem is that much Aboriginal oral historical evidence may not be available to discovery before trial in a document or in a *voir dire* and therefore the other side may not have a fair opportunity to prepare its case. A second category of problem, from the vantage point of standard practice for Aboriginal historical evidence, is that the other side can't cross-examine someone who, in legal terms, "made a statement," that is, taught an oral history to the elder or other Aboriginal person presenting that oral material on the stand. Unlike other expert witnesses, it is difficult or perhaps impossible to adequately assess the sources behind the oral historical evidence, although a Crown expert has attempted this. In the case of testimony given by a historian, for example, the opposition can examine on its own the documents and other materials on which the historian relied. Chief Justice Lamer raised this issue in his landmark *Delgamuukw III* decision: "Another feature of oral histories which creates difficulty is that they largely consist of out-of-court statements, passed on through an unbroken chain across the generations of a particular aboriginal nation to the present-day. These out-of-court statements are admitted for their truth and therefore conflict with the general rule against the admissibility of hearsay" (para. 86).

Chief Justice McLachlin pointed to the significance of the reliability of the oral historian, and, subsequently, the weight the testimony will hold:

> The second factor that must be considered in determining the admissibility of evidence in aboriginal cases is reliability: does the witness represent a reasonably reliable source of the particular people's history? The trial judge need not go so far as to find a special guarantee of reliability. However, inquiries as to the witness's ability to know and testify to orally transmitted aboriginal traditions and history may be appropriate both on the question of admissibility and the weight to be assigned the evidence if admitted. (*Mitchell*, para. 33)

Oral historians can give "oral footnoting," that is, they can tell who told them a particular piece of information and the credibility of that person in order to point to the reliability of their own testimony. Historian Keith Carlson (2007, 56) nicely described this practice among Coast Salish people:

> During the course of my research, I ultimately conducted repeat interviews with thirty-one people who had been identified for me as knowledgeable elders and cultural experts. Through their generosity and patience, I came to appreciate and expect that elders' oral traditions would not necessarily contain the elements historians used to assess the legitimacy of Western archives-based histories. Rather than referring to specific first-hand historical observations or records (something impossible in oral histories

> discussing events beyond the personal memories of the present generation), the Salish elders emphasized their relationships to both the historical actors and the various sources (earlier generation of "tellers"). Thus, in those stories that were not simply the recounting of events within the teller's own life, elders often validated their narratives by referencing the person from whom they had heard the story, and, where possible, with additional references to the antecedents of that source ("I heard this story from my great-uncle, who heard it from his uncle – who was my great-great-grandfather").
>
> On other occasions, when the links between the various generations of sources were perhaps not as well known to the teller, elders were generally careful to provide contextual information about the central figure discussed within the historical narrative, such as his or her relatives, family status, and other notable facts. In either case, the elders were providing what might best be thought of as "oral footnotes" – references that in highlighting the link between themselves and the historical actors, and/or the various intergenerational transmitters of the story, served to sustain and enhance the status of both. In this way, the validity of the historical action/actors was linked to, and in part a product of, the status of the conveyors of that historical information and vice versa.

Mr. Justice MacAulay took judicial note of Carlson's approach to oral footnoting in *R. v. Jacobs.*

However, a problem from the vantage point of litigation is that the opposition still cannot cross-examine the source of the information. And the trier of fact, judge or jury, may have a limited capacity to meaningfully evaluate this oral footnoting. The references elders make to their relations and the evaluations of their standing, and therefore the credibility of what they say, might constitute a closed system, perhaps beyond the competence of outsiders to evaluate. Ultimately, the judge or jury may simply have to rely on his or her own perceptions of the witness in giving weight to the evidence (and see Trigger 2004, 31).

This leads to a third issue regarding the use of oral historical evidence: the presiding trial judge may encounter evidence that he or she may find not believable or have no ability to comprehend. This arose in the original *Delgamuukw* case when Chief Justice Allan McEachern found oral historical testimony regarding supernatural beings to be insubstantial and to confound belief and truth. I discussed his reaction in a 1992 publication: "Another example of his confusion is his treatment of causal explanation within oral histories. He is confused by the attribution of geological events to the actions of mythological beings, noting for example, 'it is difficult to equate a land slide to a Grizzly bear'" (Miller 1992, 65, quoting *Delgamuukw*). In an especially notable passage he affirms that "the evidence does not disclose the beginnings of the Gitksan and Wet'suwet'en people. Many of them believe God gave this land to them at the beginning of time. While I have every respect for their beliefs, there is no evidence to support such a theory and much good evidence to doubt it" (62-63).

While a trial judge can make notes about the evidence being presented, and what witnesses might or might not be relied on, an appeals court judge has no such opportunity. Judges of the "courts of appeals don't see witnesses ... don't see his demeanour to know if he can be trusted [in order to] separate fiction and fact" (former justice John Bouck, interview, 2008). Sometimes the appeals court judges may ask why the trial judge didn't accept evidence. Oral historical materials, based on somewhat different epistemologies than those commonly faced by the court, become a sort of evidence weighed by judges and juries who may have difficulties evaluating the oral footnoting or even the demeanour of the oral historian. In the next round of litigation, at appeals, absent information about credibility of the witness, the oral historical evidence can be even harder to evaluate (Miller 1998; Ray 2008).

Another issue arising from oral historical evidence is that it may be difficult or even infeasible for the Crown to find a competent expert oral historian for a variety of reasons. Perhaps no member of the Aboriginal group wishes to testify against the interests of his own group, or families with different versions of an oral history may respect the version presented by a credible elder from within their own community and cultural norms may forbid creating public conflict. Or, as tribal archivist Tracey Joe pointed out in Chapter 2, someone may simply defer to another's opinion on the grounds of age or social standing. Arthur Ray (2003, 261) put it this way:

> The introduction of oral history evidence into Aboriginal rights litigation has also created a practical problem that is difficult to address adequately. Aboriginal defendants and plaintiffs control the oral histories – and often own them as hereditary rights.
>
> Understandably, First Nations are reluctant to allow opposing counsel's experts to undertake pre-trial oral history research in their communities. As a result, the Crown's lawyers and experts frequently have to rely almost exclusively on the extant scholarly literature. Several problems arise when they do, particularly the fact that most of this literature is based on field

> ethnography undertaken during the pre-claims era. This was a time when anthropologists did not address many of the issues that are central to Aboriginal rights litigation. Alfred L. Kroeber, the doyen of American anthropology at the middle of the twentieth century, made this point when he was serving as the key witness for the Indians in the USICC [US Indian Court of Claims] California claims hearings of 1955-6. He noted that most of pre-claims anthropological research had been oriented to salvage or cultural-element distribution surveys. This work had emphasized material culture, mythology, and religious beliefs; it had paid little attention to native economic systems, political organizations, or land tenure practices. Thirty years later, when the Gitksan and Wet'suwet'en filed their lawsuit, the ethnographic literatures concerning their people, and their immediate neighbours, still had the same limitations. For this reason and others, they undertook massive oral and documentary history research projects.

Ray (2008; and see Ring and Tully 2006, 16) further notes that the Crown has great difficulty in getting experts who can appear on their behalf, out of loyalty to their informants or fear that their testimony will jeopardize future research opportunities with Aboriginal communities. Ray concludes that "barred from access to this line of evidence before trial, Crown counsel has little choice but to treat oral evidence in an adversarial way at trial" (287).

Resolutions to Problems of Evidence

Evidentiary issues can be approached in several ways that may resolve some of the problems of incorporating oral traditions into mainstream law. These approaches operate at diverse levels, from simple procedure to the incorporation of features of Aboriginal law within the mainstream system. Ultimately, the strongest approach is to accept qualified oral historians as experts in their own right, free to give expert testimony. Short of that, there are other routes.

Criminal law suggests, in theory, that a line of argument for the inclusion of oral historical material is that the Crown choice to ignore oral traditions might be construed as a "wilful tort." In this argument, the government action to, for example, seize land that Aboriginal law says is owned by Aboriginal groups is construed as an intentional and wilful overlooking of Aboriginal concepts of land title. Aboriginal groups might appropriately now insist that their own legal regime regarding land be recognized by the Crown. In this approach oral traditions are linked to Aboriginal law that is "universally understood and recognized by the community." The Crown, or the state government, would then have an obligation to accommodate oral law and to take notice of those articulating it as culture experts and oral historians in the court.

A more likely scenario is one in which oral narratives might be included under exceptions to the hearsay rule not to prove the truth of evidence but, rather, to show community perceptions at the time of an event or process. This might allow the weaker party, the Aboriginal community, to present their own beliefs.

The common-law tradition could resolve the questions regarding which elders might be qualified as experts by the same means as in mainstream practice. If they are accepted by their peers in the field, and in effect peer reviewed, and if they are commonly accepted in their community, then they may be qualified as experts. This potentially addresses several difficulties, including questions of what to do about multiple versions, reliability, and validity. Experts in the common law must be reliable, their opinions provable, and generally accepted in their field. A suggestion has been made that communities themselves vet the oral traditional material before entry into the court (Simpkins 2000, 199; Hutchins et al. 2008).

An example of this arose in *Delgamuukw*. In the Canadian system, there is the possibility of allowing a reputation exception to the hearsay rule, as Chief Justice Lamer noted (para. 104). Asch and Bell (1994, 538) described the approach of the litigants to the legal concept of reputation. The principle upon which the reputation exception rests is that such a reputation may be taken to be true because, all the community being interested, it would not exist unless true. Once a reputation to a public or general right is established, they write, the evidentiary burden shifts to the other party to refute the existence of the right. The concept of reputation as an exception to the hearsay rule is long established in the English common-law tradition, dating to the late 1600s (Hopper 1990, 111, citing Wigmore 1940-88).

Asch and Bell (1994, 542; and see McLeod 1992; Davey 2007, 12) further describe the plaintiff's argument that the reasoning underlying the admission of oral narratives as evidence builds on the same grounds as the arguments for the admissibility of ancient documents (that is, documents published a given number of years ago, the number depending on jurisdiction) and reputation evidence. That is, the oral histories of the plaintiffs in *Delgamuukw* came into existence before any claim was engaged and were commonly known and exposed to contradiction and could be considered old enough to be the equivalent of ancient documents. Admissible ancient documents must be free of suspicion, produced from proper custody, and formally executed. This argument, however, didn't work in the trial court, though it remains a possibility. My concern with this approach is that it replicates the assertion introduced by the Crown: that oral narratives are merely documents, ancient or otherwise.

Common-law practices also provide a way to understand differences among versions of the same oral historical material, and the accompanying problem of reliability. Rather than holding that diversity constitutes the failure of an oral tradition through faulty transmission or through a faulty historical record, the common law allows reliability to be judged by whether the same message is contained in various accounts. Reliability of written documents is not indicated by exact sameness but by whether meaning is constant (Todd Miller, interview, 2008). An illustration might be found in the Western tradition in the various translations of the Christian Bible: the Protestant King James version and earlier versions from which it was created can be said to express the same message, despite significant differences in phrasing.

In the case of private knowledge, held only by a single family or a single person within the tribe, the problem arises of verification and corroboration by other lines of evidence. Sometimes there is no available form of corroboration or of refutation. Chief Justice Lamer, writing for the Canadian Supreme Court in *Delgamuukw III,* noted the trial judge's concerns on this point: "He also cast doubt on the authenticity of these special oral histories (at p. 181) because, inter alia, 'the verifying group is so small that they cannot safely be regarded as expressing the reputation of even the Indian community, let alone the larger community whose opportunity to dispute territorial claims would be essential to weight'" (para. 97).

If, however, the community commonly accepts the oral historian as expert, then, by analogy from conventional common-law practice, the court might accept the testimony as bearing weight. The tribe would need to make the case that the holder of otherwise unknown oral historical material has a reputation for truthfulness in the community, a standard for character witnesses, and is regarded as wise and expert. Other community members might show that the oral historian's reputation is solid. Further, as is the practice in non-Aboriginal litigation, the court can take cognizance of commonly accepted practices within the community.

Chief Justice Lamer also addressed this issue in his reasons for judgment in *Delgamuukw III,* regarding the use of chiefly oral narratives about land tenure and the trial judge's rejection of the reputation exception to the hearsay rule and, consequently, the evidence given in affidavits. Chief Justice McEachern had raised the issue of conflicting oral histories, finding the evidence of doubtful reliability as a consequence.

> The affidavits rely heavily on the declarations of deceased persons regarding the use or ownership of the lands, which are a form of oral history. But those declarations are a kind of hearsay and the appellants therefore argued that the affidavits should be admitted through the reputation exception to the hearsay rule. Although he recognized, at p. 438, that the territorial affidavits were "the best evidence [the appellants] could adduce on this question of internal boundaries," the trial judge held that this exception did not apply and refused to admit the declarations contained in the affidavits.
>
> *I am concerned by the specific reasons the trial judge gave for refusing to apply the reputation exception.* He questioned the degree to which the declarations amounted to a reputation because they were largely confined to the appellants' communities. The trial judge asserted that neighbouring aboriginal groups whose territorial claims conflicted with those of the appellants, as well as non-aboriginals who potentially possessed a legal interest in the claimed territory, were unaware of the content of the alleged reputation at all. Furthermore, the trial judge reasoned that since the subject-matter of the affidavits was disputed, its reliability was doubtful. (*Delgamuukw III*, para. 103-4, emphasis mine)

But Chief Justice Lamer further observed the consequences of rejecting evidence based on oral materials that is disputed internally or between Aboriginal nations:

> Many of the reasons relied on by the trial judge for excluding the evidence contained in the territorial affidavits are problematic because they run against this fundamental principle. *The requirement that a reputation be known in the general community, for example, ignores the fact that oral histories, as noted by the Royal Commission on Aboriginal Peoples, generally relate to particular locations, and refer to particular families and communities and may, as a result, be unknown outside of that community, even to other aboriginal nations.* Excluding the territorial affidavits because the claims to which they relate are disputed does not acknowledge that claims to aboriginal rights, and aboriginal title in particular, are almost always

> disputed and contested. Indeed, if those claims were uncontroversial, there would be no need to bring them to the courts for resolution. (*Delgamuukw III*, para. 106, emphasis mine)

The process for qualifying an oral historian addresses another lingering problem, often expressed by community members, about the cross-examination of elders. Aboriginal community norms may not sanction verbal aggressiveness toward distinguished elders as may arise in cross-examination, as Daly (2005) notes. But cross-examination might appropriately focus less on the content of the oral histories and more on the elders' background, including where they were born, the nature of instruction from their families, and so forth, which is relevant to qualifications. Elders need not face aggressive questioning on their testimony per se (Catherine Twinn, personal communication, 2008; Hutchins et al. 2008, 25; Davey 2007, 35).

One can argue that oral historians can pass peer review by the means suggested by Carlson (2007), and so be favourably regarded by the court. Pre-trial conferencing can allow information to be exchanged by an arranged date and the information to be presented by oral historians can be summarized. These elders might be prequalified as experts before the beginning of the trial, as can happen with experts in other areas. In this procedure, a motion can be filed presenting a line of evidence one side wishes to follow and why it is important to the trial. The opposition can then raise objections and demands, or agree to accept the oral historian as expert. In theory, these issues can be resolved before the beginning of the trial.

But a 2006 discussion paper on the use of experts in federal Aboriginal litigation, based on a meeting with various interested parties, concluded that elders might have a limited and prescribed role as experts:

> When specifically asked whether or not elders should be considered experts for litigation purposes, all counsel and academic experts indicated that elders should not be classified as "expert witnesses" in the litigation context. Some counsel expressed the view that two types of witnesses have very different roles and functions. Expert witnesses provide opinion evidence on particular issues to assist the Court. Elders typically give evidence of oral histories of their communities. The Courts permit elders to relay hearsay evidence because, for some First Nations, these oral histories may be the only record of their past. Some counsel noted, however, that with respect to a particular point on which opinion evidence is sought, an elder

> *may* be an "expert" *but* only if he/she is qualified as having expertise in a particular area in which an opinion is sought. (Ring and Tully 2006, 15, emphasis in original)

There is even the possibility that the concept of "expert" be rethought in order to classify Aboriginal elders as experts, not merely under the exception of the reputation rule (Hutchins 2005). Hutchins et al. (2008, 27; and see Davey 2007, 35) observe that under federal rules, elders and community experts might be deployed as *assessors:*

> Rule 52 of the Federal Courts Rules provides for the category of assessors to "(a) assist the Court in understanding technical evidence; or (b) provide a written opinion in a proceeding." To the extent that oral traditions evidence requires an understanding of a particular knowledge system, the evidence is "technical" and perhaps requires more direct dialogue between a judge and someone familiar with this knowledge. The assessor could be an Elder or another community member with knowledge of oral traditions. All communications between the assessor and the Court take place in open court and parties can make submissions as to the form and content of questions put to the assessor. Parties can call other "experts" to testify on the issues dealt with by the assessor and can respond to the assessor's opinion.

But one line of reasoning suggests that particular elders might simply be regarded as experts in common with other experts admitted by the court. Hutchins and his colleagues write,

> We submit that it is high time for our legal system to reconsider the characterization of expert evidence and who may tender such evidence. While the Supreme Court continues to direct that the aboriginal perspective is important and must be considered by the Courts, the people most equipped to provide that perspective and to instruct the Courts are still labeled "lay witnesses" while scholars, who are more often than not from another culture, are considered the "experts." (Hutchins et al. 2008, 34)

Their argument for expert status is buttressed by the notions that elders meet the *Mohan* test of necessity in that their knowledge is outside the experience of a judge or jury, and, further, that the Canadian judiciary has called for more flexibility regarding rules of evidence (32-35). In Chapter 3, I presented information about an oral historian, Sonny McHalsie, who could aptly fill the role of expert. I included this chapter in part to flesh out just what such an oral historian is.

Following another line of discussion, the Crown's argument that oral histories become historical documents once they are written down, and therefore fixed and inert, can be understood in light of community understandings of them, as suggested by Tracey Joe (in Chapter 2). On the one hand, if evidence is fluid and hence malleable and changeable, it may not be deemed dependable and valid. The judge can recognize this and instruct the jury to give the evidence the weight to which it is entitled. But fluidity is not inherently indicative of invalidity. Tracey Joe believes that fluidity is an inherent quality of oral historical materials, at least some sorts of them (and see Bahr 1993, 44). The real issues regarding the writing of oral materials are whether the meaning is changed, and is therefore wrong, and whether the meaning as indicated on paper is accepted by the oral historians and the community. The transformation into writing, like any transformation, runs the risk of generating error. The issue is less whether standard historiographic methods, and only these, can be applied to interpreting the oral narratives, as the Crown has argued, and more that community theories of the transmission of knowledge may be violated. It is also appropriate, and within the practice of the mainstream legal system, that recognized experts, academic or community, explain what such a document means.

Canadian courts face the related problem of the imprecision of oral narratives, which may not appear to directly answer historical questions of relevance to the court. Chief Justice Lamer wrote,

> In my opinion, the trial judge expected too much of the oral history of the appellants, as expressed in the recollections of aboriginal life of members of the appellant nations. He expected that evidence to provide definitive and precise evidence of pre-contact aboriginal activities on the territory in question. However, as I held in [*R. v.*] *Van der Peet,* this will be almost an impossible burden to meet. (*Delgamuukw III,* para. 101)

Oral narrative evidence, from this perspective, would have to be understood and evaluated somewhat differently than Western historical evidence, a finding later challenged by the Crown expert.

Some of the issues regarding oral traditions in court can be mitigated if, as Aboriginal legal scholar John Borrows (2002, 69) and others have argued, there is the "common law's recognition of the ancestral laws and customs" of Aboriginal peoples. One can ask what the common law by which Aboriginal communities are regulated is, in order to create accommodation within mainstream law. These Aboriginal systems must presumably meet the criteria of Western common law of having historical precedence and being universally recognized and accepted. It is less clear how the standard of being enforced could be fulfilled, given that Aboriginal communities have long since been deprived of the ability to apply many of their own law and justice practices. However, recognition of Aboriginal law is not outside of the scope of mainstream practice generally. Common law itself originated in the accommodation of local practice in the creation of a centralized legal system. Notably, the legal systems that predate and are ancestral to the common-law system, the complex tangle of Anglo-Saxon law in the several jurisdictions in the area that is now England, focused on accommodation between different legal regimes. Current examples also exist of contemporary accommodations between different jurisdictions. Pennsylvania state law, for example, has been restructured to accommodate US federal law in recent years.

The Canadian court has made a beginning in working through many of these issues in practical terms and within the scope of Canadian jurisprudence. Newman (2005) points out that until a February 2004 preliminary trial order of the British Columbia Supreme Court in *Tsilhqot'in Nation v. British Columbia,* precisely how oral narratives would be treated had not been worked out. Mr. Justice Vickers did not envision his work as a template for future cases, but the detail of his procedural order and the sorts of issues raised in *Tsilhqot'in* dictate otherwise. Newman suggests,

> The *Tsilhqot'in Nation* order is likely to help shape a standard in the use of oral history in Aboriginal law contexts more broadly, thus giving it a significance far beyond that often attached to a trial court's preliminary order ... we can appropriately take the judgment on the *Tsilhqot'in Nation* order as an important source helping to frame the debates around how to operationalize *Delgamuukw* and the resulting principles on oral history. (433)

Newman was writing before the judgment came down in this case in 2007.

In *Tsilhqot'in,* both defendants, British Columbia and Canada, and the litigants sought to clarify rules of evidence in their own favour. Canada suggested rules so that oral narrative evidence could be introduced only after the qualification of experts on oral history and through *voir dire* or preliminary inquiries. This approach meant that Aboriginal knowledge would be at the mercy of anthropological gatekeepers and interpretations. British Columbia hoped for a more complex evidence order that would permit hearsay evidence in limited areas – genealogy and traditional activities and practices – based on a *voir dire* that could establish that such evidence was needed and that it was likely to be reliable. Hearsay evidence on past events would be permitted with a hearing and with expert testimony about the context of the Aboriginal transmission of oral narratives. Meanwhile, the plaintiffs, the Tsilhqot'in, agued against such processes, holding that the oral evidence given in testimony by their own people should be determined in light of the other evidence of the case. In other words, let the evidence be entered and weighed on its own merits as with any other evidence.

Justice Vickers, sympathetic toward the Tsilhqot'in people, understood that the directions coming from the Supreme Court of Canada allowed judicial discretion. He opted to create no formal process for the admission of oral evidence but rather said that it would be considered on normal rules of evidence applied flexibly, but with the principle of reconciliation as featured in section 35(1) of the constitution in mind. He expressed a preference for non-hearsay evidence if an eyewitness was alive and available to give testimony. He set a number of guidelines that effectively created an informal process. As Newman (2005, 434) writes,

> However, he also indicated the need for a searching probe into reliability of hearsay testimony, indicating that the court "would want to know" the following:
>
> 1 some personal information concerning the [witness's] circumstances and ability to recount what others have told him or her; who it was that told the witness about the event or story;
> 2 the relationship of the witness to the person from whom he or she learned of the event or story;
> 3 the general reputation of the person from whom the witness learned of the event or story;
> 4 whether that person witnessed the event or was simply told of it; and,
> 5 any other matters that might bear on the question of whether the evidence tendered can be relied upon by the trier of fact to make critical findings of fact.

Newman had further comments about Justice Vickers' opinion:

> In order to enable such consideration of the reliability of hearsay evidence, going to both admissibility and weight, Vickers J. established two elements to the process. First, he indicated a helpful practice for the start of the trial: "At the outset of the trial it would be helpful for counsel to *outline the traditions* of the people they represent relating to the questions of: 1) how their oral history, stories, legends, customs and traditions are preserved; 2) who is entitled to relate such things and whether there is a hierarchy in that regard; 3) the community practice with respect to safeguarding the integrity of its oral history, stories, legends and traditions; 4) who will be called at trial to relate such evidence, and the reasons they are being called to testify. (*Tsilhqot'in,* para. 22)" (Newman 2005, 434-35)

There would also be a preliminary inquiry (not in the form of a *voir dire* but at the start of a witness's testimony) into the hearsay evidence a witness would present. Justice Vickers wrote:

> "Thus, assuming the test of necessity is met by the death of persons involved in the events being testified to, when a witness is called upon to give hearsay evidence counsel should give a brief outline of the nature of the hearsay evidence to be heard. Before the evidence is heard, there should be a preliminary examination of the witness concerning the following: a) Personal information concerning the attributes of the witness relating to his or her ability to recount hearsay evidence of oral history, practices, events, customs or traditions. b) In a general way, evidence of the sources of the witness, his or her relationship to those sources and the general reputation of the source. c) Any other information that might bear on the issue of reliability." (In order to enable such consideration of the reliability of hearsay evidence, going to both admissibility and weight). (*Tsilhqot'in,* para. 20, cited in Newman 2005, 435)

Justice Vickers thus called on the counsel acting for the Tsilhqot'in to create a context for later oral evidence. In itself, this requires considerable mastery of the ethnography of the nation, which seems to me to be material normally provided to the court by an expert. There could then be a challenge to the admissibility of a given witness's testimony upon the conclusion of this preliminary inquiry, or there could be arguments on the weight of particular testimony (using this contextual information, which would be part of the record) at the conclusion of the trial (*Tsilhqot'in,* para. 26, cited in Newman 2005, 435).

This is rather specific for informal guidelines, but helpful in that in many ways the procedure replicates the process that occurs inside some Aboriginal communities that I have identified, following Carlson, as oral footnoting, except that the oral narrator doesn't provide the information directly to the court but rather through an intermediary, the counsel. In particular, the idea of clarifying the sources used by the witness, who would be known to the witness as relatives and ancestors, and of showing his or her relationship to these sources, allows Aboriginal people to demonstrate their standing and gets to the reputational feature common to both the court and the community. In my experience, these are very widely practised procedures in Aboriginal communities.

Newman (2005) interprets Justice Vickers' approach highly favourably. He believes that it proceeds along the route to reconciliation between, as he says it, the values of justice and the value of a fair justice system. Said differently, he is referring, I think, to the practices of evidence law and Aboriginal peoples' approaches to justice. He believes that a dialogue is under way on evidentiary principles and substantive law. He observes, correctly, that Aboriginal oral narratives are embedded in a system that itself contains tools to work with substantive law. There are, he says, many practical difficulties still not worked out (238).

The key principles Newman (2005) believes were established in *Tsilhqot'in* include provisions for the lawyer to provide a general introduction, effectively creating room for and consciousness of oral narratives; and the testing of admissibility of each piece of oral history evidence. This latter feature is reminiscent of the onerous Canadian legal requirement for Aboriginal bands to prove right and title in each instance. Newman suggests that more tests could be added, including tests of the relationship of witnesses to the preparation of litigation. Because bands often interview knowledgeable elders on upcoming litigation, this test could prove a deterrent to the reasonable assemblage of oral narratives for communities beleaguered with the problems of undertaking litigation in a decolonizing period in national history. Napoleon (2005, 13n56) notes, for example, "In the 1970s, approximately 200 interviews were conducted with elders concerning Treaty 8 as part of the Treaty and Aboriginal Rights Research (TARR) project (a research initiative of the Indian Association of Alberta)." There have been many such projects; this project has already come under attack by the Crown, as noted by Napoleon (134n62): "The Crown's expert witness, anthropologist Dr. von Gernet, described the TARR interviews as the worst oral history project that he had ever seen. The TARR project included interviews with elders from Treaty 6 and 7, with isolated peoples that entered the treaties later, and with people who said they did not know anything. Other interviews were specific to reserve boundaries, resource rights, and mineral rights." It seems reasonable to expect further Crown attacks on Aboriginal efforts to protect their legal rights by gathering information.

Hutchins and associates express even greater concern that a broad swath of tape-recorded or transcribed oral materials held by bands could be subject to discovery under rules of disclosure. Currently, they note,

> Rule 222(2) of the Federal Court Rules sets out the meaning of a relevant document that must be disclosed to the opposing counsel:
>
> > (2) Interpretation – For the purposes of rules 223 to 232 and 295, a document of a party is relevant *if the party intends to rely on it or if the document tends to adversely affect the party's case or to support another party's case.* (Hutchins et al. 2008, 28, citing S.O.R./1998-106, emphasis mine)

They suggest that a broad interpretation of relevancy in pre-trial disclosure will force First Nations to choose between preserving knowledge for future generations and running the risk that information will be subject to discovery in litigation. Although they don't say this, this could present the humiliating prospect of having such knowledge picked apart by opposing counsel intent upon discrediting elders giving testimony, in part by finding discrepancies between oral testimony and past materials.

There are, however, yet other ways that oral narrative evidence might be used in Canadian courts without disparagement. McLeod (1992, 1284) notes that judicial notice, in which judges may use their own knowledge of the world without requiring the litigants to prove the things known by the court, and long a practice of common law, can be a vehicle for the entry of Aboriginal oral materials and perspectives into legal proceedings. However, judicial notice can also have the opposite effect, as in the original *Delgamuukw* trial. McLeod notes the 1990 judgment handed down by the Supreme Court of Canada in *R. v. Khan,* which held that the statement of a young child to its mother made out of court could be taken as trustworthy and an exception to the hearsay rule because the statement was necessary and children are inherently trustworthy. In addition, the ruling spoke of a need for flexibility in light of new situations facing the court. McLeod argues that an analogous argument could be made that the statements of tribal elders should be taken to be trustworthy.

The principle of inference, which allows for a finding of fact if it flows logically from proof of another fact, might be applied to enhance the probative value of oral histories (Milward 2009, 2). If, for example, oral traditions regarding treaty negotiations are not contained in treaties or documents, it might be inferred that the oral history contains references to those treaty terms because of what Crown officials said during negotiations.

Finally, Hopkins and Nahwegahbow (2008), on behalf of the Indigenous Bar Association (though not articulating the official position of the IBA), suggest seven protocols for the federal court concerning the treatment of elder oral testimony:

1 The Trial Judge shall consider the interest at issue from the Aboriginal customary system in conjunction with the common law system.
2 The Trial Judge shall have recourse to a cultural interpreter from the community and not solely an expert forwarded by the Crown.
3 The venue for tendering and admitting oral history evidence by an Aboriginal elder shall be done by way of a special preliminary inquiry.
4 The special preliminary inquiry shall have a court reporter and will be video-taped.
5 If the Trial Judge is of the opinion that it is in the interest of justice and/or on request of a party, the special preliminary inquiry may also include relocation to a site.
6 Where it is not possible to fully access and discuss oral history evidence, the Trial Judge shall encourage the Aboriginal group to consider alternative strategies in adducing evidence.
7 The Trial Judge shall ask the parties to formulate a list of common principles at the beginning of the special preliminary inquiry that speak to the need for a fair and equitable trial process. (3-5)

These protocols, taken as a whole, are aimed at developing mainstream legal practice that carefully acknowledges and respects Aboriginal people and culture (and in particular, their own laws and legal processes). While these don't directly address oral narratives, their concern is for the context of the delivery of the narratives. They call for the use of prayers and smudging, and for holding legal proceedings on Aboriginal lands (a circumstance that dates at least to *Delgamuukw*). They are calling for, in effect, a Canadian version of medieval English legal practice that relied on sensory procedures such as smelling the land, incense, prayers, and singing. They also take into account the surprise of Justice Addy in finding the additional depth of videotaped oral interviews as compared to written transcriptions.

6 Conclusions

The history of the Canadian legal engagement with Aboriginal oral narratives makes clear that they are understood very differently by the various practitioners of law, anthropology, and history, as well as oral historians themselves. But my argument is that these understandings need not be viewed as mutually exclusive, and that oral narratives should not be excluded by courts by virtue of various literalist understandings of what they are. By taking this position, I include myself among the widely criticized proponents of liberal, inclusive democracy. This stance has been critiqued by Aboriginal scholars such as Taiake Alfred (1999) and the anthropologist Nadasdy (2003), who argue for a general radical incommensurability between Aboriginal societies and the state. People holding this perspective frequently assert that there is little utility in attempting to find zones of mutuality and that the attempt to do so damages Aboriginal people and distorts their societies. Mainstream proponents of a view of democracy that operates by exclusion also argue a fundamental incompatibility between the epistemology, values, and practices of Western and Aboriginal societies. The archaeologist Mason is one of these. There are many others, however, whose voice appears to me to be more constructive and whose practices are incorporative rather than exclusive. The archaeologist Andrew Martindale is one, as are Cruikshank, Borrows, Mills, and others among the academics; McHalsie among Aboriginal intellectuals; and Grove among legal scholars.

However the question of the significance and feasibility of incorporating oral narratives into Western systems of knowledge and authority is understood, the adversarial legal process is clearly not the best venue to work this question out. In any case, it is failing, as evidenced by Department of Justice–sponsored conferences created specifically to work the issue through. Ray (2003) points out the problems with the current practice, noting that academics are forced into defending obsolete or simplified versions of theory by the very nature of the cross-examination process. The legal system has rejected informed and thoughtful versions of how to understand oral narratives, such as that produced for the court by Wheeler, in favour of a less informed but simpler version presented by the Crown.

I foreground Cruikshank's notion (2005) that those of us in the mainstream world must listen *for* the narrative rather than simply *to* the narrative. It's our job to help determine how Aboriginal peoples can more appropriately be included within Canadian society, just as many Aboriginal people themselves take it upon themselves to push Canada to be more responsive to them. A significant part of this project concerns the incorporation of Aboriginal modes of knowledge and the transmission of information into Canadian thinking generally. I have pointed to differences, but also to similarities in the uses of knowledge – to create predictive capacity so that life can be lived fruitfully and in proper relations with other people and other entities. The possibility of the entry of Aboriginal modes of expressive culture into legal settings through the use of oral narratives introduces an exciting effort at exchange and reciprocity. We need not reject the gift of knowledge and even wisdom offered by oral historians, as Daly (2005) suggests happened in the original *Delgamuukw v. British Columbia* trial. But, I argue, all the players still don't have a clear idea of what oral narratives mean to the others and the grounds on which we can reasonably proceed to incorporate the narratives and their speakers into legal settings.

I've extensively incorporated materials from the Canadian Crown into this book to show that the Department of Justice effort at responding to the Canadian Supreme Court's evolving position on oral narratives has been less than helpful, and perhaps less than honourable on some occasions. The emphasis remains on the strategic defence of the Crown's perceived prerogative to control resources and land, and on the tactical use of academic devices intended to discredit and dislodge the use of oral narratives in civil litigation. These legal tactics have contributed to making litigation long, expensive, and contentious, developments that are not in the best interests of Canada or Aboriginal peoples.

I have also incorporated some of my own work to give a sense of the chronology of the dispute over oral narratives as seen concretely through one person's engagement. Nobody, other than Crown personnel perhaps, has been engaged full-time or nearly full-time on this issue, but many have had their say. It has been a source of frustration for many that oral narratives, so much at the heart of Aboriginal culture, have received such a rough ride at the hands of the Crown.

I've tried to show issues that arise as a result of how Crown researchers and legal teams work, preparing storylines or narratives of their own to present to the court. Anthropologists view "the law" not just as it is enacted in courtrooms or in reasons for judgments, but also as it takes place in other, less obvious venues. These are obscure places where decisions are made regarding the framing of a case while the selection of evidence is under way. These behind-the-scenes processes transform problems facing members of society, in this case, Aboriginal people with concerns for their historical lands and resources, into legal actions recognizable by the court.

These processes are seldom focused on the intellectual issues regarding the nature of oral narratives, which ought to be of interest to a legal system professing a willingness to incorporate them. The interviews with Crown researchers in Chapter 2 show the means whereby transcriptions of oral narratives are objectified and transformed into documents that might yield raw data, "facts" that can support a Crown storyline. In some cases, the researchers are able to suggest or convince the legal team that the Crown ought to negotiate with First Nations seeking legal redress rather than entering into litigation. But in other cases, they cannot, perhaps even when it would be of considerable benefit. The research process often requires a cursory examination of massive sets of materials. In other cases, Crown researchers are able to use their extensive experience with particular archives and knowledge of the social organization of particular First Nations to make a preliminary evaluation of oral narratives as sources of information. Sometimes they have keen insights into the practices of those who have recorded oral narratives and of the people who were the speakers. They can meaningfully examine the chain of references given by oral historians, the oral footnoting, in their examination of what to them is the search for potential evidence. But one senior researcher expressed his dismay that the process is fundamentally flawed and untrue to the nature of the oral materials.

On one level, the issue of oral histories in court appears to be simply about the misuse of a particular category of evidence, which is sometimes mishandled and distorted by researchers in the process of preparing it for trial. But misuse never seems to be pointed out by the Crown as an issue regarding oral narratives entering the legal domain. Perhaps this circumstance reflects the nature of legal training, which emphasizes the downstream selection of evidence appropriate for a particular legal argument, a storyline, rather than the earlier production of evidence. This fact may parallel the disciplinary differences in fact and evidence between law, anthropology, and history. It strikes me as very partial that the story of the production of oral narratives told in court emphasizes only a small part of the whole picture: we hear, for example, of the purported problems of transmission of narratives through generations, but not of what actually happens in our own legal system to the oral narratives. Nowhere in court do we hear that the narratives are frequently butchered, cherry-picked, and misrepresented. We don't hear that key decisions about oral narratives are made long before trial by people who lack the time, and sometimes the skill, to give adequate thought to what are sometimes long, dense statements. If oral narratives are difficult for non-Aboriginals to comprehend and to make useful, part of the problem lies in our own system of "bulk processing," for lack of a better term.

Some of the problem facing courts arise from simply determining *what* oral narratives are. Cohen, Cruikshank, Rosaldo, Wheeler, Borrows and others have argued for understanding oral narratives as operating on multiple levels simultaneously. Oral narratives are not simply repositories of facts awaiting examination, an idea that has confused the court at times. Nor does the primary work by leading scholars with oral narratives focus on their "facticity." In some cases, the court has determined that oral narratives are too uncertain and too difficult to interpret to be useful. This puzzles me, because in my own experience as an expert witness I have seen the state incorporate various, sometimes strange, forms of information as evidence without any apparent difficulty in stripping data to create potential "facts." (One major case involved the introduction of evidence from a 1940s novel by a socialite living temporarily in a rural community. Her inexplicable inability to comprehend the Indigenous presence there, even though she frequently encountered them, was given as evidence that they did not exist then nor at the time the case was heard.)

The court has stumbled over the idea that oral narratives can be used to address contemporary problems in social life. This fact has led the court, following the Crown argument, to conclude that these oral narratives are products of the present, without secure connections to the past. This conclusion involves a binary, either-or proposition: oral narratives are either about the past or about the present. There are no grounds to believe that there is such an incompatibility, however, and much to suggest that both coexist.

Further, the court has grasped that some oral narratives in some First Nations in Canada have the particular distinction of being highly formalized and the prerogatives of chiefs. But there are great differences among Aboriginal communities regarding oral materials, particularly who may speak them, the occasions on which they might be delivered, and their ontological basis. Various classifications have been derived, such as those from the Coast Salish peoples, which I have included here. McHalsie (see Chapter 3) has argued that rather than employing etic categories – those of outsiders – internal, linguistically based understandings should be employed in order that overlap between the sorts of narratives be clarified and that the classifications more closely follow Aboriginal epistemologies.

This is a significant issue. Systematic eighteenth- and nineteenth-century Western thinking regarding oral narratives was conventionally built around a kind of salvage effort to save folklore before it disappeared. These efforts resulted in products such as the familiar Grimm's Fairy Tales and also faked folklore such as that of the overenthusiastic eighteenth-century Scottish writer James Macpherson. Early scholarship emphasized the diffusion of common motifs around the world and tried to set different traditions of orality into formalized comparative perspective. Arguably, this practice influenced the work of Africanists such as Vansina, whose early work (1965) on African oral narratives in turn influenced a generation of scholars, including those working in North America. This early Africanist work later came to be regarded as too rigid and literalist and based on particular formalized systems, leaving out many other forms of oral narrative. McHalsie's treatment of the oral narratives of his own community allows a more subtle understanding of his culture and enables connections between ideas to be clarified. Cruder systems of classifications obscure local understandings of personhood, ownership, and other topics that might be of interest to the court.

The Crown has argued tediously over issues of the reliability and validity of oral narratives. These are legitimate and important concerns, but the Crown's handling of them reflects an underlying understanding of oral narratives that is fundamentally not supported by the literature, and the sort of misuse Rosaldo (1980) and others have pointed out. In the interests of certainty, the Crown has intimated a view of oral historians that I call the "jukeboxes" concept, which regards them as devices that simply reproduce bits of sound given them, either through verbatim memorization or through the use of mnemonic devices to reproduce certain parts, filling in the rest. The core of my argument is that much of the legal wrangling reflects this bias.

As a counterpoint, I have introduced material by an oral historian, Sonny McHalsie, that reveals *how* cultural understandings are produced and transmitted. I use materials from McHalsie's nation – the Stó:lō – to engage other issues about oral narratives. McHalsie hasn't simply learned verbatim stories from his First Nation but, rather, he has slowly developed an interpretive capacity. He has synthesized information, assessed its validity using internal standards, and gradually become what might be called a cultural historian. His accounts have been tested at home and displayed in many public settings, including many academic conferences. McHalsie's work is a good example of what the Supreme Court may have had in mind in the 1997 ruling in *Delgamuukw v. British Columbia* on the comparability of oral histories and histories. Both sorts of historians, oral and academic, evaluate and employ multiple sources in coming to a reasoned understanding of the past. My argument is that McHalsie, and others like him, *are* experts and that if McHalsie were to give testimony on Stó:lō oral history, it would be that of an expert witness; he could be granted the standing due to experts to use various sources to create and enhance understanding. His expertise relies on his comprehension and thinking through of both oral and written material and of his clarity regarding the grounds of his knowledge – including both relational and authoritative systems. The issue is not so much whether there is a formal practice of oral historical narratives but whether there are community experts who can provide the court with information.

Part of the problem regarding oral narratives lies outside of the Canadian legal system itself, although it is reflected there. Canada, and Western societies generally, might be described as having a bias against orality, or perhaps more accurately, ambiguous feelings about the relationships between orality and other senses and orality and written expression. This old and persistent theme was captured nicely by the historian of religion Karen Armstrong. She describes the transformation from orality to writing in several locations in the period between 700 and 600 BCE, noting that the Deuteronomists (the authors of the books of the Bible with the same name)

> made Judaism a religion of the book. But it seems there was considerable opposition to this development. Literacy changed the people's relationship with their heritage, and not always for the better. In India, for example, oral transmission required a long apprenticeship, dynamic interchange with a charismatic teacher, and a disciplined, self-effacing lifestyle. But solitary

> reading encouraged a more individual and independent education. The pupil was no longer reliant on his guru, but could peruse the texts by himself and draw his own conclusions, and his knowledge might be shallower, because he might see no need to look beneath the words on the page or experience the luminous silence that took him beyond its words and concepts. (Armstrong 2006, 194)

Further, Armstrong writes, describing the prophet Jeremiah's reservations about the written Torah, "How dare you say: 'We are wise, and we possess the law of Yahweh?' he asked his opponents. 'See how it has been falsified by the lying pen of the scribes!' The written text could subvert orthodoxy by a mere sleight of the pen, and distort tradition by imparting information rather than wisdom" (ibid.).

It is this focus on information rather than wisdom (if this term is too frightening, try informed and thoughtful judgment), and the distortions present in documents (as opposed to oral narratives), that disturb many Aboriginal people. McHalsie (interview) made this point in referring to the work of anthropologists such as Wilson Duff, and his own effort to try to determine what the elder had said to Duff, and to understand the particular distortion introduced by the academic process, rather than simply receiving Duff's written words uncritically. McHalsie, here, has a little bit of Jeremiah in him, and rightfully so, I believe. It's my view that experts, anthropologists, historians, geographers, and others owe the court more than mere technical analyses that facilitate casting doubt on the evidence of the Indigenous litigants or, for that matter, anybody. Rather, since they are *experts,* they owe the court insight regarding how to proceed and how to understand Aboriginal evidence and Aboriginal perspectives that senior jurists, including the chief justices, have said are obligatory for a just society.

There are interesting contrasts in this regard between the work of an oral historian, McHalsie in this case, and the positions taken by the Crown. McHalsie makes clear the relational component of his knowledge: he reveals from whom he learned, their relationship to him as teachers or colleagues, the underlying epistemology, and the larger implications. He is responsible to and employs community notions of authority. He uses local standards of chronology and locally derived means to test historical propositions. He indicates what responsibilities oral historians bear and for whom. McHalsie primarily, but not exclusively, has learned orally. He doesn't dismiss written accounts, but evaluates them carefully and commits some of his own ideas to writing. He evaluates oral accounts carefully as well.

The Crown expert on oral traditions has written (2000) on the influences on him by his dissertation supervisor, Bruce Trigger; however, he has derived none of his understanding from working with oral narratives *in situ,* but only as he encounters them in the alien environments of the courtroom and on paper. He regards them as forms of evidence no different than any other document, despite their particularities. Although he indicates that oral narratives, once transcribed on paper, are, and must be, amenable to standard historiographic methods, he strips the context from them by treating them merely as artifacts. In so doing, the Canadian court lives once again through the anguished struggles over orality and literacy that, as I have noted, have characterized society at different points in history.

Boorstin (1999, 40) captured the sense of this passage in the other great predecessor society to the contemporary Western world, classical Greece:

> Plato lived in an age of transition in Athens when the written word was invading the world of learning. And this seems to confirm the warnings (reported by Plato) of the Egyptian god-king Thamus to Toth, the [legendary] inventor of writing. "This discovery of yours will create forgetfulness in the learners' soul, because they will not use their memories; they will trust to the external written characters and not remember of themselves. The specific which you have discovered is an aid not to memory, but to reminiscence, and you give your disciples not truth, but only the semblance of truth" *(Phaedrus).*

Boorstin points to the invention of history, and a new kind of historical conscientiousness, by Herodotus and Thucydides, who mark the transition from poetry to prose. Poetry, a characteristic of oral societies because it was an aid to memory, and singing, as methods of transmission, declined in favour of writing (134-35).

Something like this ancient transition was repeated in western European society much later on. Hibbitts (1992) creates a colourful account of the use of various senses in English and western European legal traditions into the late middle ages. Legal contracts were engaged by handshakes and other physical gestures. Law was crafted as song and meant to be sung, in some instances. Over time, these practices declined with a new and very focused emphasis on writing. My argument here is that the idea of oral narratives as evidence, and oral historians as experts, faces considerable resistance because of our societies' marked bias for the visual or written and against other sensory practices. This is so even though there have been several periods of difficult transition in our own history. We are no longer sufficiently aware of this perennial conflict and of the ways orality and literacy intertwine. They do not simply displace one another.

A considerable body of evidence indicates that oral narratives, once written down, do not simply become documents, which is the key argument used by the Crown to dislodge the narratives in court. Instead, they continue on in lives of their own. They are *still* told in communities, as the Crown is clearly aware, given the effort to disqualify oral narratives because of variation over the years and between storytellers. My claim here is that they are misused in Crown testimony by various experts, who make simplified or unsupportable propositions made about them. But band archivists and cultural historians indicate that they regard these written oral materials as having particular, "living," qualities and that they are open to revision for accuracy. They are living in that they have, in Stó:lō terminology, *shxwelí*, or a kind of life force of their own. This life force renders them ontologically distinct from other materials recorded on paper, and they are housed separately, sometimes with distinct protocols such as those used for the statue T'xwelátse (described in Chapter 3). They require distinctive handling. They have particular features of ownership. They come in particular genres but are delivered orally with distinctive styles and in response to the occasion. There are times they may be opened and others when they may not. Thus they are not simply historical documents like any others.

I emphasize *difference* because the recognition of difference is important in responding to Crown attempts to homogenize or even obliterate oral narratives. However, there is common ground between the transcripts and tapes of oral narratives and other sorts of exhibits that may be entered into the courtroom. For example, maps entered as evidence must be understood within a particular Cartesian worldview, with its own conventions. Although in the medieval period Europeans depicted east as up, today north is up, and differences in scale reflect not on-the-ground differences but distortions inherent to depicting three dimensions as two. If maps of a different sort, say those produced by archaeologists that appear as three-dimensional, are introduced, experts can explain their conventions. Similarly, forensic knowledge that requires a particular view of disease and physiology can be brought as evidence. And evidence from physicians, nurses, and psychologists, which derives from direct and intimate contact with a patient, can be tendered, and their mode of analysis accepted by the court for what it is. In none of these cases is the evidence forcibly translated and rendered inert by a foreign disciplinary gaze.

There are many other overlaps between Indigenous practice and that of Canadian society, and between legal practice and that of other disciplines, all of which can be better exploited to open courts to meaningful engagement with oral narratives. First Nations of Canada have long had what might be regarded as public institutions that are similar to courts and that undertake activities to determine something like *reputation* as it used in the English common-law system. Potlatches among several Northwest Coast nations are historically gatherings in which, in part, parties make claims to social statuses, including titles and accompanying resources. Here, oral narratives consolidate a claim and attract broad public support. These narratives are acclaimed in part based on their longevity and their history of previous support in the community, especially among the most knowledgeable. Likewise, the speakers in these gatherings themselves undergo a regular form of public examination for the accuracy, veracity, and relevance of the information they provide. These are community experts. This is just one example showing that Canadian and Aboriginal systems of law and justice are not totally different.

As in the Canadian legal system, Aboriginal oral narratives and ideas of fact, I have pointed out, derive from concrete, particular circumstances, rather than abstract, generalized notions. In both the law and in Aboriginal epistemology, a fact is not an element of raw data, but rather a finding made within a moral and normative context. Both Aboriginal epistemology and the law are based on underlying moral systems, even though they may not be explicitly referenced.

Further, the perspectives of practitioners of law, anthropology, history and other disciplines are not wholly distinct, as my experiments with showing the ethnographic film *Dead Birds* to law students and anthropology students suggest. There is considerable overlap, even though, over time, people become more familiar with and more committed to the language and perspective of their own disciplines. Legal scholar Douglas Saunders once commented that progress in Canadian Aboriginal litigation occurs in the courts of judges who are about to retire, when they feel less pressure to conform and less concern about being overturned on appeal (personal communication, 1999). This suggests that the judiciary may be attuned to Aboriginal perspectives in unexpected ways, and to representations of these perspectives by practitioners of history and anthropology. Certainly, some contemporary rulings indicate this. As I pointed out, there is a great deal of cross-training, in any case. Many lawyers have history degrees, Aboriginal lawyers have anthropology degrees, and so on.

Geertz (1983) succinctly made the point that there are overlaps at the theoretical level between anthropology and the law in his commentary on the legal emphasis on the "skeletonization of fact" in order to determine culpability and the "schematization of social action" in ethnographic analysis. These features, he writes, have "more than a passing family resemblance" (170-71). But for Geertz, law is a system of local knowledge and requires attunement to the local. In our case, legal notions of fact and Indigenous notions of fact are from separate neighbourhoods, yet needn't be entirely alien.

All of these systems of thought – law, anthropology, history, and Aboriginal thought – have both relational and authority dimensions, although the proportions may vary considerably. In each case, people learn from those who are older and more knowledgeable; in each case, they are tested at various points regarding their own capacity. These are the authoritative, transactive dimensions, but people also learn through relational and interactional practices, including sharing, accommodating, listening. Here I argue that it is important to make clear the nature of one's disciplinary knowledge in expert presentation.

Finally, all of these disciplines have a central core of narrativity, despite differences in underlying epistemology. They all depend on developing a comprehensible, convincing storyline. Potlatch speakers do this, as do litigators, researchers, and expert witnesses. Each marshals evidence to make a case, and the evidence is open to scrutiny regarding its origin, appropriateness, and importance. In some cases, the evidence is formally testable, a central feature of Western normal science, and, says Whiteley (2002) a feature of the non-mythological components of oral narratives. In humanistic versions of social science, such as that practised by Geertz, the methods of evaluation are less precise but nevertheless formal. All the disciplines depend on the gathering, management, and testing of information.

My concern here is the retreat by the court from the use of oral narratives since *Delgamuukw* – an inclination to find them foreign and an inability to include them within existing evidentiary law. As a counterpoint, I foreground the court's findings regarding their importance. Oral narratives are important in that they may be the only source of information, they integrate Aboriginal law into the common law, and their incorporation upholds the honour of the Crown. My fear is that the practices that have arisen around generating oral narratives that can survive Crown cross-examination will become onerous and overshadow the oral narratives themselves. The emerging practices described by experienced lawyers working in Aboriginal litigation require cross-checking with oral narratives from other communities, comparisons with earlier oral narratives by the same person or by others, and potentially the disqualification of the work of oral historians who have read historical and anthropological work. These developments may lead to the elimination of the most qualified oral historians because of concern about what might happen in cross-examination. In fact, it is fair to say that this already has happened: lawyers sometimes comment on the difficulties with informants or experts who are too well versed. These people may inadvertently raise complex issues that muddy the central storyline being developed by legal counsel, and open themselves to adverse cross-examination that casts doubt on their credibility.

Jurisdictions outside of Canada offer a few useful leads about the issues around oral narratives. Tribal courts in the United States, although run by tribes, themselves struggle with oral narratives. Tribes have created structures for the delivery of oral narratives by elders and community experts, and these are sometimes used. But tribal courts also have at times rejected oral narratives as mere hearsay or outside the rules of evidence. There is a debate about the extent to which tribal courts can be true to Indigenous prior practice, and the extent to which pressures to conform to mainstream legal practices restrict them. Nevertheless it is clear that to some extent they can demonstrate the relevance of oral narratives and of community tribal historians (see Nesper 2007).

In the United States, *Zuni Tribe of New Mexico v. United States* shows one means for effectively using oral narratives, but, I argued in Chapter 1, it is not a model for the future. The methodology is too committed to formalisms that are terribly difficult to reproduce and builds on a legal positivism that may derail further progress. In addition, this case did not consider the work of oral historians themselves. Finally, the openness of the recent NAGPRA *(Native American Graves Protection and Repatriation Act)* cases in the United States to the use of oral narratives in adjudication is highly appropriate, especially considering the topics at hand. As yet, however, these cases seem not to have produced new insights into how to overcome evidentiary and other problems.

Means already exist within the English common-law system and within the Canadian judiciary to implement an effective use of oral narratives. I raise this point not to present a particular resolution, which is the role of legal scholars, but to show how these might connect to a broader understanding of the nature of oral narratives. The idea of reputation is one of these means; this could include the development of practices to incorporate community experts on oral materials. Another is the ancient documents concept, the idea that documents demonstrate their truthfulness by longevity. The Canadian courts' awareness of the need for additional ways around a strict hearsay rule in light of new situations suggests that progress can be made. The strongest and most dramatic possibility lies in acknowledging Indigenous forms of knowledge and their practitioners as experts. In the end, such experts are not so different from those already known to the court. This acknowledgment will enable us to reject the inherently self-defeating claim of incommensurability between Aboriginal and mainstream societies. It will position us to listen *for* and *to* Aboriginal accounts of their own experiences and to engage the Aboriginal world directly in the Canadian experience.

References

Alfred, Taiake. 1999. *Peace, Power and Righteousness: An Indigenous Manifesto.* Don Mills, ON: Oxford University Press.

Allen, Barbara. 1979. The Personal Point of View in Orally Communicated History. *Western Folklore* 38 (2): 110-18.

Ames, Michael. 1990. Cultural Copyright and the Politics of Documents That Move and Speak. Paper delivered at the ICA Symposium on the New Media National Archives of Canada, Ottawa, 30 April–3 May.

Amsterdam, Anthony G., and Jerome Bruner. 2000. *Minding the Story.* Cambridge, MA: Harvard University Press.

Anyon, Roger, T.J. Ferguson, Loretta Jackson, and Lillie Lane. 1996. Native American Oral Traditions and Archaeology. *SAA Bulletin* 14 (2): 1-4.

Anyon, Roger, T.J. Ferguson, Loretta Jackson, Lillie Lane, and Philip Vicenti. 1997. Native American Oral Tradition and Archaeology: Issues of Structure, Relevance, and Respect. In *Native Americans and Archaeologists: Stepping Stones to Common Ground,* ed. Nina Swidler, Kurt E. Dongoske, Roger Anyon, and Alan S. Downer, 77-87. Walnut Creek, CA: AltaMira Press.

Appadurai, Arjun. 1986. *The Social Life of Things.* Cambridge: Cambridge University Press.

Arima, Eugene Y. 1976. An Assessment of the Reliability of Informant Recall. In *Inuit Land Use and Occupancy Project.* Vol. 2, *Supporting Studies,* ed. M.M.R. Freeman, 31-38. Ottawa: Department of Indian and Northern Affairs.

Armstrong, Karen. 2006. *The Great Transformation: The Beginning of Our Religious Traditions.* Toronto: Vintage Canada.

Asch, Michael. 1992. Errors in *Delgamuukw:* An Anthropological Perspective. In *Aboriginal Title in British Columbia: Delgamuukw v. the Queen,* ed. Frank

Cassidy, 221-42. Lantzville, BC, and Montreal: Oolichan Books and the Institute for Research on Public Policy.

Asch, Michael, and Catherine Bell. 1994. Definition and Interpretation of Fact in Canadian Aboriginal Title Litigation: An Analysis of *Delgamuukw*. *Queen's Law Journal* 19:503-50.

Asche, Wendy. 2004. Method, Mechanism, and Mindset: Collaborative Approaches in Native Title. In *Crossing Boundaries: Cultural, Legal, Historical, and Practice Issues in Native Title,* ed. Sandy Toussaint, 50-57. Carlton, Australia: Melbourne University Press.

Axtell, Roger. 1997. The Ethnohistory of Native America. In *Rethinking American Indian History,* ed. Donald L. Fixico, 11-27. Albuquerque: University of New Mexico Press.

Bahr, Donald. 1993. What Happened to Mythology? *Wicazo Sa Review* 9 (2): 44-49.

Barry, Michael. 2009. Standards for Oral Tradition Evidence: Guidelines from First Nations Land Claims in Canada. Presented at 7th FIG Regional Conference, Spatial Data Serving People: Land Governance and the Environment – Building the Capacity, Hanoi, Vietnam, 19-22 October.

Bartlett, F.C. 1932. *Remembering: A Study in Experimental and Social Psychology.* Cambridge: Cambridge University Press.

Basso, Keith H. 1996. *Wisdom Sits in Places.* Albuquerque: University of New Mexico Press.

Beidelman, Thomas O. 1970. Myth, Legend and Oral History: A Kaguru Traditional Text. *Anthropos* 65:74-97.

Benedict, Ruth, 1934. *Patterns of Culture.* New York: Houghton Mifflin.

Berman, Judith. 2004. "Some Mysterious Means of Fortune": A Look at North Pacific Coast Oral History. In *Coming to Shore: Northwest Coast Ethnology, Traditions, and Visions,* ed. Marie Mauzé, Michael E. Harkin, and Sergei Kan, 129-62. Lincoln: University of Nebraska Press.

Blackhawk, Julie. 2004. *Aboriginal Law: Litigation Issues – Some Thoughts on Cross-Examination of Aboriginal Elders and Oral Documents.* Ottawa: Continuing Legal Education, Canadian Bar Association.

Boissevain, Jeremy. 1974. *Friends of Friends: Networks, Manipulators and Coalitions.* Oxford: Blackwell.

Boorstin, Daniel J. 1999. *The Seekers: The Story of Man's Continuing Quest to Understand His World.* New York: Vintage Books.

Borrows, John. 2001. Listening for a Change: The Courts and Oral Tradition. *Osgoode Hall Law Journal/Revue juridique d'Osgoode Hall* 39:1-38.

–. 2002. *Recovering Canada: The Resurgence of Indigenous Law.* Toronto: University of Toronto Press.

Boxberger, Daniel T. 2004. Whither the Expert Witness: Anthropology in the Post-*Delgamuukw* Courtroom. In *Coming to Shore: Northwest Coast Ethnology, Traditions, and Visions,* ed. Marie Mauzé, Michael E. Harkin, and Sergei Kan, 323-38. Lincoln: University of Nebraska Press.

–. 2007. The Not So Common. In *"Be of Good Mind": Essays on the Coast Salish,* ed. Bruce Granville Miller, 55-81. Lincoln: University of Nebraska Press.

Brightman, Robert. 1993. *Grateful Prey: Rock Cree Human-Animal Relationships.* Berkeley: University of California Press.

Bringhurst, Robert. 2004. The Audible Light in the Eyes: In Honor of Claude Lévi-Strauss. In *Coming to Shore: Northwest Coast Ethnology, Traditions, and Visions,* ed. Marie Mauzé, Michael E. Harkin, and Sergei Kan, 163-82. Lincoln: University of Nebraska Press.

Brown, Kenneth, and Michael Roberts, eds. 1980. Introduction. Using Oral Sources: Vansina and Beyond. Special issue, *Social Analysis* 4:3-12.

Callison, Cynthia. 1995. Appropriation of Aboriginal Oral Traditions. Special issue, *UBC Law Review,* 165-81.

Carlson, Keith. 2006. Reflections on Indigenous History and Memory: Reconstructing and Reconsidering Contact. In *Making Contact Across Time and Culture,* ed. John Lutz, 46-68. Vancouver: UBC Press.

–. 2007. Toward an Indigenous Historiography: Events, Migrations, and the Formation of "Post-Contact" Coast Salish Collective Identities. In *"Be of Good Mind": Essays on the Coast Salish,* ed. Bruce Granville Miller, 138-81. Lincoln: University of Nebraska Press.

Cassidy, Frank. 1992. Rethinking British Columbia: The Challenge of Delgamuukw. In *Aboriginal Title in British Columbia: Delgamuukw v. The Queen,* ed. Frank Cassidy, 5-17. Lantzville, BC, and Montreal: Oolichan Books and the Institute for Research on Public Policy.

Chafe, Wallace. 1992. Seneca Speaking Styles and the Location of Authority. In *Responsibility and Evidence in Oral Discourse,* ed. Jane H. Hill and Judith T. Irvine, 72-87. Cambridge: Cambridge University Press.

Clifford, James. 1988. *The Predicament of Culture: Twentieth-Century Ethnography, Literature, and Art.* Cambridge, MA: Harvard University Press.

Clifton, James A. 1989. *Being and Becoming Indian.* Chicago: Dorsey Press.

Clinton, Robert N. 1986. The Curse of Relevance: An Essay on the Relationship of Historical Research to Federal Indian Litigation. *Arizona Law Review* 28:29-46.

Cohen, David William. 1989. The Undefining of Oral Tradition. *Ethnohistory* 36 (1): 9-18.

Colwell-Chathaphonh, C., and T.J. Ferguson. 2007. *The Collaborative Continuum: Archaeological Engagements with Descendant Communities.* Archaeology and Society Series. Walnut Creek, CA: AltaMira Press.

Conley, John M., and William M. O'Barr. 1998. *Just Words: Law, Language, and Power.* Chicago: University of Chicago Press.

Cruikshank, Julie. 1990. *Life Lived Like a Story.* Lincoln: University of Nebraska Press.

–. 1992. Invention of Anthropology in British Columbia's Supreme Court: Oral Tradition as Evidence in *Delgamuukw v. B.C. BC Studies* 95:25-42.

–. 1994a. Claiming Legitimacy: Prophecy Narratives from Northern Aboriginal Women. *American Indian Quarterly* 18 (2): 147-67.

–. 1994b. Oral Tradition and Oral History: Reviewing Some Issues. *Canadian Historical Review* 75 (3): 404-18.

–. 1998. *The Social Life of Stories: Narrative and Knowledge in the Yukon Territory.* Lincoln: University of Nebraska Press.

–. 2005. *Do Glaciers Listen?* Vancouver: UBC Press.

Culhane, Dara. 1998. *The Pleasure of the Crown: Anthropology, Law and First Nations.* Vancouver: Talonbooks.

Cunnison, Ian George. 1951. *History on the Luapila: An Essay on the Historical Notions of a Central Africa Tribe.* Manchester: University of Manchester Press.

Daly, Richard. 2005. *Our Box Was Full: An Ethnography for the* Delgamuukw *Plaintiffs.* Vancouver: UBC Press.

Dauenhauer, Nora M., and Richard L. Dauenhauer. 1998. Tracking "Yuwaan Gagéets": A Russian Fairy Tale in Tlingit Oral Tradition. *Oral Tradition* 13 (1): 58-91.

Davey, Jonathan. 2007. Fitting a Round Peg to a Square Hole: Native Oral History Evidence and the Canadian Judiciary. Report prepared for the Indigenous Bar Association. March 5.

Day, Gordon M. 1972. Oral History as Complement. *Ethnohistory* 19:99-107.

Deloria, Vine, Jr. 1995. *Red Earth, White Lies: Native Americans and the Myth of Scientific Fact.* New York: Scribner.

Denny, J. Peter. 1991. Rational Thought in Oral Culture and Literate Decontextualization. In *Literacy and Orality,* ed. David R. Olsen and Nancy Torrance, 66-89. Cambridge: Cambridge University Press.

Echo-Hawk, Roger C. 1997. Forging a New Ancient History for Native America. In *Native Americans and Archaeologists: Stepping Stones to Common Ground,* ed. Nina Swidler, Kurt E. Dongoske, Roger Anyon, and Alan S. Downer, 88-102. Walnut Creek, CA: AltaMira Press.

–. 2000. Ancient History in the New World: Integrating Oral Traditions and the Archaeological Record in Deep Time. *American Antiquity* 65:267-90.

Ewick, Patricia, and Susan Silbey. 1998. *The Common Place of Law: Stories from Everyday Life.* Chicago: University of Chicago Press.

Finnegan, Ruth. 1992. *Oral Traditions and the Verbal Art: A Guide to Research Practices.* London: Routledge.

–. 1996. A Note on Oral Traditions and Historical Evidence. In *Oral History: An Interdisciplinary Reader,* ed. David K. Dunaway and Willa K. Baum, 126-34. Walnut Creek, CA: AltaMira Press.

Fisher, Robin. 1992. Judging History: Reflections on the Reasons for Judgment in *Delgamuukw v. B.C.* In *Anthropology and History in the Courts,* ed. Bruce G. Miller, theme issue, *BC Studies* 95:43-54.

French, Wendy. 2004. The Evolving Law of Native Title. In *Crossing Boundaries: Cultural, Legal, Historical, and Practice Issues in Native Title,* ed. Sandy Toussaint, 86-96. Carlton, Australia: Melbourne University Press.

Friedmann, Wolfgang. 1967. *Legal Theory.* New York: Columbia University Press.

Furniss, Elizabeth. 1999. *The Burden of History: Colonialism and the Frontier Myth in a Rural Canadian Community.* Vancouver: UBC Press.

Geertz, Clifford. 1983. *Local Knowledge: Further Essays in Interpretive Anthropology.* New York: Basic Books.

Goldenweiser, Alexander A. 1915. The Heuristic Value of Traditional Records. *American Anthropologist* 17:763-64.

Goody, Jack. 1987. *The Interface between the Written and the Oral.* Cambridge: Cambridge University Press.

Goody, Jack, and I. Watt. 1968. The Consequences of Literacy. In *Literacy in Traditional Societies,* ed. Jack Goody, 27-68. Cambridge: Cambridge University Press.

Gordillo, Gaston. 2004. *Landscapes of Devils: Tensions of Place and Memory in the Argentinean Chaco.* Durham: Duke University Press.

Goulet, Jean-Guy. 1998. *Ways of Knowing: Experiences, Knowledge, and Power among the Dene Tha.* Lincoln: University of Nebraska Press.

Goulet, Jean-Guy, and Bruce Granville Miller. 2007. Embodied Knowledge: Steps toward a Radical Anthropology of Cross-Cultural Encounters. In *Extraordinary Anthropology: Transformations in the Field,* ed. Jean-Guy Goulet and Bruce Granville Miller, 1-14. Lincoln: University of Nebraska Press.

Gover, Brian J., and Mary L. Macaulay. 1996. "Snow Houses Leave No Ruins": Unique Evidence Issues in Aboriginal and Treaty Rights Cases. *Saskatchewan Law Review* 60:47-89.

Hagan, William T. 1978. Archival Captive – The American Indian. *American Archivist* 41 (2): 135-42.

Hallowell, A. Irving. 1937. Temporal Orientation in Western Civilization and in a Pre-Literate Society. *American Anthropologist* 39:647-70.

Hanson, F. Allan. 1997. Empirical Anthropology, Postmodernism, and the Invention of Tradition. In *Present Is Past: Some Uses of Tradition in Native Societies,* ed. Marie Mauzé, 195-214. Lanham, MD: University Press of America.

Harkin, Michael. 1997. A Tradition of Invention: Modern Ceremonialism on the Northwest Coast. In *Present Is Past: Some Uses of Tradition in Native Societies,* ed. Marie Mauzé, 97-111. Lanham, MD: University Press of America.

Harris, Cole. 2005/06. Do Glaciers Really Listen? *BC Studies* 148:25-54.

Henige, David. 1974. *The Chronology of Oral Tradition: The Quest for a Chimera.* Oxford: Clarendon Press.

–. 1980. "In the Possession of the Author": The Problem of Source Monopoly in Oral Historiography. *International Journal of Oral History* 1 (3): 181-94.

–. 1982. *Oral Historiography.* London: Longman.

Hibbitts, Bernard J. 1992. Coming to Our Senses. *Emory Law Journal* 41:873-960.

Hilbert, Vi, ed. 1985. *Haboo: Native American Stories from Puget Sound.* Seattle: University of Washington Press.

Hobsbawm, Eric, and Terence Ranger. 1983. *The Invention of Tradition.* Cambridge: Cambridge University Press.

Hoffman, Alice. 1984. Reliability and Validity in Oral History. In *Oral History: An Interdisciplinary Anthology,* ed. David K. Dunaway and Willa K. Baum, 67-73. Nashville, TN: American Association for State and Local History.

Hopkins, James, and David Nahwegahbow. 2008. Federal Court Draft Protocol/ Practice Direction on the Oral Testimony of Aboriginal Elders. Indigenous Bar Association for presentation to the Federal Court–Indigenous Bar–Aboriginal Law Bar Liaison Committee, February 20, Yellowknife, NWT.

Hopper, Kim. 1990. Research Findings as Testimony: A Note on the Ethnographer as Expert Witness. *Human Organization* 49 (2): 110-14.

Hornborg, Anne-Christine. 2002. "Readbacks" or Tradition? The Kluskap Stories among Modern Canadian Mi'kmaq. *European Review of Native American Studies* 16 (1): 9-16.

Howes, David. 2005. Introduction: Culture in the Domains of Law. Special issue, *Canadian Journal of Law and Society* 20 (1): 9-29.

Hutchins, Peter W. 2005. Should the Expert Be a Mediator? Pre-trial and Trial Management of Expert Evidence. Presented at National Judicial Institute Federal Education Seminar, 14-16 September, Montebello, QC.

Hutchins, Peter W., Lysane Cree, and Jameela Jeeroburkhan, Hutchins Caron and Associés. 2008. The Role of Elders and Oral History Evidence in the Courts. Paper prepared for consideration by the Canadian Bar Association.

Hymes, Dell. 1981. The "Wife" Who "Goes Out" Like a Man: Reinterpretation of a Clackamas Chinook Myth. In *"In Vain I Tried to Tell You": Essays in North American Ethnopoetics,* ed. Dell Hymes, 274-308. Philadelphia: University of Pennsylvania Press.

IBA. 2009. Federal Court–Indigenous Bar–Aboriginal Law Bar Liaison Committee. Draft Proposal for Aboriginal Practice Guidelines. Phase II: Oral History Evidence (not an official paper of the Department of Justice).

Jackson, Michael. 2005. Foreword to *Our Box Was Full: An Ethnography for the* Delgamuukw *Plaintiffs,* by Richard Daly, xi-xvi. Vancouver: UBC Press.

Jeffrey, Laura. 2006. Historical Narrative and Legal Evidence: Judging Chagossians' High Court Testimonies. *PoLAR: Political and Legal Anthropology Review* 29 (2): 228-53.

Jennings, Katie. 1997. *Huchoosedah: Traditions of the Heart.* Video recording, Seattle. KCTS/BBC Wales.

Kandel, Randy Frances. 1992. How Lawyers and Anthropologists Think Differently. In *Double Vision: Anthropologists at Law,* ed. Randy Frances Kandel, 1-4. NAPA Bulletin 11. American Anthropological Association.

Keesing, Roger M. 1986. The Young Dick Attack: Oral and Documentary History on the Colonial Frontier. *Ethnohistory* 33 (3): 268-92.

–. 1992. *Custom and Confrontation: The Kwaio Struggle for Cultural Autonomy.* Chicago: University of Chicago Press.

Kidwell, Clara Sue. 1991. Systems of Knowledge. In *American in 1492: The World of Indian People before the Arrival of Columbus,* ed. Alvin Josephy Jr., 369-404. New York: Vintage Books.

Krech, Shepard, III. 1991. The State of Ethnohistory. *Annual Review of Anthropology* 20:345-75.

Lowie, Robert. 1915. Oral Tradition and History. *American Anthropologist* 17 (5): 597-99.

–. 1917. Oral Tradition and History. *Journal of American Folk-Lore* 30 (106): 161-67.

Malinowski, Bronislaw. [1926] 1948. Myth in Primitive Psychology. In *Magic, Science and Religion and Other Essays,* 72-124. Boston: Beacon Press.

Martindale, Andrew. 2006. Methodological Issues in the Use of Tsimshian Oral Tradition *(Adawx)* in Archaeology. *Canadian Journal of Archaeology* 30:159-93.

Mason, Ronald J. 2000. Archaeology and Native North American Oral Traditions. *American Antiquity* 65 (2): 239-66.

–. 2006. *Inconstant Companions: Archaeology and North American Indian Oral Traditions.* Tuscaloosa: University of Alabama Press.

McFeat, Tom. 1974. *Small-Group Cultures.* New York: Pergamon Press.

McGhee, Robert. 2008. Aboriginalism and the Problems of Indigenous Archaeology. *American Antiquity* 73 (4): 579-98.

McGuire, R.H. 1992. Archeology and the First Americans. *American Anthropologist* 94:816-36.

McHalsie, Albert (Naxaxalhts'i, Sonny). 2007. We Have to Take Care of Everything That Belongs to Us. In *"Be of Good Mind": Essays on the Coast Salish,* ed. Bruce Granville Miller, 82-130. Lincoln: University of Nebraska Press.

McLeod, Clay. 1992. The Oral Histories of Canada's Northern People, Anglo-Saxon Evidence Law, and Canadian Fiduciary Duty to First Nations: Breaking Down the Barriers of the Past. *Alberta Law Review* 30 (4): 1276-90.

Mildon, Drew. 2008. A Bad Connection: First Nations Oral Histories in the Canadian Courts. In *Aboriginal Oral Traditions: Theory, Practice, and Ethics,* ed. Renée Hulan and Renate Eigenbrod, 79-88. Halifax and Winnipeg: Fernwood Publishing with Gorsebrook Research Institute.

Miller, Bruce G. 1992a. Common Sense and Plain Language. In *Anthropology and History in the Courts,* ed. Bruce G. Miller, theme issue, *BC Studies* 95:55-65.

–. 1992b. Introduction. In *Anthropology and History in the Courts,* ed. Bruce G. Miller, theme issue, *BC Studies* 95:3-6.

–. 1998. Culture as Cultural Defence: An American Indian Sacred Site in Court. *American Indian Quarterly* 22 (1): 83-97.

–. 2001. *The Problem of Justice: Tradition and Law in the Coast Salish World.* Lincoln: University of Nebraska Press.

–. 2004. *Invisible Indigenes: The Politics of Nonrecognition.* Lincoln: University of Nebraska Press.

–, ed. 2007. *"Be of Good Mind": Essays on the Coast Salish.* Vancouver: UBC Press.

Miller, Jay. 1998. Tsimshian Ethno-Ethnohistory: A "Real" Indigenous Chronology. *Ethnohistory* 45:657-74.

Miller, Joseph C., ed. 1980. *The African Past Speaks: Essays on Oral Tradition and History.* Folkestone, UK: W. Dawson.

Mills, Antonia. 1994. *Eagle Down Is Our Law: Witsuwit'en Law, Feasts, and Land Claims.* Vancouver: UBC Press.

–. 1996. Problems of Establishing Authority in Testifying on Behalf of the Witsuwit'en. *Political and Legal Anthropology Review* 19 (2): 39-52.

–, ed. 2005. *"Hang onto These Words": Johnny David's* Delgamuukw *Evidence.* Toronto: University of Toronto Press.

Milward, David. 2009. Document in possession of author.

Morantz, Toby. 1984. Oral and Recorded History in James Bay. In *Papers of the Fifteenth Algonquian Conference,* ed. William Cowan, 171-91. Ottawa: Carleton University.

–. 1992. Old Texts, Old Questions: Another Look at the Issue of Continuity and the Early Fur Trade Period. *Canadian Historical Review* 73 (2): 166-93.

Moss, William W. 1974. *Oral History Program Manual.* New York: Praeger.

Moss, William W., and Peter C. Mazikana. 1986. *Archives, Oral History and Oral Tradition: A RAMP Study.* Paris: United Nations Educational Scientific and Cultural Organization.

Nadasdy, Paul. 2003. *Hunters and Bureaucrats: Power, Knowledge, and Aboriginal-State Relations in the Southwest Yukon.* Vancouver: UBC Press.

Napoleon, Val. 2005. *Delgamuukw:* A Legal Straitjacket for Oral Histories? *Canadian Journal of Law and Society/Revue Canadienne Droit et Société* 20 (2): 123-55.

–. 2009. Ayook: Gitksan Legal Order, Law, and Legal Theory. PhD dissertation, Faculty of Law, University of Victoria.

Naranjo, Tessie. 1995. Thoughts on Migration by Santa Clara Pueblo. *Journal of American Archaeology* 14:247-50.

Nesper, Larry. 2002. *The Walleye War: the Struggle for Ojibwe Spearfishing and Treaty Rights.* Lincoln: University of Nebraska Press.

–. 2007. Negotiating Jurisprudence in a Tribal Court and the Emergence of a Tribal State. *Current Anthropology* 48 (5): 675-99.

Newman, Dwight G. 2005. *Tsilhqot'in Nation v. British Columbia* and Civil Justice: Analyzing the Procedural Interaction of Evidentiary Principles and Aboriginal Oral History. *Alberta Law Review* 43:433-49.

Niezen, Ronald. 2003. Culture and the Judiciary: The Meaning of Culture Concept as a Source of Aboriginal Rights in Canada. *Canadian Journal of Law and Society* 18 (2): 1-26.

Njal's Saga. 1997. Trans. Robert Cook. London: Penguin Books.

Nurse, Andrew. 2006. Marius Barbeau and the Methodology of Salvage Ethnography in Canada, 1911-1951. In *Historicizing Canadian Anthropology,* ed. Julia Harrison and Regna Darnel, 52-64. Vancouver: UBC Press.

Ogot, Bothwell A. 2001. The Construction of Luo Identity and History. In *African Words, African Voices: Critical Practices in Oral History,* ed. Louise White, Stephan F. Miescher and David Cohen, 31-52. Bloomington and Indianapolis: Indiana University Press.

Paine, Robert, ed. 1985. *Advocacy and Anthropology, First Encounters.* St. John's, NL: Memorial University Press.

–. 1996. In Chief Justice McEachern's Shoes: Anthropology's Ineffectiveness in Court. *PoLAR: Political and Legal Anthropology Review* 19 (2): 59-70.

Palmer, Andie Diane. 2000. Evidence "Not in a Form Familiar to Common Law Courts": Assessing Oral Histories in Land Claims Testimony after *Delgamuukw v. B.C. Alberta Law Review* 38:1040-50.

Parker, Arthur C. 1989. *Seneca Myths and Folktales.* Lincoln: University of Nebraska Press.

Partnow, Patricia H. 1995. The Days of Yore: Alutiiq Mythical Time. In *When Our Words Return: Writing, Hearing, and Remembering Oral Traditions of Alaska and the Yukon,* ed. Phyllis Morrow and William Schneider, 139-83. Logan: Utah State University Press.

Paul, Mandy. 2004. Reflecting on Past Practice: The Alice Springs Arrente Claim. In *Crossing Boundaries: Cultural, Legal, Historical, and Practice Issues in Native Title,* ed. Sandy Toussaint, 142-51. Carlton, Australia: Melbourne University Press.

Pommersheim, Frank. 1995. *Braid of Feathers: American Indian Law and Contemporary Tribal Life.* Berkeley: University of California Press.

Prins, Harald. 1994. Neo-Traditions in Native Communities: Sweat Lodge and Sun Dance Among the Micmac Today. In *Actes du vingt-cinquième congrès des Algonquinistes,* ed. William Cowan, 383-94. Ottawa: Carleton University.

Raglan, Lord. 1956. *The Hero: A Study in Tradition, Myth, and Drama.* New York: Vintage Books.

Ray, Arthur J. 2003. Native History on Trial: Confessions of an Expert Witness. *Canadian Historical Review* 84 (2): 255-73.

–. 2008. "History Wars" and Treaty Rights in Canada: A Canadian Case Study. In *The Power of Promises: Rethinking Indian Treaties in the Pacific Northwest,* ed. Alexandra Harmon, 279-96. Seattle: University of Washington Press.

Richland, Justin B. 2008. Sovereign Time, Storied Moments: The Temporalities of Law, Tradition, and Ethnography in Hopi Tribal Court. *Political and Legal Anthropology Review* 31 (1): 8-20.

Ridington, Robin. 1990. *Little Bit Know Something: Stories in the Language of Anthropology.* Vancouver: Douglas and McIntyre.

–. 1992. Fieldwork in Court 53: A Witness to *Delgamuukw v. B.C. BC Studies* 95: 12-24.

Rigby, Peter, and Peter Sevareid. 1992. Lawyers, Anthropologists, and the Knowledge of Facts. In *Double Vision: Anthropologists at Law,* ed. Randy Frances Kandel, 5-21. NAPA Bulletin 11. American Anthropological Association.

Ring, Kathy, and Erin Tully. 2006. Discussion paper on the Use of Experts in Aboriginal Litigation in the Federal Court. Prepared by Aboriginal Law Section, Litigation Services, Vancouver Regional Office, Department of Justice (Canada) for presentation at the Federal Court Bench and Aboriginal Law Liaison Committee Meeting, October 21.

Roness, Lori Ann, and Kent McNeil. 2000. Legalizing Oral History: Proving Aboriginal Title in Canadian Courts. *Journal of the West* 39 (3): 66-74.

Rosaldo, Renato. 1980. Doing Oral History. *Social Analysis* 4:89-99.

–. 1989. *Culture and Truth: The Remaking of Social Analysis.* Boston: Beacon Press.

Rosen, Lawrence. 2006. *Law as Culture: An Invitation.* Princeton: Princeton University Press.

Royal Commission on Aboriginal Peoples. 1996. Vol. 1, *Looking Forward, Looking Back.* Ottawa: Minister of Supply and Services.

Russell, Dan. 2000. *A People's Dream: Aboriginal Self-Government in Canada.* Vancouver: UBC Press.

Sahlins, Marshall. 1983. Other Times, Other Cultures: The Anthropology of History. *American Anthropologist* 85:517-43.

Schaepe, David. 2006. Rock Fortifications: Archaeological Insights into Precontact Warfare and Sociopolitical Organization among the Stó:lō of the Lower Fraser River Canyon, B.C. *American Antiquity* 4 (71): 671-705.

–. 2007a. Learning to Live Together in a Good Way: Lessons on Repatriation from Stone *T'xwelátse. The Midden* 39 (2): 9-17.

–. 2007b. Stó:lō Identity and the Cultural Landscape of S'ólh Téméxw. In *"Be of Good Mind": Essays on the Coast Salish,* ed. Bruce G. Miller, 234-59. Vancouver: UBC Press.

Schneider, William. 1995. Lessons from Alaska Natives about Oral Tradition and Recordings. In *When Our Words Return: Writing, Hearing, and Remembering Oral Traditions of Alaska and the Yukon,* ed. Phyllis Morrow and William Schneider, 185-204. Logan: Utah State University Press.

Schreiber, Dorothee. 2008. Glaciers Listen: A Review Essay and Response to Cole Harris. *BC Studies* 159:131-39.

Sider, Gerald M. 1993. *Lumbee Indian Histories: Race, Ethnicity, and Indian Identity in the Southern United States.* Cambridge: Cambridge University Press.

Simpkins, Maureen Ann. 2000. After *Delgamuukw:* Aboriginal Oral Tradition as Evidence in Aboriginal Rights and Title Litigation. PhD dissertation, Department of Adult Education, Counselling Psychology, and Community Development, Ontario Institute for the Study of Education, University of Toronto.

Smith, Barbara Hernstein. 2005. *Scandalous Knowledge: Science, Truth, and the Human.* Durham, NC: Duke University Press.

Sopinka, John, and Sidney N. Lederman. 1974. *The Law of Evidence in Civil Cases.* Toronto: Butterworths.

Stohr, Glen. 1999. The Repercussions of Orality in Federal Indian Law. *Arizona State Law Journal* 31 (679): 1-30.

Strang, Veronica. 2006. Happy Coincidence: Symbiosis, Synthesis in Anthropological and Indigenous Knowledge. *Current Anthropology* 47 (6): 981-1008.

Street, Eloise. 1963. *Sepass Poems: The Songs of Y-Ail-Mihth.* New York: Vantage Press.

Sui Generis. 2007. *Sui Generis* Litigation Reconciling History and Law. 22-23 February, First Nations House of Learning, UBC. Statement of conference theme and agenda in possession of author.

Terkel, Studs. 1974. *Working: People Talk about What They Do All Day and How They Feel about What They Do.* New York: Pantheon/Random House.

–. 1978. *Hard Times: An Oral History of the Great Depression.* New York: Pantheon.

Thompson, Paul. 1988. *The Voice of the Past: Oral History.* 2nd ed. Oxford: Oxford University Press.

Thornton, Thomas. 2008. *Being and Place among the Tlingit.* Seattle: University of Washington Press.

Trigger, David. 2004. Anthropology in Native Title Court Cases: "Mere Pleading, Expert Opinion or Hearsay." In *Crossing Boundaries: Cultural, Legal, Historical, and Practice Issues in Native Title,* ed. Sandy Toussaint, 24-33. Carlton, Australia: Melbourne University Press.

Twinning, William. 1984. Taking Facts Seriously. *Journal of Legal Education* 34:22-42.

Vansina, Jan. 1965. *Oral Tradition: A Study in Historical Methodology.* Trans. H.M. Wright. London: Routledge and Kegan Paul.

–. 1985. *Oral Tradition as History.* Madison: University of Wisconsin Press.

Voget, Fred W. 1975. *A History of Ethnology.* New York: Holt, Rinehart, and Winston.

von Gernet, Alexander. 1996. *Oral Narratives and Aboriginal Pasts: An Interdisciplinary Review of the Literature on Oral Traditions and Oral Histories.* Ottawa: Research and Analysis Directorate, Indian and Northern Affairs Canada. http://www.ainc-inac.gc.ca.

–. 2000. What My Elders Taught Me: Oral Traditions as Evidence in Aboriginal Litigations. In *Beyond the Nass Valley,* ed. Owen Lippert, 174-93. Vancouver: Fraser Institute.

–. 2006a. *Sawridge Band v. The Queen.* Edmonton, T-66-86A, Alberta, Federal Court. And *Tsuu T'ina First Nation v. The Queen.* Edmonton, T-66-86B, Alberta, Federal Court (Evidence, Dr. von Gernet's expert report).

–. 2006b. Oral History and Oral Tradition Evidence in the Forensic Reconstruction of Aboriginal History and Practices. Report prepared for Department of Justice (Aboriginal Law Section) in relation to *Roger William (Xeni Gwet'in First Nations and Tsilhqot'in Nation) v. B.C.* (SCBC Nos. 900913 and 984847, Victoria Registry), May.

–. 2007. Reconstructing Tsimshian Culture and History Using Oral Traditions: A Brief Assessment of Two Expert Opinions. Report prepared for Department of Justice in relation to *Lax Kw'alaams Indian Band v. Canada (A.G.),* February.

Watkins, Joe. 2000. *Indigenous Archaeology: American Indian Values and Scientific Practice.* Walnut Creek, CA: AltaMira Press.

–. 2005. Through Wary Eyes: Indigenous Perspectives on Archaeology. *Annual Review of Archaeology* 34:429-94.

Wheeler, Winona. 2001. Indigenous Oral Histories, An Academic Predicament. Report prepared for plaintiffs in *Chief Victor Buffalo et al. v. Her Majesty et al.* (Case cited in the text as *Samson Indian Nation and Band v. Canada.*)

Whiteley, Peter M. 2002. Archaeology and Oral Tradition: The Scientific Importance of Dialogue. *American Antiquity* 67 (3): 405-15.

Widdowson, Frances, and Albert Howard. 2008. *Disrobing the Aboriginal Industry.* Montreal and Kingston: McGill-Queen's University Press.

Wiget, Andrew. 1982. Truth and the Hopi: An Historiographic Study of Documented Oral Tradition Concerning the Coming of the Spanish. *Ethnohistory* 29 (3): 181-99.

–. 1995. Recovering the Remembered Past: Folklore and Oral History in the Zuni Trust Lands Damages Case. In *Zuni and the Courts: A Struggle for Sovereign Land Rights,* ed. E. Richard Hart, 172-87. Lawrence: University Press of Kansas.

–. 1996. Father Juan Greyrobe: Reconstructing Tradition Histories, and the Reliability and Validity of Uncorroborated Oral Tradition. *Ethnohistory* 43 (3): 459-82.

Wigmore, John Henry. 1940-88. *Evidence in Trials at Common Law,* 10 vols. Boston: Little, Brown and Company.

Williams, Paul. 1996. Oral Tradition on Trial. In *Gin Das Winan: Documenting Aboriginal History in Ontario,* ed. Dale Standen and David McNab, 29-34. Occasional Papers 2. Toronto: Champlain Society.

Willis, Roy. 1980. The Literalist Fallacy and the Problems of Oral Traditions. Special issue, Using Oral Sources: Vansina and Beyond. *Social Analysis* 4:51-73.

Wilson, Angela Cavender. 1997. "Power of the Spoken Word": Native Oral Traditions in American Indian History. In *Rethinking American Indian History,* ed. Donald L. Fixico, 101-16. Albuquerque: University of New Mexico Press.

Wolf, Eric. 1982. *People without History.* Berkeley and Los Angeles: University of California Press.

Wylie, Kenneth C. 1973. The Uses and Misuses of Ethnohistory. *Journal of Interdisciplinary Studies* 3 (4): 707-20.

LEGAL DECISIONS CITED

Assiniboine Indian Tribe v. United States, 77 Ct. Cl. 347 (1933).

Benoit v. Canada (2003), 242 F.T.R. 159, 2003 FCA 236.

Blueberry River Indian Band v. Canada (Department of Indian Affairs and Northern Development), [1988] 3 F.C. 20.

Coos Bay Indian Tribe v. United States, 87 Ct. Cl. 143 (1938).

Delgamuukw v. British Columbia, [1991] 3 W.W.R. 97 (B.C.S.C.).

Delgamuukw v. British Columbia, [1997] 3 S.C.R. 1010 [*Delgamuukw III*].

Hamlet of Baker Lake v. Canada (Minister of Indian Affairs and Northern Development), [1980] 1 F.C. 518.

Hwiltsum First Nation v. Canada (Minister of Fisheries and Oceans), [2001] 4 F.C. D-48, 2001 FCT 936.

Kartinyeri v. The Commonwealth, [1998] A.I.L.R. 15, 1998 HCA 22.

Klahoose First Nation v. Sunshine Coast Forest District (District Manager) (2009), 1 C.N.L.R. 110 (B.C.S.C.).

Lax Kw'alaams Indian Band v. Canada (A.G.), [2008] 166 A.C.W.S. (3d) 407, 2008 BCSC 447.

Mashpee Tribe v. New Seabury Corporation, 427 F. Supp. 899 (D. Mass. 1978).

Mikisew Cree First Nation v. Canada (Minister of Canadian Heritage), [2005] 3 S.C.R. 388, 2005 SCC 69.

Mitchell v. M.N.R., [2001] 1 S.C.R. 911, 2001 SCC 33.

Ontario (A.G.) v. Bear Island Foundation, [1985] 49 O.R. (2d) 353 (Ont. S.C.).

Ontario (A.G.) v. Bear Island Foundation, [1989] 68 O.R. (2d) 394, (Ont. C.A.).

Pueblo de Zia v. United States, 11-A Ind. Cl. Comm. 131 (1962).

R. v. Breaker, [2001] 3 C.N.L.R. 213 (Alta. Prov. Ct.).

R. v. Catarat, [1998] 4 C.N.L.R. 115, 1998 SKPC 13338.

R. v. Goodon, [2008] 234 Man R. (2d) 278, 2008 MBPC 59.

R. v. Haines, [2003] 1 C.N.L.R. 191 (B.C. Prov. Ct.).

R. v. Horse, [1988] 1 S.C.R. 187.

R. v. Jacobs, [1999] 3 C.N.L.R. 239, 1998 BCSC 3988.
R. v. Khan, [1990] 2 S.C.R. 531.
R. v. Kruger, [1978] 1 S.C.R. 104.
R. v. Marshall, [1999] 3 S.C.R. 456.
R. v. Mohan, [1994] 2 S.C.R. 9.
R. v. Morris, [2004] 2 C.N.L.R. 219, 2004 BCCA 121.
R. v. Taylor (1982), 62 C.C.C. (2d) 227.
R. v. Van der Peet, [1996] 2 S.C.R. 507.
R. v. Willison, [2005] 3 C.N.L.R. 278, 2005 BCPC 131.
Samson Indian Nation and Band v. Canada (2005), 269 F.T.R. 1, 2005 FC 1622.
Tsilhqot'in Nation v. British Columbia, [2008] 1 C.N.L.R. 112, 2007 BCSC 1700.
United States v. Washington, 384 F. Supp. 312 (W.D. Wash. 1974).
Warm Springs Reservation v. United States, 177 Cl. Ct. 184 (1966).
Zuni Tribe of New Mexico v. United States, 12 Cl. Ct. 607 (1987).

Index

Printed and bound in Canada

Set in Futura Condensed and Warnock Pro by Artegraphica Design Co. Ltd.

Copy editor: Sarah Wight

Proofreader: Helen Godolphin